1969

‡

JOHN GIELGUD *Directs*

RICHARD BURTON *in*

Hamlet

RICHARD L. STERNE

John Gielgud
Directs
Richard Burton
in
HAMLET

A Journal of Rehearsals

RANDOM HOUSE · NEW YORK

‡

FIRST PRINTING

Library of Congress Catalog Card Number: 67–12759

‡

TO

John Gielgud

✝

CONTENTS

‡

JOHN GIELGUD *Directs*

RICHARD BURTON *in*

Hamlet

———————————

Foreword

JOHN GIELGUD's production of *Hamlet* with Richard Burton was presented on Broadway in 1964 as part of the celebration of Shakespeare's four-hundredth birthday. Though Burton had distinguished himself ten years prior as a leading player with London's revered Old Vic Company, he made his first American appearance in a classic play with the production. He chose as his director the man whose own Hamlet he had most admired —the actor-director most associated with the role—Sir John Gielgud.

In the summer of 1963, while both men were in England making the film *Becket*, Burton asked Gielgud if he would direct him in Shakespeare's play. Gielgud told him that for some time he had harbored the idea of doing *Hamlet* as a rehearsal run-through, without costumes or scenery. This revolutionary idea appealed to Burton, the two agreed on the collaboration, and they were signed to bring the production to New York by one of Broadway's most successful producers, Alexander H. Cohen.

A storm of publicity heralded the show when it was announced during the height of Burton's romance with actress Elizabeth Taylor. Throughout the rehearsal period in Toronto, the performances in that city (during which the two were married), the runs in Boston and New York, literally thousands of people mobbed the streets of the theatres and the lobbies of the hotels and airline terminals, hoping to get a glimpse of the famous pair.

A sellout for the entire run, despite its critical controversy, the production went on to become Broadway's longest running and most profitable *Hamlet* in stage history, with tickets priced at a record top of $9.90. It was also the first Broadway production to be filmed while in performance before an audience. A month after the play closed the film was exhibited in a thousand motion picture houses all over the United States.

My own association with the production came about under somewhat unusual circumstances. I first met John Gielgud in 1962, while he was touring the United States with his production of *The School for Scandal*. At the time I was studying acting in the theatre school of a large midwestern university and I wrote to Gielgud, my long-time idol, asking if I might see him for some advice.

Before he could reply I hurried home for my Christmas vacation to Philadelphia, where he was playing. After seeing his performance I went backstage and met Sir John. We talked a bit about the play, about some of the work I'd done and hoped to do, and then I asked him if he would hear me do some Shakespeare. He told me to come back to the theatre on Saturday between the matinée and the evening performance when the stage would be free.

Saturday came and I returned, having prepared four speeches from the plays. Sir John listened patiently from the auditorium as I ran through the full twenty minutes worth; then he came up on the stage when I had finished and gave me some helpful pointers. To further demonstrate his instructions, to my amazement, he performed all of the passages for me from memory. "You're very promising," he told me. "I think you should go on with acting."

The following summer I worked at the Oregon Shakespeare Festival and was cast in the role of Romeo. Just three days before the festival closed I received a letter from Sir John:

Dear Richard,
    Glad to hear Oregon is so much to your liking. I will be di-
recting Richard Burton in *Hamlet* for Broadway this season,
and if you want to be in it I will have a part for you. I will be
in New York for auditions in five or six weeks, come see me
then. Only please do not tell too many other actors, as I imagine when the news comes out we shall be snowed under with
applications. Hope to see you in the fall—
                                              Yours, in haste
                                              J G

At the audition Sir John had me read the small role of the
Gentleman and told me that in addition to playing that part
he wanted me to do several other small roles and to understudy
Laertes.
    Before rehearsals began I decided that I would take down
every word Gielgud said about the play, since I believe he knows
more about the part of Hamlet and the play than any living
actor. Through all the rehearsals I kept next to me a long-
playing portable tape recorder concealed in a large briefcase.
I had asked Gielgud for permission to keep notes of what went
on, which he readily gave. But I did not tell him about the tape
recorder for fear it might be an inhibiting factor to him or the
actors.
    I attended all rehearsals, including those for which the gen-
eral company had not been called. I kept a pen and note pad
always in my pocket and during the breaks I jotted down action
notes. Meanwhile the tape recorder was silently rolling in my
briefcase at the side of the room. The machine could run for
three hours continuously, though several times I had to make
a quick trip to the men's room to change reels. Though the
other actors must have regarded me as some sort of crank who
always lugged around a huge briefcase, I managed to get the
machine through rehearsals without its being discovered.
    One afternoon during the second week of rehearsals, Alfred
Drake suddenly stopped in the middle of one of his speeches
and pointed to where I was sitting next to the briefcase at the
side of the rehearsal hall. "How did that get in here?" he de-

manded. I froze. Surely he had seen the microphone through
the hole in the side of the briefcase and I would be found out
and dismissed. He walked toward me and then said, "I wish
they'd sent it to the hotel." It was with great relief that I
realized he had been referring to his wardrobe trunk, on which
I was sitting.

There was a closed rehearsal which the cast was asked not to
attend during the third week in Toronto. It was a two-hour
rehearsal with Gielgud and Burton only—all others were locked
out. I arrived at the rehearsal hall two hours before the private
session began, climbed under the rehearsal platform and pulled
a cloth over the tape recorder and myself. I was able to record
most of what was said, and I think it turned out to be one of
the most valuable parts of the notes I collected, because it was
then that Gielgud stated what he felt the play meant.

After Gielgud and Burton left the room, I was about to climb
out when the stage manager came into the room and started
editing the sound tapes for the show. He stayed an hour and a
half. Finally, after six hours of remaining motionless, I emerged
stiff and aching from my hideout and limped back to the hotel
to transcribe the prize tape I had just recorded.

In later weeks I told Gielgud and Burton of the tapes I had
made. Both reacted favorably, surprised and amused that such
a project had been carried out.

At first I had hoped to present this material exactly as taken,
as a transcription. But with approximately one hundred and
twenty hours of tape and more than one hundred pages of
notes, a great deal of editing and summarizing was necessary
to avoid repetition. I have retained, however, as much of the
actual rehearsal conversations as possible to add a kind of pro-
pinquity. Also included are a prompt-script of the production as
it was played, and two interviews, one with Gielgud and one
with Burton, both recorded after the production had opened
in New York.

I wish to extend my thanks to the members of the cast and
many friends who have expressed interest and encouragement
for this undertaking, with a special note of indebtedness to the

following persons: Benjamin F. Ricker, my acting and writing teacher, who helped organize, revise, and correct this material; Lorraine Sterne, my mother, who typed most of the manuscript; Joseph R. L. Sterne of the *Baltimore Sun*, who suggested several improvements; Dr. John Van Meter, who proofread part of the manuscript; Hume Cronyn, who lent me the letter quoted in Chapter V (a gift to him from Burton); Professor Theodore Fuchs of Northwestern University, for his helpful understanding of the problems of authorship, and Joann Rose, my wife, whose gentle encouragement brought about the completion of this work.

Here, then, is the drama of rehearsal—the inspiration, intuition, experimentation, and ingenuity that created this unforgettable production.

Richard L. Sterne

PART ONE

A Journal of
Rehearsals

---

‡　　‡　　‡

CHAPTER I

The First Week of Rehearsals

THURSDAY, JANUARY 30, 1964

9:00 A.M.	Company leaves New York for Toronto by plane
12:00 NOON	Company arrives in Toronto
3:00 P.M.	Press conference, lobby of O'Keefe Centre
3:30 P.M.	Read-through of Act I

AT 9:00 THE COMPANY assembled in New York City in front of the office of Alexander H. Cohen, the producer. They were then driven by bus to Kennedy Airport and put on board a plane for Toronto. Mr. Cohen and his press representatives met the company at the Canadian airport at noon.

When the company arrived at the King Edward-Sheraton Hotel they found the lobby filled with several hundred teen-agers, gawkers, and photographers, all waiting for Richard Burton or Elizabeth Taylor to appear. But the pair had checked into their five-room suite (Room 850 at $65 daily rate) two days before. By 1:30 the members of the company were all checked into their rooms and informed that the first call would be at the O'Keefe Centre in an hour and a half.

After pushing through another crowd at the O'Keefe stage door, the company members were checked in by the doorman and directed to the rehearsal hall. Here Miss Jessica Levy, assistant to the director, introduced the cast members who had arrived previously in Toronto, including Richard Burton and Hume Cronyn. At 3:00 sharp director John Gielgud arrived wearing a brown tweed overcoat and a black Russian fur hat, his face sunburned from his previous week in Jamaica.

The company was then asked to meet in the theatre lobby, where they were confronted by a mass of photographers and reporters—well over fifty of them. The newsmen clustered around Burton, who answered their questions calmly and quietly, sipping vending-machine coffee from a paper cup. (When the news articles hit the stands the next day one interviewer described Burton as a "burly Welsh actor cradling a drink.")

At 3:30 P.M. the company returned to the rehearsal hall. The O'Keefe rehearsal room is large; it fully duplicates the dimensions of its vast stage. Along one wall of the room was a row of full-length mirrors, used for dance rehearsals and now curtained. Two long folding tables had been set up at one end of the room. Behind the tables and filling up most of the 35-by-60-foot room were the actual platforms and stairways of the set, which in less than four weeks would be painted and moved upstairs to the stage for the opening night.

The company was seated around the tables. Twenty-four members were present—all but George Rose, George Voskovec, and Dillon Evans,* who were called for later rehearsals. After a greeting by Mr. Cohen, Sir John began his introductory remarks:

GIELGUD This afternoon I want to read through the first act, but I thought I'd begin by telling you a little of what I had in mind. When Richard asked me to do the play for him, I already had the idea that a Shakespeare play might be done

* See the cast list on page 156 for roles played by the actors.

as a run-through. So often it has been my experience in many plays that we have been through the whole play for the last time (in rehearsal) without interruptions; then, all of a sudden, the scenery and the lighting come, and everybody is thrown to pieces. And even after we have seen the sets, however beautiful they are, they sort of cramp the imagination and the poetry—and they are also apt to destroy the pace. So we are going to act the play as if it were the final run-through before the technical rehearsals begin, and play it in rehearsal clothes, stripped of all extraneous trappings.

I looked at this play very carefully and it seemed to me that by avoiding changes of scenery and by improvising all the accessories, we might force the audience to imagine a great deal that would be limited otherwise by specific scenery and properties.

Of course, we can't really have no lighting and no scenery. Ben Edwards has designed a set which looks like the walls of an empty theatre, with high, double-dock doors in the center at the back, and ropes and weights hanging from the grid. Some plain, rough rostrums will be arranged in front of the back wall, giving various levels and steps and ramps leading to exits left and right. The lighting must seem to be ordinary rehearsal lighting. But actually, as the play begins at night in the first scene, then goes to day for the court scene, then to evening for Ophelia, then back to the next night for the platform scene, then back to day again—so we propose to have the lights fade from day to night and rise from night to day, probably taking a quarter of an hour. But from the audience's point of view, there'll be no sudden blackouts, no sudden changes of light to startle them and disturb their concentration. I once saw a Shakespearean production done all through under white light, but I thought this became tedious after a few scenes.

Often, in rehearsal, one sees an actor pick up a piece of material for a cloak, as it were, and fling it over his shoulder convincingly, and he seems to believe it more than when he has the final costume. Actors seize on things that they need. If they suddenly think they must have a cloak or a dagger or a sword, they snatch a substitute from somewhere or even pretend to do so.

We will have a few beautiful period props—an inkstand on the table, a portfolio for the King, and a showy hat for Osric—these things we can use, and since the people onstage will be dressed in ordinary clothes, perhaps these things will suddenly seem more interesting. And we shall take care with the colors used for the clothing of the principals so that they will stand out in exactly the same way that the royal family in England stand out when they appear in public.

But I would like you to imagine that if there had been costumes for this performance they would have been Renaissance clothes of the time of Holbein—but you see, you won't have the ruffs or the tights or the wigs or the beards. I think it might be good if some of the men grow their hair long, as if they were getting ready to wear a costume—it would be effective, and most actors like their hair long. Too, if people want to have beards, we may decide that beards are good. Alfred [Drake] has a splendid beard already. George Rose might have a beard. I don't think Polonius [Hume Cronyn] needs a beard because when Hamlet says "It shall to the barber's with your beard!" he can simply flick his fingers rather than pull Polonius' beard.

But I want the actors to help by using their imaginations. Everybody must try to find what he would feel. I want the acting to be strong and broad and spoken out with all the poetry of the play. It should be realistic but strongly projected.

We have had brilliant productions of many of the classics in modern dress, but I have always felt that when the actors begin to have revolvers, cigarette holders, umbrellas, and all sorts of things which the audience associates with other periods, these are distractions. Yet if we have a sword strapped round us as we do at rehearsal while we are wearing trousers instead of tights, after a few minutes nobody will notice the trousers.

Now let's have a look at the model of the set. The rear doors are used only when we have entrances from the outside —when the Players come, when the Ghost appears, or in the Fortinbras scene. There will be different directions for the movement of the actors in the platform scenes from those in the court scenes, in order to give an illusion of different locale when the scene changes. For example, the first platform scene moves diagonally across the stage, and the first court scene moves straight up and down, or horizontally. For the costuming, I am going to have Jane [Greenwood], the costumer, watch very closely at rehearsals to see if we should wear duffle coats and fur hats and boots and things, and if we see people wearing something effective, we'll try to copy them, or have people use their own clothes. I'm always fascinated by the way actors try to get into a part. Don't feel that you must dress in rehearsal clothes that make you *look* the part, but dress in the clothes that help to make you *feel* the part.

Well, now let's start reading and see how far we get this afternoon. If anybody feels strongly about cuts, or if there are things that I've cut out that they would love to have back, I will do my best to put them back. The play should begin like a pistol shot. We don't want the usual striking bells and wind to give atmosphere. Francisco believes he has seen the Ghost and shouts out "Who's there?" suddenly and with great force. All right, let's begin. . . .

During the read-through Gielgud sat back in his folding chair and followed the play in both the mimeographed copy of the cutting he had provided for the company and in a printed text of the complete Cambridge edition. Now and then he would close his eyes and drift back into a cloud of smoke from the English Oval cigarette hanging from his lip; a long precarious ash fell unnoticed on his brown corduroy suit while his lips moved silently to follow a passage as the actor read. Gielgud read the role of the Ghost and also read in for Reynaldo.

For the most part the actors read without too much emotion —rather straightforwardly—being concerned with saying the lines with proper emphasis and phrasing as Gielgud followed along. Burton read with great emotion and great speed, shouting many of the passages and not holding back as most actors do during their first readings. All of his readings were energetic and dynamic—no melancholic or soggy ones. This was an active Hamlet—no whining.

Gielgud briefly interrupted the readings for the following comments:

GIELGUD For Hamlet's first entrance we will have him walk down the steps as everyone waits and watches. When I did it with George Rylands directing, he had me sitting as if for a photograph, staring at the audience. But Granville-Barker suggested another way: this is the first meeting of the Privy Council. I think it will be more effective to give Hamlet a late entrance after the King has made an impressive start for himself. Then Hamlet comes in like the bad boy at the party. . . .

Concerning the murder, I don't see the Queen as conniving in any way. She is totally ignorant of any funny business. (Eileen Herlie, the Queen, agrees.) Polonius is suspicious but immediately moves with the power, and takes sides with the new King.

Horatio must be scholarly in contrast to Hamlet. Marcellus and Bernardo, old soldiers who had been employed at the time of the old King and loved him, know something is wrong. And it's more moving that it is the older men who ask the younger men about the Ghost.

BURTON John, what if at the end of the court scene, Ophelia comes on early for her first scene so that I see her and take the lines "Foul deeds will rise, though all the earth o'erwhelm them to men's eyes" to her?

GIELGUD We could bring Ophelia on early so that she sees *you*. But I don't think Hamlet would see her. He's thinking of other things. . . .

Gielgud was concerned with the timings of the act and had the stage manager keep a stopwatch on the readings.

GIELGUD We've got to keep the timing in mind at all rehearsals so that we don't spread it too much. Let's stop now—it's 5:30 —and tomorrow at 10:30 we'll begin reading Act Two. Thank you all very much.

FRIDAY, JANUARY 31

> 10:30 A.M.   Read-through of Acts II and III
> (scenes 8-16)
>
> 2:00 P.M.   Block scenes 1, 2, and 3

THE CAST MET AT the long tables and sat as before. Sir John asked for a consensus on lunch-break time.

GIELGUD We'll try to make it 1:00 and then be back at 2:30, and I'll try not to keep you all hanging about in scenes that don't concern you. And I think when we come to the Ghost scene and the nunnery scene and the closet scene,* it might be a good idea to do them at night alone. I think sometimes you get much more feeling for it that way. . . . I don't think you should worry too much about being heard, even though this is such an enormous theatre. My theory—I don't want to start lecturing at this point—my theory about speaking Shakespeare is that phrasing and diction are much more important than declamation. If one puts the commas and full stops in the right place and phrases the thing as it's written, and the players are not tempted, as I noticed a lot of people were tending to do yesterday, to jump their bridges, it will all go better.

I want it to be swift, but if you give away the fact that you know what's coming next, it gives an effect of memorization or gabbling. You must try to empty your minds of the next

* See *Scene Designations*, p. 159.

phrase before it comes, and then place it accurately in the right position as it follows. Do you know what I mean? As in real life, one often doesn't know quite what one is going to say next; but at the same time in a poetic text one mustn't pause and make great holes in the play in order to appear natural—that one cannot do. Somehow it must be so carefully rehearsed that the thoughts are ready to come into your mind before the words so that you sew the speech behind your thought, so that it doesn't appear glib—then it will somehow seem to have a freshness. But I think I can show you, as we go, what I mean. It's only a question of spacing it and not rushing too much. But let's go on now. We begin the second act with "Speak the speech."

The read-through continued. There were halts for a few comments:

GIELGUD Guildenstern, can you find some other word for "cess of majesty"? [III, iii, 15] I don't want the audience to spend the next four lines worrying about what it means. I think "cease of majesty" would be better.

Rosencrantz and Guildenstern, you both are so good and clear in your readings, let's put back some of your speeches which I cut. These parts are never very interesting if they're played by very young men, and I'm so delighted in this production to have two interesting actors instead of college boys. The parts so often have to be cut to shreds.

Alfred, you know a lot about music. Can you find some soldiers' whistling song for the Fortinbras scene? I want an Elizabethan song like "Let Me the Canniken Clink," obviously a dirty song. Someone will whistle it and the troops will take it up, so that when Fortinbras' army is passing we get the same effect as in "Bridge on the River Kwai." And finally, if they are all whistling and the feet are tramping, we should get the effect of marching men which has been characteristic of armies all through history, even in Caesar's time.

I remember once I was playing that scene and right in the

middle of the Fortinbras soliloquy, some man in the front row took out an enormous watch and wound it up very loudly. In the front row! I thought I would brain him.

How was our timing, by the way? Thirty-six minutes? Well, it will probably take about forty-five. So, counting yesterday, we are up to two hours and fifteen minutes. We have to be careful so that we give them time to catch their trains. Well, let's take a ten-minute break and then we'll go on and read the last act.

The cast took a break, and then Gielgud resumed.

GIELGUD I know this is a difficult place to begin the act after an intermission, but it's really a question of how the vitality of the play holds up. Still, it's very hard for poor Ophelia to have to open the third act, but there isn't any other place to break it. The Fortinbras scene makes a marvelous curtain for the second act. I have an idea about Ophelia's mad scene. I thought we could get the idea that she was shut up in the castle. And you, Gertrude, come down the grand stairway saying "I won't speak with her, I won't speak with her." But then they let Ophelia in—and her one idea is to get out into the open air. And so she keeps on going to the center doors trying to find a way to open them. Gertrude knows it's dangerous and that Ophelia mustn't be let out. Finally she does find the door and she rushes out, which alarms the Queen.

Then the riot begins with Laertes, and Ophelia, coming back, hears all the noise. She has been down by the river already and her dress is stained with weeds and muck. And she thinks of the flowers. She's come back, she thinks, for the funeral—to offer the flowers for her father; she can't find the body because the King has done "but greenly in hugger-mugger to inter him." And I don't think she ever saw him after he was dead. So that when she's come back the second time and Laertes is there, she's looking for poor Polonius' body, and for Hamlet, too, who went away, and she can't find either of them. She's distracted and looks about, under the rostrum and everywhere. Then finally, when she sees it's no good and she's given away the flowers and doesn't know where she is because there is no funeral, she kisses the Queen suddenly, and then very slyly, seeing the door is open, makes a dash for it and goes rushing out. The Queen rushes out after her, so we are prepared to hear the description of Ophelia's death at the end of the scene.

I'm rather sick of the wild indecency that has been put into the scene in recent productions, with Ophelia tearing off her clothes and clutching all the gentlemen. I don't think Shakespeare meant it. It must be a touching scene. You see, I think in Shakespeare's time people always laughed at lunatics. They visited madhouses right up to the eighteenth century in England as we visit the zoo today. And Shakespeare knew that the only way to make madness pitiful, as is obvious with Lady Macbeth and Ophelia, was to give them a poignant, agonized, though not sentimental, scene. If that was not intended by Shakespeare, Laertes would never say "Thought and affliction, passion, hell itself she turns to favor and to prettiness." And to suddenly make Ophelia openly lewd onstage is against the intention of the writing. In this other way you can be just as strong. I don't want to make it sentimental and Victorian.

I think we must all play not as though we were going to put this poor creature in prison or to lock her up, but as though we were going to restrain her in the castle. After all, "Denmark's a prison," as Hamlet says and as our set conveys. Even Hamlet himself is trying to break away to get to the outer world. All the people in the play are shut up in this castle. You play that, really, all through the play. There is this curious feeling, except on the battlements and in the churchyard, that they are all really locked in the castle, in a miasma of corruption and sensuality. It isn't until Fortinbras comes at the end that the whole thing opens and all are free. I had an idea to use a lute for Ophelia as we once did in another production of mine. It was beautiful to have her play it. But it's such a big prop to manage and it's such an Eliza-

bethan prop. It would really only work well if the actress
could play it properly herself. I originally thought a lady-in-
waiting might play it sitting in a chair, but that was no good.

HERLIE Do you want the Queen's speech about Ophelia's
death to be "read" or "acted"?

GIELGUD It must be frantic. But also, it has to be spoken very
beautifully. It's like the description of an automobile crash,
"Oh, there they were, all covered with blood and it was horrible." Only the Queen describes the romantic aspect of it
with her own rather limited romantic attitude even toward
disaster.

During the reading of Act Three there were a few discussions
about cuttings and the possibilities of alternate line readings.
Sir John had a comment on the Hamlet-Horatio conversation
at the beginning of the last scene.

GIELGUD This scene is so difficult, following the big drama at
the end of the grave scene. It's such an anticlimax. I never
know how to make it interesting up to the entrance of Osric.
This is where they get restless and start to cough. Let's cut
all the lines about the letters—who cares about that? You
just told Horatio *offstage* that Rosencrantz and Guildenstern
are dead. We don't care particularly how you did it. Anything belabored at this point, when both the actor playing
Hamlet and the audience are tired, is very dangerous.

After finishing the reading Gielgud again called for the timing. The third act took forty-two minutes to read.

GIELGUD That makes a total of three hours and a quarter. I
think we'd better have an eight-o'clock curtain so we get
them out on time.

‡   ‡   ‡

Following an hour and a half lunch break, the company
returned to the rehearsal hall to spend the four hours of the

afternoon session blocking* the first three scenes of the play. Gielgud staged the production entirely from his head. He did not use a prompt-script except for an occasional referral to his sparse notes on a few entrance and exit positions. He invented most of the blocking as he went along, and *never* stopped improving on movements.

Gielgud knew every line in the play. He was his own prompter and would correct an actor for the slightest change in the text. He picked up even the misquotes made by the actors in the bit parts. He seemed to be everywhere at once—out front watching from every angle, always on his toes, and always moving about. At the same time that he was watching the play, he was also acting all the parts with the actors, mouthing the lines, reflecting the emotions in his facial expressions, and kinesthetically making all the gestures.

Sometimes he found it most expedient in dictating the moves to dash up on the set and guide the actor bodily where he wanted him to be placed. "Move over there. Cross back. No, no, go right," he would call. Yet one could not tell whether he meant stage right or audience right.† It didn't matter, because before the actor had time to question this, Gielgud was taking him by the shoulders and moving him bodily to where he wanted him. Gielgud did not hesitate to demonstrate while directing, so as not to waste time in needless theorizing. He had the actor stand in front of the set while he himself demonstrated lines in the passage on which he was working. Yet he would let people try any gesture or reading they felt strongly about. But once Sir John decided that something was not right, it was out.

Often, while he directed, he would be holding a glass of milk in his hand, or be popping Life Savers into his mouth. He would frequently squint during his close scrutiny of scenes. He demanded everything from his actors at that first blocking. For

---

* Process of setting the actors' movement patterns.

† In the English theatre stage right means the right side as one looks at the stage from the auditorium. In America, the opposite is the case; a curious example of the differences in stage jargon in the two countries.

most, it was impossible to keep up with all his suggestions and criticisms, no matter how furiously the actor would write notations in his script or how accurately he could memorize the direction. Sir John pushed on rapidly with a minimum of discussion or review, expecting the actor to retain much. He would speak constant encouragement to his actors. "Much better!" "Beautiful!" "I like what you're doing with that speech."

Richard Burton walked through the first blocking rehearsals with the complete Cambridge text in his hand. He made no notes at rehearsals. Obviously, he had noted Gielgud's cuts in his script. As soon as a scene was run a second time, Burton discarded the book at once. Yet he did not duplicate the moves exactly as before; rather he felt his way through the scenes, making changes each time. He engrossed himself completely in some speeches and gave a plain, straightforward reading in others. He turned to Gielgud for help at some points and almost became annoyed with his suggestions at others. Burton would not try to imitate Gielgud's demonstrations and would sometimes go out of his way to be different. The Hamlet he played was his own, and Sir John only made suggestions to Burton and did not demand strict adherence to them. When not on set, Burton buried himself in the text and whispered his lines to himself.

Hume Cronyn constantly amused the company with his characterizations. His work had polish and distinction. He was careful and precise in all that he did. His pencil was poised constantly and he would write furiously immediately after leaving the set, to jot down all that he did or was given to do. Often he would remain an hour or two after rehearsals were over, continuing his notations while walking through the movements.

‡　　‡　　‡

Before starting the actual blocking of the first scene, in which the Ghost appears to Horatio and the soldiers, Sir John had Horatio, Marcellus, Bernardo, and Francisco put on their overcoats to help them to feel the atmosphere of a cold night. He gave Bernardo and Francisco their entrance positions and then let them start their lines. They got as far as the fourth line when Sir John interrupted to demonstrate the exact tempo and vocal contrasts he wanted.

GIELGUD The words of these opening lines must have height to give the sense of the open air. As it must be dark, the words must be pitched very clearly or they will not be heard. (Gielgud repeats the opening lines four times.) Don't set your readings. You've got to listen and refresh your ear each time. Keep the feeling of the cold. You've got to walk about to keep your circulation going. They all know there is something in the woodshed, yet they won't speak of it openly. There is so much they *don't* say in this scene. That's what's interesting—what is understood. People still go about their business, doing what they have to do, but with a terrible shadow hanging over them—like in the war. One does it with a heavy heart and this must be conveyed.

Then Horatio comes in. He's the young philosopher-student without fear, and the old men have gone to him for help. I think that's very moving.

At the entrance of the Ghost Gielgud first had an actor walk across the platform to give the actors in the scene the proper timing for following the moving shaft of light that would be used instead of a "live" Ghost. When the actor walking for the Spirit could not get the right timing for the cross, Gielgud walked it himself. He would occasionally break his ghostly mien to turn to an actor and paraphrase a line or give a description of the surrounding mist.

Gielgud hammered away, building tension in Bernardo's speech preceding the Ghost's first entrance. Three times he demonstrated the lines.

GIELGUD Each phrase must top the preceding one, as in a musical crescendo. "Last night of all,/ When yond same star that's westward from the pole/ Had made his course t'illume that part of heaven/ Where now it burns, Marcellus and myself,/ The bell then beating one—" Each phrase is a little louder and a little more excited and tense. Then at that point we hear the bell. *Dong!* And when you hear that bell you're terrified that the Ghost may come again—and it does. . . .

When the Ghost disappears after his second appearance, the lights begin to change so that Marcellus' speech about "the season wherein our Savior's birth is celebrated" has a kind of benediction. And on Horatio's line, "But look the morn, in russet mantle clad/ Walks o'er the dew of yon high eastern hill," everything must drop away to beauty and relief.

Be careful not to move on that line, Bob Milli [Horatio]. Let's take it again, and Courtiers and Polonius be ready for the next scene because we go right on so that there is no break whatsoever between the scenes.

Seven times Gielgud ran the entrance of the court, each time taking the final lines of the preceding first platform scene so that the entrances of the court nearly overlapped with the exit of Horatio and the soldiers. Gielgud directed the seven Courtiers and the principals to their entrance positions. Prior to the entrance of the King and Queen, he inserted business* of Courtiers greeting each other along with Polonius and Laertes. While the Courtiers were coming on, Gielgud ran about, pushing them into their positions and groupings, demonstrating bows, changing them and readjusting them each time the entrance was repeated.

GIELGUD   I want you all to talk when you're coming on, but I don't want to understand what you say. I want it to be a lively and a decadent court. . . . More voices. It's much too soft. I can't hear a word. Sweep on, look at one another. Talk much louder so that we can have a hush when the King comes. I want this instead of the usual trumpet fanfare. More talking! Louder. Take some lines from any speech in the play. Then if the audience hears any of the words distinctly they will be Shakespearean lines, not modern ones. Polonius must be a busybody in this scene, and then he hushes everyone for

* Any detailed pantomimic action other than movement about the stage.

the King's entrance, and then you all bow. . . . The King's
first speech must be affable for the court. This is the first
Privy Council meeting. You don't want anyone to think
you're not sorry about the old King's death. Then Hamlet,
after the King says "for all, our thanks," you come in. And
everyone be aware of Hamlet's late entrance. Hamlet, you
come down the stairway any way you like and sit at the end
of the council table. So we're all waiting and the King doesn't
know what to do, of course. He can't go on with the Prince
behaving like that—Polonius tries to speak to Hamlet as he
passes him on the way in, but Hamlet ignores him. Then
Eileen [Queen], you go to him and touch him when you say
"Good Hamlet, cast thy nightly color off," but he doesn't
like it and so he gets up and moves away. Then Richard,
when you say "Seems, madam? Nay it is. I know not seems,"
all through that speech there should be regret at having
moved away from her, as if to say "I really love you but I
can't do anything." But show some kind of tenderness. I
would keep moving away from the King, too. You don't like
the King but you don't think he is a murderer. He's only a
bastard who cheated you out of the kingdom, and he sleeps
with your mother, which you hate. But it isn't the same hate
you've got to keep up your sleeve until after the Ghost tells
you he's murdered your father. So we don't want too much
reaction toward the King as yet.

Sir John had been working for an hour and a half on this
court scene. He decided to take a five-minute break before
tackling the exit of the court. After the break he started the
scene over from the beginning. This time Ben Edwards, the
scene designer, pointed out to him that actors would not be
visible at the top of the stairway, which was out of sightlines;
and so some further rearrangement was necessary. At the end
of the scene Gielgud pondered over the exit of the court.

GIELGUD This is where Tony Guthrie is so good at getting
everyone off in one second.

BURTON　John, do you suppose I could start the "too, too solid flesh" before the court leaves?

GIELGUD　No, no. This is the most realistic of the soliloquies and it would seem odd that the Courtiers would fail to hear it if they were there.

BURTON　I would like to be close to the audience for this. (Burton moves downstage and says the soliloquy with great energy and passion.)

GIELGUD　That's fine, but I think it's too active. Keep it sad and simple. Soft. He's down—a very sad boy, but not morose.

Before going on to the last part of the scene between Hamlet, Horatio, and the soldiers, Gielgud dismissed the rest of the company. Most of them stayed on, however, to watch the proceedings.

Gielgud worked through the last section of the scene. He told Horatio, Marcellus, and Bernardo not to wear their coats now. "They've left them in the hall," he said. He concentrated on line interpretations as well as movements. When Burton spoke sharply the line "I prithee do not mock me, fellow student," Gielgud said it should be read warmly. When Burton shouted out "The King, my Father!" Gielgud felt the line should be said with quiet amazement. At the points in the scene where the text indicated that the soldiers speak in unison, Gielgud divided the lines between them to avoid a humorous "Tweedle-dee and Tweedledum" effect. Burton took his closing soliloquy, "My Father's spirit in arms, all is not well," very softly. Gielgud asked for it to be done louder to show a change of mood now that Hamlet had heard of the Ghost. The scene was repeated a second time without interruptions, except for a few minor changes and adjustments in the blocking.

The Laertes farewell scene, in which Polonius gives the famous parting advice to his son, was rehearsed in the same manner: worked through for movements and interpretation slowly, and then repeated with few interruptions. Gielgud gave the following directions during the first working:

GIELGUD   Ophelia [Linda Marsh], be more jaunty and playful in this opening scene. Laertes [John Cullum], be careful of sounding too colloquial. You mustn't ignore the verse. I like the ease, but sustain the poetry. First Laertes gives Ophelia a lecture, and then she lectures him on "Do not, as some ungracious pastors do." And then Pop comes in and gives another one. They're a most terrible family for lecturing one another. Then when Polonius comes in, Laertes should have a little more humorous attitude toward his father. He said goodbye in the hall but here he comes again.

Polonius [Hume Cronyn], can you give us more fluster and busy-ness on your entrance? You're very anxious to get him off.

CRONYN   John, I'm having trouble establishing that Polonius is in a high position as chief of state. I want to retain the dignity and not start being cute too soon.

GIELGUD   Oh yes, I agree. But he is a shrewd man. And shrewd men can sometimes be awfully tricky. And I think he's fond of both children in a very selfish way. But I think the scene is comic in that you are annoyed that Laertes is late and yet you give him a long lecture.

SATURDAY, FEBRUARY 1

10:30 A.M.   Block scenes 4 and 5

2:00 P.M.   Block half of scene 6 (to entrance of Players)

BURTON ARRIVED EARLY to rehearsal, as was his practice. He was accompanied by Bobby, an ex-prizefighter and part of the Burton entourage made up of a chauffeur, a dresser, and two secretaries. He chatted informally with members of the cast while Bobby hung up his coat. Gielgud arrived promptly at 10:30 and began work with the second platform scene in which the Ghost confronts Hamlet.

During rehearsal of this scene Gielgud shouted the offstage effects of the drunken Courtiers loudly and with great spirit at the appropriate cues and walked the part of the Ghost (with a glass of milk in his hand). He also gave these descriptions:

GIELGUD   At the beginning of this scene Horatio is trying to be calm, but I think that underneath he's terrified and anxious. You should play it as if you're on the top of a big wall and looking down into the courtyard—that's where you hear the cannon and the shouting. The offstage rouse is the real world breaking in on something that is very sacred—a supernatural waking, like someone screaming in a very solemn sermon. It disturbs the whole feeling and prepares us for the coming of the Ghost for the third time.

I think the "So oft it chances in particular men" speech comes rapidly and impatiently. He *must* say it—it comes fast and nervously. He is almost talking to himself just in an effort to say something, anything. Keep it simple and not too profound or you give the impression of an older man. It needs a boyish discovery, not a mature thinker. A young man not really quite sure. It must have the doubt of youth. It's all about youth and what becomes of you because of your background.

BURTON   What version of this very celebrated line, "the dram of eale," should I use? The one I rather favor is the incomplete sentence.

GIELGUD   So do I.

BURTON   John, is there some way you can contrive it so that I have my back to the audience when the Ghost appears?

GIELGUD   Why don't you come downstage during the "So oft it chances" speech? Then when you get to the line "That these men, carrying, I say, the stamp of one defect," Hamlet remembers they are listening and turns back to talk to them. Can we have a switch on Marcellus' lantern which he could turn off when he sees the Ghost, so it looks as if the light has been blown out by the Ghost?

BURTON   I'm not sure what to do when I see the Ghost at this point.

GIELGUD   I'm not either. Let's wait. Something will come when we play it.

BURTON   How tall is this Ghost?

GIELGUD   My height. . . . I think you've got to be more hushed and awed when you talk to the Ghost. Save your outbursts for the soliloquy after the next scene when the Ghost is gone.

BURTON   Is the line "I say away" spoken to the Ghost?

GIELGUD   No, it's to them. . . . Now let's play this Ghost tape. I've left spaces for your lines. Let's see how it works.

For the production, a tape recording of Gielgud's voice was to be used for the Ghost. Sir John had recorded the Ghost's awesome lines in a studio the day before. Everyone waited while stage manager Harry Young set up the rehearsal print of the tape on the recording machine. When the tape was ready to roll, Burton started with his lines to the Ghost: "Whither wilt thou lead me? Speak, I'll go no further." "Cock-a-doodle-doo!" crowed the tape recorder, and everyone collapsed into gales of laughter. Harry Young then backed up the tape to the right cue; the pauses left between the Ghost's lines for Hamlet's lines did not time out to Burton's readings. Notes were made on this and the tape was sent out for re-editing.

The scene in which Polonius instructs his servant Reynaldo to keep an eye an Laertes was blocked roughly with the understudy standing in for Reynaldo.

GIELGUD   The set is too big for this scene; it dissipates the intimacy. Let's go on with Ophelia's entrance. Linda, come down the stairs and give a little cry to get your father's attention. She really doesn't want to tell him what happened.

Gielgud worked with Ophelia on the correct phrasing of her opening speech in this scene. There was some discussion on Polonius' line, "Mad for thy love!" Gielgud felt it should be a statement, though Cronyn preferred to keep it a question so that his later line, "That hath made him mad," could be delivered as a concluding statement. At the end of Ophelia's closet speech, Cronyn started angrily for the exit as if to go tell the King what had happened; then he turned back to say to Ophelia, "Come, go with me, I will go see the King." Gielgud modified this action to have Polonius start for the stairway from which Ophelia had just entered, as if going off after *Hamlet*, and then, changing his mind, turned back to go to the King.

After Polonius' question, "Have you given him any hard words of late?" Linda Marsh gave an angry reading of her reply, "No, my good lord."

GIELGUD   No, no, dear. You mustn't be spiteful. She's sadly reproachful. Of course, she didn't like what he made her do, but she's too good a daughter to disobey. Do you agree? Well, try it. . . . I want to have Polonius lead the exit. In each scene we'll have Ophelia left alone at the end. They don't need her, and here she is walking about and nobody cares.

For the first time in rehearsals Gielgud consulted his prompt-script to check where to have Ophelia and Polonius exit. He then reran the previous scene.

In the afternoon Gielgud began staging the play's sixth and longest scene (II, ii) which begins with the entrance of Rosencrantz and Guildenstern, who are brought by the King and Queen to spy on Hamlet; the scene continues for some six hundred lines to Hamlet's self-deprecation soliloquy, "O what a rogue and peasant slave am I."

Gielgud spent the first half hour working on the entrance of Rosencrantz and Guildenstern and of the King and Queen. He finally settled on his fifth arrangement of positions. After the exit of Rosencrantz and Guildenstern, Drake asked Gielgud to put in a "lecherous thing" between the King and Queen, in the moment they are alone just before the entrance of the ambassadors. Gielgud complied and added the business of having Polonius catch them in their intimacies.

Burton suggested that he take an early entrance cue on this scene to overhear the Polonius plot to "loose my daughter to him." Gielgud agreed to try it, though in his own book of notes on the play, written in 1937 while he was performing the title role, he wrote:

> Dr. Dover Wilson has evolved a clever theory that Hamlet's entrance should take place some lines earlier than when the Queen's "but look where sadly the poor wretch comes reading" heralds his appearance. Both in my own production and in Mr. McClintic's I have tried different cues for the entrance in the hope that Hamlet's overhearing the last lines of Polonius to the King and Queen would make clearer the lines in his scene with Polonius, as well as his subsequent treatment of Ophelia in the nunnery scene.
>
> One or two people have noticed this treatment, but on the whole I do not think it clarified the meaning sufficiently to warrant the trouble we took with it at rehearsals. I was also afraid that the audience might mistake my meaning or wonder what was happening (whether one had made a mistake and come on too early) and, while they were speculating, thus miss what followed. I was constantly struck with the feeling when playing this scene that if Shakespeare had meant Hamlet to overhear something, he would surely have made it clear in the text. The play has much spying in it, and two or three of the most vital moments in subsequent scenes are built around this device, but in each case it is Hamlet who is spied upon. I think it unlikely that Shakespeare would weaken this characteristic feature of his play by making Hamlet spy on, or overhear, any other character before the more important point in his enemies' spying on him had been definitely registered with the audience. (John Gielgud, "The Hamlet Tradition," from Rosamond Gilder, *John Gielgud's Hamlet*, New York, 1937, pp. 51-52.)

In the scene between Polonius and Hamlet, Burton suggested that Hamlet and Polonius walk in step during the first few lines. The business of Hamlet ripping a page out of his book and handing it to Polonius was suggested by Gielgud. Gielgud suggested that the line "into my grave" be read sadly as a preparation for the "To be or not to be" soliloquy.

This much of the scene was then reviewed. When Cronyn got to the letter scene, he had great difficulty remembering the blocking as modified for the latest restaging. "I wish that someone would remind us," he yelled angrily. From that time on assistant stage manager Nat White kept his pencil and eraser busy recording all blocking and modifications.

It was during this repeat that Gielgud demonstrated the anticipated entrance to Burton. He came on to overhear Polonius say "I'll loose my daughter," smiled knowingly, and leaned on the railing of the stairway to strike a listening attitude. When the Queen saw him on her line, "But look where sadly the poor wretch comes reading," he quickly hid his face in his book and continued walking down the stairway.

Proceeding to the section of the scene between Hamlet and Rosencrantz and Guildenstern, Gielgud made these comments:

GIELGUD Hamlet hasn't seen them for years, so it takes him a moment to recognize them. He is very surprised to see them and is friendly toward them until the point that he catches them conferring behind his back. I think the reading should be "*Many* confines, wards and dungeons," Richard. (Burton goes back and says the line the same way without emphasizing "many.") No! no! Richard, "*Many* confines, wards and dungeons."

BURTON (Half joking, half in earnest, he snaps.) Don't you *dare* give me a line reading. (He goes back and then reads it using Gielgud's emphasis.)

GIELGUD You mustn't be too sharp with Rosencrantz and Guildenstern in their first scene or else the recorder scene will be anticipated. When Hamlet says "What a piece of work is a man," *they* are the men he is referring to, and he plays it to them as an expression of what he wants them to represent. Otherwise, they just stand there with nothing to do and look like supers. Then Hamlet gets angry when they laugh at the end on "Man delights not me." Rosencrantz quickly changes the subject and thinks of the Players. He gets this idea suddenly. Then the whole tone of the scene changes. Everyone is relieved and happy. The Players are coming. We'll have Polonius come in and read the "comical pastoral" list from a playbill.

The scene was reviewed from the Hamlet-Polonius scene up to the entrance of the Players. It was 4:30 and the company was dismissed. After the rehearsal Gielgud chatted informally with the actors playing Rosencrantz and Guildenstern:

GIELGUD How curious that Shakespeare always uses three young men; in *Romeo and Juliet* there are Romeo, Mercutio, and Benvolio; and in *The Merchant of Venice* it's Lorenzo, Bassanio, and Gratiano. But each must be an individual with a separate identity and personality. Unfortunately, Rosencrantz and Guildenstern have become a twin-brother act over the years. But let's make Rosencrantz attempt to be terribly subtle and intelligent like Claudius, and Guildenstern can be more like the Queen—not too bright, lazy, yet kindly.

During the above discussion Burton had a tray of Scotch and sodas brought in for the group.

SUNDAY, FEBRUARY 2

10:30 A.M. Review of scenes 1-6

4:30 P.M. Block second half of scene 6 and scene 7

THE MORNING REHEARSAL began with a review of scenes already blocked. Gielgud kept a small white note pad in front of him, his glasses down on his nose, peering over them at the scene. For these scenes most of the actors did not have the script. Gielgud prompted them when necessary. A rehearsal tape of sound effects was used. Gielgud made some comments after the first scene:

GIELGUD That looks very promising. Horatio, when you see the Ghost, you must be galvanized. *Your* reaction is the most important, because the others have seen it before. I'd like to feel all of your backs go up like cats when the Ghost first appears behind you. It must be chilling. You feel something unnatural and your hair bristles and you break into a cold sweat. Feel the thing's breath sere your stomachs. Your voices came in too soon after the cock crew. Suddenly the real world comes in, and you need a pause, and then your voices change. It's such a marvelous thing. The old boy really knew what he was doing. Horatio, can you work it so that you have your back to the audience just before you say "But look, the morn in russet mantle clad"? That way you can feel the warmth of the sun, as it rises, on the back of your neck, and then you turn and open out on the line, giving it great beauty and solemnity.

Many adjustments were made in the court scene. The entrance was repeated over and over and new positions were given to everyone in the scene. Polonius was placed closer to the Queen, Gielgud describing them as "great cronies who probably play bridge together on Saturday."

Hamlet's "too, too solid flesh" soliloquy was put aside for the time. In the Laertes farewell scene Gielgud added an overcoat for Laertes which Polonius helped him get into while hustling him off.

During the second platform scene Sir John rehearsed the offstage rouses with five of the Courtiers.

GIELGUD On the last rouse I want it to sound as if they're breaking up the party. We'll have you all call back as you go off to your dressing rooms. Then perhaps one lonesome drunken laugh can trail off in the distance.

The Ghost scene was put aside too, for scenes 3 and 4 to be reblocked before breaking for lunch.

During the afternoon session Gielgud decided the business of Polonius catching the King and Queen embracing was too comic for the scene and cut it. After working through the scene between Hamlet, Rosencrantz, and Guildenstern and the entrance of the Players (sketched through in Voscovec's absence), Gielgud worked with Burton on the "rogue and peasant slave" soliloquy.

GIELGUD What do you think, Richard, if the Players left a prop-sword onstage which you could plunge into some sort of prop-throne on "O vengeance!"

BURTON I wouldn't like to rely on a prop, John, in case I change my mind in performance.

GIELGUD Well, we don't really need to have an actual sword, then.

BURTON Do you think I'm too far from the audience? I'd like to speak it to them.

GIELGUD It's such a phony Shakespearean technique to come out on the apron in a proscenium theatre. It seems to me it's more realistic to keep it within the scene. . . . At the end of the soliloquy I want you to see the King offstage coming on just before you say "The play's the thing." And you point to him when you see him coming, and that's why you exit. There's only one more scene in the act, and I want to try to prevent applause here so that it doesn't come until the end of the act. Then, Alfred, you come right in before Richard leaves.

DRAKE I don't want to enter on Richard's line.

GIELGUD Well, hold, then, until just after he's finished.

At 5:00 work began on the nunnery scene, in which Hamlet breaks with Ophelia.

GIELGUD Before Hamlet comes on, I think the Queen should kiss Ophelia on the cheek, and then we can somehow do the reverse of that in the mad scene. Let's have Ophelia do a full curtsy to the floor to the Queen.

Burton began the "To be or not to be" soliloquy upstage on the platform.

GIELGUD Do you think you're too far away?

BURTON Well, you know me, John. I'd be out in the audience if you'd let me do it.

GIELGUD (Walking through the moves.) Begin the speech as you're coming on and then try coming down the steps at the beginning. Then you can go back up to the platform on "thus conscience doth make cowards of us all," and get settled at the end of the speech.

BURTON (He goes through the speech entirely, whispering it, feeling out the movement.) Do you want me to say "Nymph in thy orisons" directly to Ophelia, John, or to myself?

GIELGUD She's supposed to be kneeling at a *prie-dieu* (he pronounces it with over-elaborate French through pursed lips) but we haven't got a *prie-dieu*, so I don't know what we can do.

BURTON Can she have a prayer book?

GIELGUD Yes. Let's have her go off during "To be or not to be." Then she can come back on from the right at the end of the soliloquy so Hamlet won't see Polonius and the King hiding on the left just yet. I think she comes right back to Hamlet and tries to kiss him. Then before Ophelia speaks, Hamlet should look around and check to see that they are alone.

BURTON Do you think, John, I could take her prayer book from her when she approaches me, and put it down?

GIELGUD   Very good. Very nice. I like that very much. Very good. You could even hold the book for a few lines before you put it down. Then Ophelia, you put your arms on his shoulder just before you return the bracelet on "I pray you now receive them." . . . You'll have to say it louder, dear. Then after you give back the bracelet and say "there my Lord," you've done your job and you turn away to go. Now if you want, Richard, you can see Polonius and the King at this point. When I played it, I knew they were spying from the beginning of the scene.

BURTON   Well, I think it's more interesting if Hamlet discovers it now.

GIELGUD   Yes, I quite agree. And Ophelia sees that he has seen them and she's in a terrible state. Then, Richard, when you say "Now the time gives it proof," you take her very forcefully by the arm so that she gives a squeal. . . . Make it a loud cry, dear. . . . No, no, much louder—a yell. That can make "I did love you once" very moving because she's been hurt. Now, Linda, sink to your knees on "I was the more deceived." . . . Good. Now let's go on with "Get thee to a nunnery."

BURTON   Did you know that nunnery meant whorehouse? I didn't. Played for years and I never knew.

GIELGUD   I was brought up in one, so I knew. (There is general laughter.) I think before you say "Where's your father?" you take a pause as if you think "Dare I ask her," because you're giving her the most terrible test. You almost don't say it to her. (Burton does the line flippantly and takes the following line, "Let the doors be shut on him," vehemently.) I think it's much more chilling, Richard, if you say "Where's your father?" straight out, deliberately and forcefully. But take it slowly so that we get all the irony and bitterness. Then when Ophelia gives him the lie, he says to himself "That's done it." Try to leave without saying anything at all and then suddenly say the line "Let the doors be shut on him" back to Ophelia quickly and quietly.

In the last section of the scene between Polonius and the King, Cronyn suggested that he have Ophelia on his arm and pay little attention to her. Gielgud wanted her left lying on the steps where Hamlet left her; Polonius, seeing her, speaks off-handedly to her and goes on his way, leaving Ophelia behind to drag herself up the steps as the curtain falls.

With the conclusion of this rehearsal Gielgud had blocked the entire first act (roughly half the play) in four days.

MONDAY, FEBRUARY 3

10:30 A.M.   Block scene 8 (play within-the-play scene)

2:00 P.M.   Block scenes 9-13

GIELGUD SPENT THE entire two-hour morning session working on the play-within-the-play scene. Gielgud asked if anyone minded if he cut the dumb show, that it would hold up the play and that he saw no purpose in doing it. Alfred Drake asked that it be left in, feeling that it was very important for the King's build-up to "Give me some light. Away." The growing anxiety could come more gradually as Claudius realized that words were about to be set to the play. And so it was left in.

In the recorder scene, in which Hamlet attempts to force Guildenstern to play a recorder, Gielgud worked toward a lightness and ease; Burton tended to play the scene with a lot of shouting. Gielgud wanted the scene ironic and bitter, yet mocking.

In the afternoon, work resumed with the King's prayer scene.

Burton asked if he might use a dagger, but Gielgud pointed out that the line "Up, sword, and know thou a more horrid hent" called for a sword. Gielgud then hit on the idea of Hamlet picking up the sword which the King put down just before praying, using it in the scene and also in the following closet scene to kill Polonius. Drake asked for a stool to kneel on while praying, though Gielgud preferred to use a bare stage.

During the closet scene, in which Hamlet inveighs Queen Gertrude and slays Polonius, Gielgud worked toward getting the Queen to start in a low key; Miss Herlie tended to play the opening hysterically. A clothes rack was brought in to represent the arras behind which Polonius would hide. Cronyn suggested falling out from behind the arras when he was killed. After some discussion it was decided that Hamlet and the Queen would not actually wear the portrait miniatures of Hamlet's father and his uncle, but rather pantomime the business with them. At the end of the scene, when Claudius entered, Gielgud told Gertrude to "sit apathetic, like a dead duck, failing the King when he needs her and is full of plans." The scene was run three times.

Burton gave an introspective and reflective reading to the "How all occasions do inform against me" soliloquy, which Hamlet gives after seeing Fortinbras' troops pass.

BURTON   Should I sit for this one, John? I've stood for all the others.

GIELGUD   I don't think you should. It's a war. I thought we'd use the marching. It's a big climax to the act. It must be a very determined speech—getting more and more convincing. He decides. (The scene was repeated.) Well, I'm exhausted, I don't know about everyone else. I think we should stop today. It's been a long day. Let's can it for today and run Act Two tomorrow morning.

BURTON   Can we come early and work on the Ghost scene?

GIELGUD   Sure. But that's all for now. We've got on awfully well.

Exhausted or not, late that night there was some commotion for the company back at the King Edward-Sheraton Hotel as a drunk tried to force his way into Burton's suite. Bobby, the bodyguard, came out and asked the intruder to leave. When he refused, a resounding thud brought members of the cast in neighboring rooms out into the hall. There they found the drunk flattened on the floor with Bobby pacing nervously around him. Everyone looked to Bobby for an explanation but all he said was "Fainted!"

TUESDAY, FEBRUARY 4

10:30 A.M.   Review scenes 8-13 (Act II)

2:30 P.M.   Review scenes 1-7 (Act I)

BURTON ARRIVED HALF an hour early to work with the Ghost tape.

At 10:30 the review of Act Two began. Gielgud demonstrated the exaggerated style he wanted the actors to use in the play-within-the-play scene. He then described the Queen's reaction to the play.

GIELGUD   Even the Queen, dumb as she is, must see some parallel between the play and her remarriage. I think she looks at her son as if the play is in the worst of taste.

In the King's prayer scene, to prevent a comic effect of Polonius being startled by the King's sword, Cronyn was cautioned to keep a good distance from the King.

Gielgud made the following notes on the closet scene:

GIELGUD   Keep Hamlet more ironic at the beginning of the scene. Maintain suspense but don't shout. He has a purpose, a strong attitude. We see two people close together for the

first time. At the beginning they are taking each other's meas-
ure. You're both rushing this too much. Let's have a great
feeling of tension at the beginning. It's the night, don't forget. We've had a great shemozel after the dazzling play scene
with all the hubbub. Then there are two scenes which are
two huge, haunted shadows. And then the dramatic closet
scene. . . .

Hume, I don't think you really ought to say "*Oh*, I am
slain." Just give a cry. And be sure there's no pause before
or after the cry, or the audience will laugh.

Richard, don't be tempted to shout too much. It's a long
scene. Find the climaxes, but change the key a lot. It needs
variety, more color. Then after Hamlet drags Polonius out,
the scenes must go fast. There is a great rush to find Hamlet
and the body and to ship Hamlet off.

In the politic worms scene, in which the King captures Hamlet and sends him off to England, Gielgud suggested that Hamlet run up and kiss the King on the cheek just before saying
"Farewell, dear Mother." (This became one of Burton's favorite
bits of business.)

The afternoon review of Act One ran smoother, with a minimum of interruptions and changes.

WEDNESDAY, FEBRUARY 5

10:30 A.M. Block scene 14, second half of scene
15, second half of scene 16.

2:30 P.M. Rehearse entrance of players scene (6)
and play within-the-play scene (8)

GIELGUD DID NOT set any specific blocking in his first working of Ophelia's mad scene, but rather let the actress feel her

way through it, trying various movements and business. He blocked the last half of the graveyard scene and roughly blocked the final scene. Gielgud discussed with Burton the possibilities for Hamlet's death. In his own performance Gielgud fell into Horatio's arms. He suggested using the Forbes-Robertson staging of dying, in which Hamlet sits on the throne, with the possible variation of getting up at the last minute and finally falling to the ground.

Burton appeared at the afternoon rehearsal wearing a black V-neck sweater. Gielgud liked it and told him to wear it for the performance. A tailor took Burton's measurements and made five duplicates of the sweater.

In the scene in which the Players enter Gielgud told Cronyn to *whisper* his line "This is too long" which interrupts the First Player's long Hecuba speech.

GIELGUD Whisper it to Hamlet, like those awful people who whisper in theatres. I think the line "He's for a jig, or a tale of bawdry, or he sleeps" will be funnier, Richard, if those are separate thoughts. "He's for a jig. Or a tale of bawdry. Or he sleeps."

Elaborate business was given to the Players at the beginning of the play scene. As the scene started, they were discovered setting up scenery, putting on make-up, lighting lanterns, and getting into their costumes. Then Hamlet came on with the First Player, at the same time giving him the advice to the players, and the others stopped what they were doing to listen. After working through the scene twice, Gielgud stopped for the afternoon.

GIELGUD We're awfully well advanced. We've almost got the whole play except for the Gravedigger scene. I don't want to tire any of you with great run-throughs. I'm planning to have the theatre on Sunday. We'll run the whole play then. That will be for continuity, so we get used to entrances and exits and the pace. So we'll begin doing solo scenes tomorrow. Third act in the morning. In the afternoon we'll do the

closet scene and the nunnery scene with only the people involved. Will the others please not come so that the principals
can work alone? Let's do Laertes' farewell scene too. Then
on Friday let's do the Players' entrance scene. Would you
like Friday afternoon off, Richard?

BURTON   No! I feel nervous if I'm away.

GIELGUD   Then we'll do the platform scenes and the prayer
scene in the afternoon. That's all for now. Thank you everyone.

CHAPTER 11

The Second Week of Rehearsals

THURSDAY, FEBRUARY 6

10:30 A.M.   Scene 14.

2:30 P.M.   Scenes 3, 7, 10

WITH THE SHOW completely blocked except for one scene, Sir John began detailed work-throughs of special scenes. The first half of the morning session was spent on Ophelia's mad scene. Sir John decided that an entrance on the platform would be stronger for her, as she could have a more sudden appearance from there than by coming up the ramp formerly used for her entrance. He also decided to discover the Queen onstage at the beginning of the scene and eliminate her long entrance down the grand stairway.

Gielgud tried a new approach for Ophelia in this scene. He now felt that there should be some sudden outbursts and a quality of strangeness. "Not too elegant or balletic," were his instructions to Linda Marsh. "She should be somewhat awkward and odd." He still allowed the actress to find her own business and actions. Rather than plot her movements, he gave her freedom to wander through the scene and do as she felt. When she struck an attitude or position that he liked, he told

her to keep it and would throw in suggestions as they seemed
to fit her own tendencies.

GIELGUD   When you sit there, can you cry as a child who has
just had a doll taken from her? Very good. Excellent.

The rest of the morning was spent on the remainder of the
act up to the graveyard scene. Crosses and positions were juggled a great deal and assistant stage manager Nat White wore
down three erasers keeping track of all the changes.

After rehearsal Gielgud remained for half an hour listening
to the Ghost tape played on the new multichannel speaker sys-
tem. He experimented with shifting directions of the sound so
that it seemed to rotate all about the set and to give a sense of
omnipresence.

The afternoon rehearsal was a private session which company members were asked not to attend. Only Hamlet, Ophelia,
Gertrude, Polonius, and Laertes were present. The closet scene
was worked on first. Gielgud asked Cronyn to build more initial
tension at the beginning of the scene by adding the element
that Hamlet might come in at any moment. He then got the
idea of having Polonius peek through the curtain on his line
"Pray you be round to him" for a deliberate comic effect in
contrast to the weighty scene about to follow.

He worked especially for an innocent reaction from the Queen
on her line "As kill a King?"—to show that Gertrude had nothing to do with the murder of Hamlet's father. He asked for a
slower, more pointed, and astonished reading of the line, which
would also provide a contrast to Hamlet's agitation.

GIELGUD   Richard, you've got to keep more agitation and movement in the scene immediately after you kill Polonius. Follow
through. It takes a while for Hamlet to settle down. When
you say "What judgment would step from this to this?" be
sure you inflect the first "this" favorably to indicate your
father and color the final "this" repulsively to indicate Claudius. I think you ought to whisper the line "O Shame, where
is thy blush?" and take the following lines in a hushed quality
to give a variety of color.

Eileen, when you say "Oh Hamlet, speak no more," use more self-reproach. The Queen suddenly begins to realize she's been a bad woman. Richard, I think you ought to see the Ghost out toward the audience; it will give a better picture. I just had an idea. Suppose while the Ghost is talking to you, you were to pick up the sword you dropped when you killed Polonius, as a sort of reminder of what you must do. Could you try that and let me see it? (Burton does this.) No, no, it doesn't work. Forget it, the idea was silly. This scene is coming very well. It's still a bit jerky and some of the pauses are too Chekovian—but it will gain the proper pace as we work on it.

The nunnery scene was next.

GIELGUD   I think Hamlet should be soft and truthful the first time he says "Get thee to a nunnery," so in that whole speech we get a recollection of Hamlet and Ophelia as they were before—both very much in love, though she more than he. Richard, you tend to be terribly violent there, and I think it should have a softness for contrast to the outburst which should come after Ophelia gives Hamlet the deliberate lie on "Where's your father?" "At home my lord." At this point Hamlet completely loses his head and goes into a near state of madness which is no longer assumed. He's out of control here, not merely playing for the King and Polonius.

Gielgud gave Hamlet a long exit up the grand stairway so that Ophelia could begin her "O, what a noble mind" speech before he was out of sight, thereby killing any applause which might interrupt the scene before its conclusion. He worked with the actress on this speech, demonstrating how the first half of the speech must have a "major-key quality taken all in one breath, with the images suspended and built on top of one another; then shift into a minor key on the second sentence, speaking slower and with downward inflections."

The afternoon concluded with the Laertes farewell scene. It was run only once, mainly for review. Gielgud suggested that

Ophelia place a flower in Laertes' buttonhole before he left, in order to identify her with flowers. Miss Marsh added that perhaps this action could then be repeated later in the mad scene.

FRIDAY, FEBRUARY 7

10:30 A.M.   Review play scene (8)
              Block first half of scene 15

2:30 P.M.   Scenes 9, 6, and 2

THE PLAYERS WERE called for the morning session and George Voskovec, the Player King, worked with Gielgud to find movement for the speech about Priam's slaughter. Gielgud asked that the action of the dumb show be somewhat puzzling to the watching Courtiers, thus saving the revelation for the play-with-words afterward. "It should have the stylized movements of the Chinese theatre." Sir John looked extremely comical as he demonstrated the type of exaggerated movements he wanted. It was something like a Mary Pickford silent film, and he left the Players howling with laughter. Gielgud suggested that the Player King and Player Queen go off by themselves and see what they could come up with.

With the arrival of George Rose (First Gravedigger) work began on the graveyard scene. Gielgud explained to Rose how he proposed setting the scene, using an upturned table to represent the grave. Gielgud suggested that the two Gravediggers have lunch on the steps during their first speeches. Apples, chicken, and bananas were eliminated in favor of bread and cheese for lunch.

GIELGUD   What if, when you get into the grave, you polished one of those skulls that you pick up?

ROSE Well, John, I don't think he'd be so careful with them, but rather more casual, and would probably throw them down without a second thought.

GIELGUD Ah, yes.

As Hamlet and Horatio entered the scene, Gielgud first kept them some distance from the grave. As the scene is traditionally staged, the Gravedigger does not see Hamlet until the Prince says to him, "Whose grave's this, sirrah?" Gielgud directed Hamlet to cross to him before this on "the hand of little employment hath the daintier sense." In this way the Gravedigger performed the second verse of his song directly to Hamlet and then enjoyed Hamlet's wry comments about the characters who might have possessed the skulls.

BURTON This is a great help, John. It's usually so awkward for me to wait while he sings, and for him to wait while I speak, when we are not supposed to hear each other.

GIELGUD Yes. It gives a nice intimacy to Hamlet's conversation with him, because they can already be making friends before they begin talking with one another properly. (At George Rose's request this much of the scene was repeated.) This is beautiful! Here we have the old man talking to the young with the dead in between—which so relates them both. It gives a sort of Ages of Man effect. (Gielgud then moved on to the Yorick section.) I've often wondered how this Gravedigger knows it's Yorick's skull, and if he does, why he digs it up in the first place. But anyhow, do you suppose we could assume that he and Yorick were very great friends? They are about the same age.

Gielgud made some comments on Burton's reading of the Yorick speech:

GIELGUD It's very nice, Richard, but I don't get the feeling of the little boy riding on the back of the jester. It must have the reminiscent quality one feels as he looks back on his childhood. I think it's just a question of the picture in your mind.

Then in the last part of the speech when you say "Now get you to my lady's chamber," you can be sharper and recall the "frailty, thy name is woman" and the "I have heard of your paintings" lines. I think this is a sudden change and should be against womankind as a sex, showing their fickleness, not just against Hamlet's mother personally.

The King's prayer scene was first on the afternoon agenda, but Burton arrived early, and finding Rosencrantz and Guildenstern also ahead of schedule, Burton ran his first scene with them. As soon as Sir John arrived, he watched them play the scene. He made only one interruption. At the line "those who would make mows at him," he apologized for stopping the scene and turned to Alfred Drake:

GIELGUD Something just occurred to me, Alfred. Hamlet indicates in this line that Rosencrantz and Guildenstern didn't like Claudius before he was King and I think *he* probably hated *them*. So he might be rather delighted when he gets the news of their death later in the play. And this shows how phony and shallow everyone is in the play—just fawning and toadying to the King, turning with the tide. And it makes you a subtle villain by appearing so kind to Rosencrantz and Guildenstern at first.

During the King's prayer scene, Gielgud suggested some new crosses for Claudius. Burton stopped after his entrance on the upstage platform.

BURTON John, couldn't we put a step here on the edge of the platform? It's so awkward climbing off this high level.

GIELGUD Yes, but it looks awfully good that way. It's very suspenseful—like a burglar climbing in at a window.

The afternoon ended with intensive work on the first court scene. Gielgud concentrated on the Courtiers, carefully and specifically setting their movements and reactions.

GIELGUD Gianini, turn to Harz after the King's line and say "You're looking very well this season." Sterne, bow to the

Queen when she passes you and offer her your place. These actions must all be done wholeheartedly. Don't sneak through them as if you were apologizing to the principals for distracting from them. Then that's what it looks like. But take your moment, play it fully, and then throw the action back on the scene. In this way you supplement the main action. What we don't want is the usual Shakespearean arrangement of the principals declaiming while everybody else stands about as scenery—dumb. I know it's difficult playing these Courtiers, but you will find it much less tedious if you will invent complete characters for yourselves—which are as important to the scene as the principals. You do so much with improvisation and method in America, here is the time to use it. Be real in your reactions. If you dislike another actor onstage, let it show. Perhaps you smirk at him or show you are jealous of him. If we can only make the crowds alive, it would be a great feather in my cap and not a bad one in yours.

SATURDAY, FEBRUARY 8

10:30 A.M.   Run scenes 1-13 (Acts I and II)

No afternoon rehearsal

REHEARSAL BEGAN PROMPTLY with the full company called. It was announced that the entire play would be run for continuity and review of movement. Gielgud promised the company he would not interrupt, and except for two or three prompts, he kept his word. The first act ran one hour and twenty-five minutes. "Jolly good," said Sir John, "it could even run ten minutes longer."

After a ten-minute break, Act Two began. It ran forty-eight minutes. The run-through was unusually smooth. Only one part of the second act was uncertain—the fragmentary scenes after the closet scene, which had been rehearsed only once. The stage manager quickly ironed out the difficulties and no time was lost. All actors were off book and little prompting was needed.

Gielgud kept a note pad on his table through the entire run; by the end this was all he had written:

> *Hamlet—Sit King's chair aft 1st soliloquy*
>
> *"But what in faith make you at Wittenberg"—left this out*
>
> *"In the secret parts of fortune"*
>
> *Pronunc.—"Plautus"*
>
> *Hume—Shiver coming in from outside*

During the run Sir John was entirely caught up with the performance. He leaned forward in the tense moments, reflected the expressions of the actors in his own countenance, and silently lipped the speeches along with the actors. If one looked very closely he could see Gielgud secretly wipe a tear away after Hamlet had spoken with the Ghost.

Sir John was more than pleased. He thanked and congratulated everybody. Rather than run the third act, he gave the company a much appreciated afternoon off.

It was also on this day that headlines began hitting the Toronto papers about some U.S. Congressman who was seeking legislation to keep Richard Burton out of the United States. Rumors began buzzing around the company. "The show is going to close in Toronto." "The show is being sent to London." "Burton is being replaced." Burton couldn't have been less concerned. He jokingly said to Gielgud before the next rehearsal, "You'd better start learning the lines, John."

SUNDAY, FEBRUARY 9

11:00 A.M.   Scenes 1 and 2 onstage

2:30 P.M.   Scenes 3, 4, and 5

WHILE *Hamlet* WAS REHEARSING in the basement of the O'Keefe Centre, Sid Caesar and Company were performing *Little Me* on the stage. Because the musical had no Sunday performance, Burton and company moved all their rehearsal props and equipment up on the stage to try the play in the enormous theatre. The platforms were hauled up from downstairs and placed in front of the *Little Me* set.

With this first onstage session, Gielgud began looking at the show with a fresh eye and hearing it with a new ear. It was announced originally that the entire play would be run, starting at 11:00 A.M. By 6:00 P.M. less than three quarters of the first act had been rehearsed. One hour and fifteen minutes were spent on the first scene alone, the opening twenty lines of which Gielgud repeated not less than eight times.

GIELGUD   You've got to throw your voices more, as one does on a cold, windy night in an open space. It must have more toughness, wildness—fury and frostlike speaking on the deck of a battleship. And still be conscious of variety. Don't all shout with the same tone and pick up each other's pitch. Each line must have its own little tune. Then they are all woven together.

Over and over he demonstrated the line readings as he walked about the huge auditorium, calling them out from every corner. He also cautioned the actors to make the exposition clear:

GIELGUD   Emphasize the names Horatio and Marcellus when you first speak them. They are two new characters to the audience. We know the play backwards and forwards, but we mustn't assume they do.

To everyone's surprise, the first court scene went smoothly and a minimum of regrouping was necessary. At 1:00 the rehearsal broke for lunch. The afternoon rehearsal began with the third scene, Laertes' farewell:

GIELGUD　Laertes, you mustn't put false stops in your long speech. It makes the audience think you've come to the end of it, and then when you go on, it seems long and labored. Overlap your ideas so that they carry through. Suspend the end of lines to telegraph that there is more to come. It has to be brash and have all the confidence of youth—like undergraduates telling each other how to live life. Be confident that the words will carry you. Don't try to naturalize them; use them. If Shakespeare had wanted it in everyday speech he would have written it that way. But it's poetry and you must speak it as such. Both you and Ophelia must make the scene lighter and more vibrant. Show us a young brother and sister who have the whole world before them.

Gielgud eliminated his previously staged business of having two servants run through the scene with Laertes' trunk just before Polonius said "Your servants tend." Upon seeing this onstage he decided it was too elaborate and distracting. He eliminated also the formerly inserted business of having Ophelia sewing during the scene—he thought it was lost on stage.

Gielgud spent over an hour on this scene. He reworked all the entrances and exits, changing patterns for crossing the stage, and then changing them back. In general he found that crosses had to be made farther so that more space could be utilized in the huge theatre. Too, distance between players had to be expanded to accommodate the wide sightlines of the auditorium.

Work progressed to the second platform scene, during which the following conversation occurred:

BURTON　John, this scene is so long. Do you think we could cut the "So oft it chances in particular men" speech?

GIELGUD   Yes, I think you're right. I hate to see it go and I know you do. You can get away with it at the Old Vic with all the students and scholars in the audience, but I think it's too much for the general public. I'm going to cut twenty lines from my Ghost speech, too. I think it's too long to hold with just a recording.

When Burton first saw the Ghost, he shouted out on the lines "O, answer me!" and "What should we do?"

GIELGUD   It's best to keep a hushed voice through all this. You can get just as much effect. Save your loud moments for the play scene and for leaping into the grave. That was the marvelous thing about Paul Scofield's Lear. Peter Brook kept him so in range that he never appeared to be working hard. But when you go too loud and fast, you tend to let your emotion carry you through a speech and I don't believe you think of all the phrases.

Burton repeated the scene following Gielgud's suggestions.

GIELGUD   Beautiful! Don't you find that's better?

BURTON   Oh, yes. Much easier, too.

The scene between Hamlet and the Ghost was put off until the shortened version of the Ghost tape could be prepared. Gielgud went on working with the section of the scene immediately following the Ghost's exit—in which Hamlet swears Horatio and Marcellus to secrecy.

GIELGUD   Be sure you don't anticipate the Ghost below. Let it come as a surprise. When you first ask them to swear, hold the sword up higher so that you can have a bigger reaction to the Ghost below. Remember that the Ghost is in hell, and you must mix pity and sorrow for him with the comic and weird effect of his burrowing through the earth. After you say you are going to "put an antic disposition on," wait for a beat to see if they understand what you mean, and then demonstrate it for them. Do the next few lines in a comic way, and just as you almost get carried away with the anticipation, come back earnestly when you ask them to swear.

After "Rest, rest, perturbed spirit," Hamlet is tired. Start putting your cloak on, but then let it droop to the ground. Then walk upstage and isolate yourself for "The time is out of joint," so that we see Hamlet very lonely, forgetting for a moment that Horatio and Marcellus are still behind. Then turn back to them on "Nay, come. Let's go together."

The remainder of the afternoon was spent working on Ophelia's scene with Polonius after Hamlet has frightened her. Linda Marsh was asked to repeat her entrance several times.

GIELGUD Make it frantic, more out of breath. You can begin preparing for the mad scene here. You speak it well, but she's got to be hysterical—much more turbulent and sensational. Act it all out as if you were describing a terrible accident you'd just seen in the street. Make it more startling. It must have all the fervor of life. You should almost trip on your skirt, you come in so fast. Now it's too pretty and controlled. Ophelia wouldn't even worry about falling down.

MONDAY, FEBRUARY 10

> 10:30 A.M.   Scenes 7, 5, 15, and 16 onstage
>
> 2:30 P.M.   Scenes 8 and 9 in the rehearsal hall

IN A DEPARTURE FROM the usual closed-rehearsal procedure, theatre critics from the Toronto newspapers were invited by Alexander Cohen to attend the morning rehearsal.

Gielgud gave some notes to Rosencrantz and Guildenstern about the scene in which they report to the King and Queen:

GIELGUD   You both can afford to be more cunning in this scene. They now can deliver the goods that they know the King and Queen want. I thought we might have the King drink in this scene, but I'm afraid it would be too distracting. Hamlet is always saying what a drunkard he is, but we never see him drink. We'll have him drink in the play scene, though.

With the arrival of Dillon Evans (Reynaldo and Osric), Gielgud blocked him into the Reynaldo scene. After running it twice Gielgud called Evans down into the auditorium:

GIELGUD   Make Reynaldo a civil servant, foreign office, enormously condescending. The bored feeling of someone who knows everything—not servile. He does his business with condescension. Make him terribly supercilious, like me. Now go off and work on it with Hume.

Gielgud experimented with the setup for the graveyard scene. At first he had the two Gravediggers silently set the table on end to represent the side of the grave and make a hiding place for the spade and skulls before the scene began. He then tried it with them running dialogue as they moved the objects. He decided the first way was better. The scene progressed to the point where Laertes leapt into the grave. When it came time for Burton to leap in with him, he vaulted over the edge of the table as Gielgud instructed.

BURTON   (Calling out into the house) I don't think that will work, John!

GIELGUD   (Shouting out of the blackness) It looks all right. Use your hand to help you over.

BURTON   (Hesitating) John, you don't think we could fight outside the grave? There's such a danger of this being comic.

GIELGUD   No. Hamlet is competing with Laertes. It's in the text and the lines require it. Try it again.

BURTON   (Firmly) No, John! (He paces about the set, thinking.) What if I came in from above and jumped off the platform?

GIELGUD   That might work.

Immediately Gielgud set about rearranging the positions of the Courtiers in the scene and changing Hamlet's and Horatio's position to observe the funeral procession. On the line, "It is I, Hamlet, the Dane!" Burton did an exciting leap from the platform into the grave which both he and Gielgud thought worked well.

Osric was blocked into the final scene, Gielgud explaining to Evans that he conceived of Osric as a spy sent by the King, and that his affected manner was only assumed as a trick.

GIELGUD   He's not just a camp as he's usually played. The King has told him to play the fop. Underneath, he's steel.

In the afternoon the second act was run through the King's prayer scene. The play scene needed major alterations for the large stage. All the Players were regrouped for the speech of advice Hamlet gives them. During the entrance of the court the Players were instructed to peek out from behind the scenery they had set up, to get a look at the King and Queen:

GIELGUD   Actors can never resist peeking at royalty arriving to see a play. I've even done it myself.

During the play-within-the-play scene Gielgud restaged Hamlet's position so that he was lying on the steps directly in front of where the King was sitting. He made this observation on the exit of the King:

GIELGUD   He is afraid to go off in the dark so he covers his eyes and calls for light. When the lights surround him, he removes his hands and regains his courage.

In the prayer scene, Gielgud cut the startled reaction Polonius had on seeing the King with a drawn sword, for fear of a "cheap laugh." After the scene he made these remarks to Burton:

GIELGUD I think you are playing the speech too slowly and
deliberately. You give the audience too long to puzzle over
why you don't kill him there. I think it must all go very
swiftly. You suddenly see the King, grab the sword he's left
behind, and go to kill him quickly before he notices what's
going on. And then just as rapidly you decide it's not the best
time and run off.

TUESDAY, FEBRUARY 11

10:30 A.M. Scene 8 in the rehearsal hall

2:00 P.M. Scenes 14, 15, and 16

BACK IN THE REHEARSAL hall an anonymous member of the
company had posted the following newspaper editorial on the
call board as a final word on the subject of Burton's entry into
the United States:

SLINGS AND ARROWS

Congressman Michael A. Feighan of Ohio strongly feels that
the State Department ought to show its regard for propriety
by revoking the visa issued to Mr. Richard Burton, the British
actor. Mr. Feighan points out, correctly, that publicity has attended Mr. Burton's friendship with Miss Elizabeth Taylor.
The American people's deep moral repugnance toward this entire episode may be measured by the minute and voluminous
detail in which the American press has described every aspect
of it. The Department announces that it will "reexamine the
case."

Both Mr. Feighan and the Department have missed the more
substantial threat to our national morals. If Mr. Feighan thinks
that the past publicity is deleterious, what will he think of the
perfectly shocking play that Mr. Burton proposes to bring to
New York in April? Reeking with scandal and passion, it re-
volves around an eccentric young man whose mother is guilty

of incest and whose uncle, a politician, won power by poisoning his rival. His fiancée commits suicide. The script is sown
with off-color jokes. In the last act there is a duel; the viscious
custom of dueling is fortunately illegal here, whatever may be
the law in the notoriously wild and bloody Kingdom of Denmark. The play ends with four more murders. The tone
throughout is one of unbridled violence and pessimism.

Worse still, this play reflects political ideas wholly foreign to
our American democracy. No doubt Mr. Feighan and the State
Department will, upon reflection, find it more profitable to
leave the actor to his own devices, and instead investigate the
playwright. (*The Washington Post*, February 9, 1964.)

The morning was spent working on the play scene. Gielgud
first listened to some music from the record album *Sweet Pipes**
and chose two sixteenth-century Spanish villancicos to be played
as background music to the play. There was a lively melody
("Fata La Parte") for the dumb show and a lyrical melody
("Triste España") for the *Murder of Gonzago* play.

GIELGUD The dumb show must be very much in a stylized
Chinese theatre kind of invention. We don't want the King
to really know what it's about. His reaction will probably
be to laugh at it.

VOSKOVEC Suppose, John, we did the poisoning behind the
scenery.

GIELGUD Yes. That's a wonderful idea! We'll have Lucianus
run in behind the screen, like Felix the Cat. First he'll hold
up a little vial which he can use for the poisoning in the
word play. And then he can run behind the screen with it
and return triumphantly, having administered it out of sight.

Afternoon work continued almost to the end of the play,
including the little-rehearsed final court scene.

Gielgud made this comment on the graveyard scene:

GIELGUD Richard, don't recognize Yorick too quickly. And
Hamlet must have a strange distance and detachment here.
Think the passage over rationally and come to the recogni-
tion gradually. . . . And let him admire Alexander. Hamlet

* Columbia ML 5875.

admires him as a great leader and he is thinking of his own inadequate leadership in contrast to it.

Gielgud had an idea for the scene between Osric, Hamlet, and Horatio:

GIELGUD   Do you think, Richard, you could show just a flash of thought of killing the King on "let the foils be brought"? This might be the chance to do it.

When a thorough rehearsal of the final court scene began, everything went wrong. Gielgud started by placing the Queen on one side of the stage and the King on the platform above her. When this was arranged, the King gave the line "Give me the cups," but the wine cups were on the opposite side of the stage. "Oh, what a terrible director I am!" Gielgud said in desperation. He started from the beginning with a complete restaging, only to have similar problems arise.

Drake asked that he be placed closer to the Queen after she takes the cup.

DRAKE   He never betrays her, and I think he would be with her after she accidentally gets the poison.

Gielgud asked Drake what he thought of having the King at the end of the scene accept his imminent death openly, realizing that there was no escaping it, but Drake pointed out that this was counter to his line "O yet defend me, friends."

Returning to the duel between Laertes and Hamlet, Burton suggested that in the exchange of rapiers the traditional staging of having Hamlet violently beat the poisoned rapier out of Laertes' hand be eliminated. He preferred that Hamlet very quietly and with no struggle should simply walk up to Laertes and take the weapon from him deliberately.

DURING WORK ON THE play scene, Gielgud remarked he had seen a particularly effective piece of business in the production in which Alec Guiness played Hamlet:

GIELGUD   When he said to Ophelia in the play scene, "That's a fair thought to lie between a maid's legs," he reached right up her skirts in front of the whole court.

BURTON   Well, John, that's good for Alec, but I'm liable to get a sexy reputation.

GIELGUD   I could add a program note.

Gielgud finally was pleased with the scene after spending an hour and a half on it.

In the recorder scene he worked for a gradual acceleration as Hamlet's anger with Guildenstern increases.

In the prayer scene Gielgud demonstrated to Burton two possible ways of raising the sword above the King in the "Now might I do it, pat" speech. Burton stood in front and watched while Gielgud first brought the sword straight above the King, holding it with both hands as if to plunge it straight down. The second method was to swing the sword back in an arc with one hand, as if to hack the King's head off. Burton chose the latter method. (Note: During performances in Boston, Burton switched to the two-handed plunge and after two weeks in New York he cut the sword raising altogether.)"

The lines of the speech go as follows: "Now might I do it, pat, now he is praying;/ And now I'll do't: and so he goes to

heaven;/ And so am I revenged. That would be scanned. . . ."
Gielgud raised the sword on "so he goes to heaven" and then
lowered it on "And so am I revenged." Burton, when he did
the business, raised the sword and lowered it after "And now
I'll do't." Gielgud again emphasized the importance of performing the action rapidly.

GIELGUD Hamlet is hurrying to his mother and stumbles on
the King, and in a frenzy grabs the sword and almost kills
him without reflecting. The lines and business must all go
rapidly. I think you should whisper the speech.

In the afternoon working of the closet scene, Gielgud gave
the following instructions to Gertrude:

GIELGUD You mustn't weep too much on "O Hamlet, speak
no more, thou turnst mine eyes into my very soul." Be more
bewildered. Otherwise there's no climax to build to. And if
Gertrude fully realized what she'd done at this point, Hamlet
wouldn't continue. This is the first time we begin to see what
she really is; not just a charming front.

Concluding the act Gielgud again stated that he felt the
soliloquy after Fortinbras' scene should not be delivered con-
templatively, but rather "full, angry, and grand."
In the first platform scene, sound-man Charlie Bellin watched
as Gielgud walked the part of the Ghost, timing and counting
the steps for the sound effects tape.
Burton put up a tremendous struggle in the second platform
scene in his attempt to break away from Horatio and Marcellus
to follow the Ghost.

GIELGUD Save your energy. It's very important that you let
them do the work in restraining you. Otherwise you'll tire
too quickly. It's dark and the audience can only get a general
impression of what's going on, so fake your part of the struggle.

The cut version of the Ghost tape was played and Burton
implored Gielgud not to cut any of his marvelous readings. But

Sir John felt the shortened version was better, the speech being "too difficult to hold with just a voice." During the scene Burton was placed on the stairway so that on the Ghost's exit he could fall down the stairs before beginning the "O all you host of heaven" soliloquy. (Note: This was cut when it was found that Burton's position on the stairs was out of sightlines in the theatre.)

CHAPTER III

The Third Week
of Rehearsals

THURSDAY, FEBRUARY 13

    10:30 A.M.   Scenes 1, 2, 3, 5, 6, and 7

    3:00 P.M.   Private session—Gielgud and Burton
                      only

STARTING ON THIS DAY, Burton and John Cullum began coming to the rehearsal hall at 9:00 A.M. to practice the duel between Hamlet and Laertes with fencing master Charlie Bellin. In this first session they exercised thrusts and lunges for half an hour and then set the choreography of the first two bouts in the scene.

During the morning rehearsal most of the first-act scenes were run. A significant change was made in the long sixth scene, just after Polonius reads the letter to the King and Queen. Gielgud decided to cut the business of Hamlet taking an early entrance cue to overhear Polonius say "I'll loose my daughter to him."*

GIELGUD   If Shakespeare wanted to have Hamlet overhear that he would have given some indication in the lines.

* See page 32.

BURTON Yes, I think you're right, John. It would be better to
learn of the spying in the nunnery scene when it happens.

‡   ‡   ‡

The doors of the rehearsal hall were locked for the afternoon
with Bobby the bodyguard placed on duty to allow no one to
enter but Gielgud and Burton. Both men arrived at 3:00,
greeted each other, and hung up their coats. Burton walked
over to the platform and sat on the edge while Gielgud went
over to a table and picked up his script, then sat on the end
of the table. After reflecting a few seconds he began speaking:

GIELGUD It seems to me, Richard, and I found in playing the
part, that in the concern with details in each single scene one
forgets the main motivation which must progress through the
part as a whole. You said you felt this and I've felt it so
often, too. But somehow you must force yourself to think of
the actual action of the play. And I don't agree with Larry
[Olivier], who said in the film that this is a play about a man
who can't make up his mind. Surely it's about a man who
cannot reconcile his own conscience with the world as he
sees it, but who is able to come to this reconciliation by the
end of the play. In all the play he goes through a deluded
world, putting up with the persecution which one inevitably
finds; and it isn't until the end of the play, after he's assembled and solidified his action, that he is able to relieve all
the difficulty. And he comes back, having solved it in England.
    The fight with the pirates and Hamlet's departure are in
the play to show the feeling of a journey. Shakespeare does
the same in *Winter's Tale* and *Tempest*. He was fascinated
by journeys because they were so much more important then
and took so much longer. And it has a tremendous effect on
Hamlet in this play because he comes back fantastically ready
to carry out his mission without complications. It's only the
sight of Ophelia's body and Laertes jumping into the grave,
in which Hamlet suddenly sees this young man whom he
always had liked behaving exactly as *he* had done when *his*

father died, in a sort of hysteria of grief. That makes him jump in and do all that violent stuff.

And immediately after he's so ashamed of his behavior, he becomes completely open and doesn't suspect any of the treachery. And Horatio, who is not a very communicative man, does suspect that there is something wrong, but doesn't seem to have the courage to deflect Hamlet from the duel because Hamlet has always been a prince and has done what he wants. Horatio is there to obey and to serve and to listen; he doesn't seem to have much closer a personal relationship. But you feel that Hamlet wants really to die, in a way, if he can kill the King in doing it, he will have accomplished his purpose. He's made a spiritual progression and feels at ease with himself. But what is so hard in the first act is to mix all the motives and keep the true line of what he's plotting to do. He obviously begins apathetically and he can't rouse himself to any action, although he hates and resents the King. Then his friends come and tell him they've seen the Ghost; something begins to happen to him, and he says he'll watch that night with them. Now the Ghost tells him about the murder, and this must be something absolutely new when he hears it. Then he's in a frenzy from the point after the Ghost disappears. All sorts of thoughts occur to him. "Shall I tell my friends?" "Should I run and kill the King?" "No. There's more to be done. I must be quite sure that it was a real spirit." And remember, you must give yourself time to put over to the audience the awful thing in your mind—which is "What shall I do next?"

Then Hamlet goes from the ramparts, and the next thing he does is to terrify Ophelia so that they'll all think that he's mad and he will be left alone to do what he has to do. You hate being alone. You're so terribly lonely in the first scene and in the "too, too solid flesh." But if one is used to thinking that one is lonely, one is also infuriated by not being left alone. When he says "Leave me friends," before the "rogue and peasant slave" soliloquy, it's with great impatience. But from the time you hear the Old Player's speech, you've got

some vague idea of what to do. You can't think exactly what
it is. You'll have a play and put in some extra speeches of
"a dozen or sixteen lines." In your head you're ready to write
a speech, but Rosencrantz and Guildenstern are still there.
So it's "Go away! I want to be alone to think this out!" And
then you try to think of a speech, as one does when one's
alone. You think there's time to write that letter you must
write. And then instead of writing a letter and getting it done,
you say "The Old Player was acting." "It's so terrible!" and
"I can't do it!" and all this. And all your inside falls out,
instead of getting anything accomplished. All these thoughts
crowd in so strongly that you have to go through a maze of
self-communing and building up all the things that come
between you and your interest.

Then in the next scene you come back and you're in a
deep depression. But somehow that's wonderful musically.
"To be or not to be" in the nunnery scene is like an andante
after the violent rhythms of the "rogue and peasant slave"
soliloquy. Like most people, Hamlet probably has a low-key
reaction after all the emotion of "The play's the thing."

BURTON Well, I think that's terribly right, you know, John.
Because I know myself that one day I'm absolutely bubbling
over and making jokes and being rather coarse and jumping
about, and the next day I'm very down. And I think that's
Hamlet's problem, too.

GIELGUD Yes. First he lashes himself for his own stupidity
and then he becomes despondent and feels that he doesn't
care one way or another and tries to determine if everything
is worth it. "Shall I kill myself and get rid of the problem?"
And then he decides at the end of the speech that he *will*
go on living in spite of all the drawbacks of life—the fears,
the doubts, and the sufferings. He seems to doubt the Ghost
a little, doesn't he? But the Ghost is a bit of a tyrant. Obviously, Hamlet was greatly in awe of him, just as Ophelia
fears *her* father. But when Ophelia comes, and I think this
scene is going awfully well, could we not consider it as a

second development? I feel more and more that the first off-stage scene when you went to her with "your doublet all unbraced" must have been an attempt to seduce her forcibly. But when you see her the second time you have another desire. You know you frightened her the last time, and I think both of you should begin it by remembering that first scene.

BURTON I think that from the practical point, John, what we're playing at the moment is a perfect extension of "To be or not to be." It's gentle now. And particularly because I'm so rough, the more gentle I can be whenever possible, the better. Then Hamlet won't seem to be a maniac.

GIELGUD Yes, that's true. And sometimes, Richard you're inclined to shout out very loudly on one word, rather than to build a speech to a climax of a shout on three or four lines, which to me is more effective. You keep one word high and all the rest are lost to it. And if you do this too often, it becomes dull and coarse. It's only a question of holding your own strength.

That's what is so marvelous about Edith [Evans] when she acts. She doesn't open her soul to the audience quite, except for three or four moments in the play. And in these moments she opens this window with intense feeling. It is something like a child who can hardly wait to show you something. And you lean forward and are eager to see more, and then she slams the window shut! I marvel at the way she selects the vitally telling moments. She never weeps a lot or indulges in superfluous emotion. She hits the nail on the head for every correct mood and feeling. I think you need to select your effects precisely as she does. Find the places for them and make a scaffold to build your speeches on.

BURTON I do have a tendency, as you tell me, John, to shout.

GIELGUD It's very dangerous—as dangerous as speaking too beautifully. But to get back to the play. After the scene with

Ophelia, again there is a break. What I find so fascinating about the part is that Hamlet always begins a scene one way and has to end it in another because something has happened in the course of the scene. Rosencrantz and Guildenstern's spying doesn't occur to him until he catches them. The arrival of the Players causes another enormous change. He meets Ophelia in the nunnery scene and he doesn't know how she'll react to him. Then he realizes they are spying on him and there's another change. He goes to his mother, hears a voice, and kills Polonius, and this changes the whole course of his life. You never know in real life the actual time or moment when your whole life may be changed—when you meet someone who is going to be important to you, or somebody dies, or somebody forgets something vitally important. You know, I found all through my life how extraordinarily some people make certain effects on you, such as you have; and others come and go in your life and you don't have anything to do with them, really, and you forget them. And it's so important in this play to show the extraordinary way in which Hamlet responds so sensitively to characters around him. It's as if he has antennae which feel the contacts and the business and the emotion going on around him. And things happen which we do not follow clearly unless the actor playing Hamlet indicates the various stages of his disappointments. He always tries to recover himself and go on—like a man on a tightrope who's continually being knocked off his balance and then regains it. You have to create a line which is perfectly straight and then allow him to wobble on it. You continually destroy yourself and then recover from it, as when he comes back in the "How all occasions," which is a summing up of strength for the last section of the play. That should have a firmness because now he's no longer distracted by the surroundings of the court. And on that plain, watching Fortinbras, whom he doesn't know at all, who is just a figure passing with an army, he suddenly realizes he has a mission as great as the war and reassesses the whole of his life.

BURTON   John, the other problem that I have with speaking Shakespeare, which you know about better than anybody in the world, is speaking the verse too flatly.

GIELGUD   You just have to be careful not to jump your images, so that you don't put three images in two lines and jump on to the next image two lines away when there are other images in between. If you don't mind me telling you these things, it's simply that sometimes you go too quickly for the audience to believe you really are thinking of what you say, that's all.

BURTON   Let's start and work on the "rogue and peasant slave." I'd rather not use any sort of physical violence on the "O vengeance" because they always think I'm going to smash the throne to bits or something. I did a thing in *Henry the Fifth* which got an enormous laugh, but which would not be funny in this play. In the scene where I was trying to talk French to the girl, I got very fancy and my arms went right up in the air, like this (Burton raises his arms over his head), and then I just simply dropped them. Perhaps we could do that with "O vengeance!" But stabbing the chair is so distinctive. They'd know.

GIELGUD   It is an awful cliché. It doesn't really go with this kind of production.

BURTON   That's what I think. You see, John, because of the nature of this production, there are things in this which would never work in any other.

GIELGUD   Yes, quite right.

BURTON   For instance, seeing the Ghost—which you've carefully taught me. At the back of my head I think when I play it, I'm not going to have a costume on—which I'm not. So that the simpler you make me, the better. Elizabeth's a very clever girl about such things. She said, "It was absolutely marvelous to see how John made you better, made you easier," just like that.

GIELGUD You are very clever, too, at taking what I give you and making it your own. There are some things I think of that don't work for you, and if you did them they'd come off badly, and so you don't do them. And that's what I'm thankful for. The moment I feel that I'm giving you too much what I myself would do, then I shrink from making any comment.

BURTON But it works for me, which is why I told you I think it was dangerous for Peter [O'Toole] to act Hamlet with Larry [Olivier] directing, because he could so obviously be tempted to mimic him. And I would be just as bad with Larry, because my build is so like Larry. We have the same kind of squatness and strength, and it wouldn't have worked.

GIELGUD Well, let's start on this speech now. Do you think you can show more impatience in clearing the room before you start?

BURTON Would it be too much if I made Rosencrantz and Guildenstern scurry off by sounding vicious on "Aye, so God be with you"?

GIELGUD Good! I like that. (Burton begins with this line and then takes a pause before "now I am alone.") I think there must be more relief here. You mustn't seem tired or sad because that's all coming in "To be or not to be." Keep it energetic and perhaps follow a little where they've gone off. (Burton does twenty lines of the speech—from "O what a rogue" to "And can say nothing") I don't like it. I think it should all be quicker—your mind is so busy. The beginning was beautiful. But then it's got to come faster up to "And can say nothing." That's the first movement of the speech. Now you're taking too long with the images. If you keep them clear and make the commas right, you can go so much faster. (Burton repeats the section more rapidly.) Much better. Do you think you could put your head in your hands for "and can say nothing"? Or do you think it's too sad? (Gielgud demonstrates this action.)

BURTON It's marvelous, John. Anything like that. What I should love to do, if you approve, is to take all the well-known passages so that the audience are not aware of them as famous speeches.

GIELGUD Sometimes you still shout too much, like you shouted a bit too much when you said "What would *he* do"—as if you were asking somebody really there. You're alone; you needn't take it so outwardly. Then it won't seem as if you are talking to the audience. Try to conceal the fact that it's soliloquy by making it more to yourself. Don't use quite so much voice, because the moment you shout, we feel "Who's he talking to? Is somebody up there?" It's coming very well, though.
(Burton runs through the lines softly. When Burton comes to the line "Who does me this, Ha?" he does a great yell on the last word.) I think that's too showy. I would make it simpler. I think it's awfully good. But save your climax for the "O vengeance." Can you give the impression of stabbing him on that line? Try the same gesture you use in the prayer scene of the sword over your head. Then try sinking on the arm of the chair, exhausted, for "Why, what an ass am I." (Burton does this.) That's good. Now stay sitting for "about my brain!" You've already thought of it once before the scene. Suddenly, at last, you're back to your first thesis. That's why the whole speech mustn't be slow. Because we must get the impression that you think of the play and then go into the rogue speech. The less you wander about during it, the better. And I think at the end of it, you must be wonderfully roguish on "The play's the thing." You almost have to take that to the audience.

The soliloquy was repeated three more times until both men felt satisfied with it.

GIELGUD I think it's much better now. What shall we do next? "Too, too solid flesh"?

BURTON Fine. By the way, John, we will get these platforms fixed, won't we? In the quiet scenes they creak terribly!

GIELGUD Yes. I'll tell them.

During work on the "too, too solid flesh" soliloquy, Gielgud had Burton bring out the time references "two months dead," "within a month," and "a little month."

GIELGUD You can afford more voice on "O most wicked speed to post with such dexterity to incestuous sheets." Play that rather high so that you have something to come down from on "It is not, nor it cannot come to good." Now, what shall we do with "To be or not to be"? That must be very simple, too.

BURTON There's something I've been meaning to tell you, John, but I didn't want to stop rehearsals. At the end of "To be or not to be" it's an awfully long walk to Ophelia. Does she have to come on from the opposite side of the stage? If she came on over here, it would be terribly good.

GIELGUD Yes, I hadn't thought of that. Of course. It'd be much easier if she had been hiding there on your side.

Gielgud worked to put more movement into "To be or not to be," getting Burton to feel his way through it and "walk in time to the thought."

BURTON I must stop for a minute, John, to tell you something that you did when I was a young man. I saw you play the first Hamlet I ever saw. I was at the University at the time and you were playing at Oxford. But in this speech, when you came to "when we have shuffled off this mortal coil," you did such a magnificent gesture that the friend I was with completely gave up drinking! (They both laugh.)

The speech was run two more times.

GIELGUD   That's fine. Would you like to try the Fortinbras soliloquy? I think this should be a stated four-square box that sums up the whole of the first part of the play. It would be wonderful if we could play right through to this speech. It is a legato finish, like the end of a Bach fugue. (He sings) Da dee da da daaah! It slows down and finishes.

BURTON   John, I think one of the things that's fascinating about the way you're directing me, where I normally went "YAH!" you've toned me down quite rightly. And this speech, which before I spoke absolutely dead quiet, we've run into—as you suggested—a rhythm. I never thought of it before as declamatory, and yet the sense says, "From this time forth, my thoughts be bloody or be nothing worth." The whole climax is that Hamlet is going forth to kill.

GIELGUD   And it's so extraordinary. You've come out of Denmark, and here you are on the plain and you're out in the air for the first time. You're away from the "confines" and "dungeons" and "prisons." And I think you come in thinking that this is glorious to see the troops going by and the snow and all that. But suddenly even this, which you thought was a wonderful change, is a terrible blow to your character because you feel that you're going off to England and escaping all that you're supposed to do. So you think "I must do something about it," and "I bloody well will, too," by the end of the speech, and "What's the matter with me?"
   The death of twenty thousand men doesn't matter to you except in a grand compassionate way. It's an impersonal attitude toward it—"Five people killed in China," "fifteen in an earthquake," or "sixteen in an air crash." There is something so much more impersonal about this speech. It's away from personalities altogether. The rest of the play is a struggle between personalities—your uncle, your mother—but this is the whole world going by. And it's an example to you and a reproach to you. At the same time it's a sort of glory.

BURTON　Then I think that I should change my attitude with the Norwegian Captain. Instead of being kind, I should be indifferent.

GIELGUD　No. I think Hamlet is very interested. Suddenly you come into a new world. You've not been aware of politics or Fortinbras. This is the first time Hamlet apprehends that people are coming through the country without fighting a war. And he thinks "Where are they going to?" And "Who are they?" It's a sudden return to the interest of the world, as when you've had a private grief, or have been rehearsing a play for three weeks, and you suddenly go out and see people in the shops and you think "My goodness, this is interesting. I'd forgotten all about it."

They worked on the speech for twenty minutes. Gielgud prompted for exact readings and also played the Captain so that Burton could work into the soliloquy more easily. He suggested starting the speech with a heroic laugh, as if Hamlet were saying, "What a fool I've been."

GIELGUD　You've got to suddenly discover the army and then stop and watch it. Then it starts in a major key so that you can go back and be thoughtful during "What is a man." And when he says "Sure, He that made us," I think he recalls the same marvelous mixture of willingness to believe, combined with the terrible doubt that he had in the "What a piece of work is a man" speech. And finally it works up to a major-key climax for the end of it.

I think that's enough for today. It will be easier to apply all this when we put the drums with it tomorrow. Thank you so much, Richard.

BURTON　No. Thank you, John.

FRIDAY, FEBRUARY 14

10:30 A.M.   Scenes 5 and 15

2:00 P.M.   Run-through of scenes 1-13 (Acts I and II)

GIELGUD DID NOT come to the morning rehearsal, but left the hall free for any actors who wanted to work on their own. Hume Cronyn and Dillon Evans rehearsed the Reynaldo scene. George Rose ran the Gravediggers' scene twice and then George Voskovec ran through his Player's speech.

The afternoon was a nervous time. It was to be the first full run-through of the entire play and it would show how much work was needed in the last week before opening night, as Gielgud had previously announced that the weekend would be free.

Before starting the run, Gielgud took Linda Marsh through the new entrance at the beginning of the nunnery scene. "Let's begin," he called. "Harry, keep time. And I really won't stop."

He kept to his word. It was necessary to correct one or two crosses and three times he threw a prompt but did not stop the run. The first act ran one hour and twenty-nine minutes. Gielgud had written many notes and the company gathered in a circle around him to receive them:

GIELGUD   That was very good. A beautiful performance. Marvelous! Now let me give these notes. Bernardo, you are getting too sonorous—it sounds Shakespearean and phony. And in that first scene, Horatio, you tended to chop up your lines instead of reading straight through them; especially when you spoke to the Ghost on "What art thou, that usurp'st this time of night." Harry, that recording for the Ghost's footsteps will have to go. It sounded more like a railway train. Marcellus, the fear was good. Can you lift that line, "twice before and jump at this dead hour," and bring it out a little more? That whole scene needs more poetry. It lacks the splendor of the play.

In the court scene, Hume, don't forget the new business of beckoning the ambassador forward. Eileen, lift your line, "Thou knowest 'tis common." Richard, the soliloquy was excellent, but you had a few misquotes, and with such a famous text they're bound to be noticed.

BURTON Yes, John. I went through the lines this morning and I was surprised at several things I'd changed. I thought *he* was wrong!

GIELGUD Your line "weary, stale, flat and unprofitable"—I think you've got to find each of those words out of the other. You can't take them all as one phrase. Think of each word before you say it. I don't think "I prithee do not mock me, fellow student, I think it was to see my mother's wedding" should be so forceful and petulent. He's sad there, with just a touch of bitterness. "He was a man." That needs a full stop at the end.

Laertes, you were terribly down in the farewell scene. It needs to be dashing, impulsive, and fiery. You were much too timid and it sounded long-winded and boring. I know that's a difficult first speech, and if it's too difficult I'll cut part of it, though I'd rather not. It's your only scene of introduction—then you spend two hours in the dressing room —so it's got to make an effect. It's still too colloquial and modern. Make it more exciting and young. It should have all the life and flourish of the Renaissance. Show us the young man off on an exciting trip to Paris. Keep him fiery and impulsive and dashing.

Hume, you can afford to play more with the word "tender." That's the first of Polonius' characteristic word elaborations and it should get a laugh.

Richard, try saying "Angels and minister of Grace" *before*

you kneel. And you made such an enormous pause on "I'll call thee . . . Hamlet!" I thought for a moment you were going to say "John Gielgud." "Now to my word" needs to be more conclusive. Let's see the decision to carry out the revenge. Don't smile on "Oh, wonderful!" I think Hamlet should be sort of ecstatic and mad—very excited. You were just very pleasant.

BURTON I have a terrible disease about that, John. The first time I played it, they said I was charmless, so I feel I have to give a little smile every so often.

GIELGUD When you say "heartily, yes, faith, heartily," you must give a new color to the repeated word; otherwise there's no reason for saying it. Don't rush the changes of ground when the Ghost is moving about below. They seem perfunctory. You miss the realization that he has moved somewhere, and you have to search a bit before you can locate him. On "Rest, rest, perturbed spirit" kiss the ground with just your fingertips. If you use your whole hand, it looks as if you're spitting.

Linda, the scene was wonderful, but don't break your verse. Read through to the ends of the lines.

Polonius, when you report to the King and Queen, you can be much more amused yourself at the delightful way you phrase things like "effect–defect," "effect–defective," and and "tis pity–pity tis." Relish your own dialectic.

I think the fishmonger scene needs to start much lighter. It's a comedy scene. Richard, try doing some elfin things. Enjoy it at first. Use the madness as a kind of relief—which will keep returning—and then toward the end you can grow weary of the game. Show us that you are inventing the "old men have grey beards" speech. "No, nor woman, neither" needs to be much more savage. Apart from the beauty of the performance, I find that in principle, Richard, you don't chastise yourself enough. It needs an athletic despair, a self-flagellation. But it must never be self-indulgent sorrow. Rosencrantz, when Hamlet points to your medal, be sure you look at your lapel and not at your flies.

George [Voskovec], the First Player's speech was much too much in the same style as the rest of the play. I love the reality of it and I don't want you to lose that, but make it more old-fashioned with exaggerated gestures and great sonorous sound. All of the Players must get very excited when Hamlet says "We'll hear a play tomorrow." It means you're going to have a job.

Richard, you can still afford more impatience in getting rid of the Players. Get everybody off quickly and then go right into the "rogue and peasant slave" soliloquy. Be more suspenseful in "I have heard that guilty creatures sitting at a play," and then be absolutely certain on "I know my course." "Abuses me to damn me" has no pause. You left out a lot in "To be or not to be." Be sure you prepare for the long list starting at "whips and scorns of time" so that it all comes out as one thought.

I found the nunnery scene intensely moving. I think in the tirade to Ophelia at the end, Richard, you played too strongly too soon. Keep it in as long as you can—up to "it hath made me mad." You came in just right, Linda, with "O, what a noble mind." If you do it that way, we'll kill the risk of applause on Richard's exit and they'll hold it till the end of the act. Otherwise, the interruption will make your speech which follows very much more difficult to sustain.

That was excellent, everybody. Now I'm going to leave it up to you what you want to do in the time remaining. Shall we have runs or stops? Which do you find more helpful?

BURTON   What I'd like to do, John, is run the whole play every day. Do, say, Act One and Act Two in the morning and then start with Act Three in the afternoon, and use the remaining time for whatever scenes you think it necessary to spend more time on.

GIELGUD   That's fine with me. Will that suit everyone? All right. Let's take a ten-minute break and then at four o'clock we'll go on with Act Two.

During the break an announcement was posted that because of the enormous advance sale at the box office, the Toronto engagement would be extended for a week. This brought a general groan from the company. Alfred Drake pondered whether he should take out Canadian citizenship.

Gielgud gave more notes after the run of the second act.

GIELGUD　That took forty-eight minutes. Very good. It went very fast. I have only a few notes.

Hamlet, when you see Horatio after the advice to the Players, show more relief. And can you be more tender with him? He is the only one you can rely on.

The whole play scene was chilling! I was in a terrible state! Alfred, I think you must be very loud on "Give me some light—away!" Use less voice though in the prayer scene when you say "Help, angels." In that same scene, Hamlet, look at your sword just before you say "Up sword."

Eileen, in the closet scene you can still take longer with "As kill a king?" The emotion wasn't right. The Queen must be terribly bewildered, and slowly realize that Hamlet thinks he's killed Claudius. Richard, can you show a little shame on "At your age the heyday in the blood is tame"? Even though it's said in such a terrible rage, it is agonizing to say those things to one's mother.

Eileen, I think we must put back the line "Forth at your eyes your spirits wildly peep."

Richard, what do you think if in the politic worms scene you pointed at Claudius when you say "fat King" and at Guildenstern when you say "lean beggar"?

That act looked so good. It would be terrible now to do the third act and have it fall apart. I think we'll begin with that on Monday. I want to congratulate you all. It's a joy to work with such a company. You all work so well together and are so punctual. I'm most touched by the way it's gone. Now let's keep our wits about us next week so that we don't all wind up hating each other.

Though the play was yet to have a continuous run-through, it was put to rest for two days, except for an understudy rehearsal Saturday morning of Acts One and Two conducted by the stage manager. Other company members went to New York for the weekend.

MONDAY, FEBRUARY 17

2:30 P.M.   Scenes 14 and 8

THE CAST WAS OBVIOUSLY glad to get back and eager to resume work. Light designer Jean Rosenthal had arrived and Gielgud began explaining the set to her, pointing out the path of the Ghost's light.

The stage manager called places for Act Three and the run began. Gielgud let the mad scene run without stopping. But the going became hopeless in the plotting scene between Laertes and the King. Neither Drake nor Cullum could remember the blocking, as the scene had been done only twice before and had been completely changed the second time.

GIELGUD   Well, it's obvious we're not going to do this without stopping. This whole act needs a great deal of work. Even the mad scene positions were wrong. What I want to do now is to run the play scene for Miss Rosenthal, and then we'll come back and work on the last act.

The play scene ran smoothly and Gielgud looked a little more encouraged.

GIELGUD   Now let's get back to Act Three. The first scene must start with much more energy. It was terribly dull and no one's going to pay the least bit of attention to it. It's got to begin with much more intensity.

Gielgud was on his feet now, and he worked rapidly, running through all the moves, altering them, and giving the actors line readings. He tried eliminating the Gentleman's entrance when Ophelia came on, but then decided to put him back into that section of the scene. The business of having the Gentleman kneel for mercy in front of Laertes when the latter entered was altered so that the Gentleman attempted to obstruct Laertes' entrance. Laertes then grabbed the Gentleman and threw him aside, giving more strength to his entrance.

When Ophelia re-entered the scene, Gielgud asked that she be given something to carry, other than the ropes she had been using, as a substitute prop for her flowers.

GIELGUD I want to avoid real flowers, but perhaps we'll have to use them. The ropes don't say anything. I want something that looks like weeds. (His eye is caught by a pile of plastic recording tape, unraveled on the floor under the stage manager's desk.) Couldn't we get a large bunch of this?

YOUNG (Who had been splicing tape all weekend to have the rehearsal tape ready) Oh, we've got plenty of that.

GIELGUD Well, let's try it.

DRAKE John, what if at the end of this scene I picked up Laertes' sword and gave it back to him on "Let the great axe fall."

GIELGUD Excellent, excellent. We'll use that.

The scene was put in good order and Gielgud then spent the rest of the afternoon working on a complete restaging of the Laertes-King plotting scene.

GIELGUD Somebody write this down. Otherwise I shall forget it and change it all again.

He ran the scene twice and then gave the actors notes.

GIELGUD Alfred, can you take more delight in Laertes' plot to use the poisoned rapier? Claudius is a professional poisoner, and as soon as Laertes mentions it, we should see him already planning to go one better.

Eileen, the willow speech was marvelous. But there is a danger now of it becoming too like a messenger from a Greek play. Play it more to the King and Laertes. Lean on Alfred's chest when you come in. Take a pause after "dead men's fingers" as if to ask yourself, "Why did I say that? It hasn't anything to do with anything!" Then start in a different key and play the rest of it to Laertes. I think we must give you some piece of material—perhaps something that might have been torn from Ophelia's dress—and it could fall from your hand as you describe her falling in the brook.

This whole scene looks much better now. Does it feel better? (All affirm this.) Good! It should.

He stayed after the rehearsal to listen to samples of five different funeral drums that had been collected by sound-man Charlie Bellin. Gielgud chose the most appropriate and then left to confer with Jean Rosenthal and Ben Edwards.

TUESDAY, FEBRUARY 18

10:30 A.M.   Scenes 15 and 16

2:30 P.M.   Complete run-through (to 7:00 P.M.)

IN THE GRAVEYARD SCENE, Gielgud decided to eliminate the business of the Gravediggers eating at the start of the scene, since there wasn't enough time for it. He suggested that Hamlet imitate Osric on his line "a courtier, which could say 'good morrow sweet lord.'" The section of the scene where the Courtiers haul Hamlet and Laertes from the grave was worked and reworked until the Courtiers stopped falling over one another and the scene ran smoothly.

At the end of the scene Gielgud spent much time in trying to decide the best point at which to remove the graveyard

properties and set the stage for the final court scene. He experimented by trying the shift first at the end of the graveyard
scene, then during the section of the final scene in which Osric
appears, and then at the entrance of the court. Since shifting
during the Osric scene proved too distracting, the final solution
was to remove the grave props between the scenes and set up
the chairs and tables for the court just before the entrance of
the court. He gave this note on the Hamlet-Horatio section of
the final scene:

GIELGUD   This scene must start in a light mood, as if it's the
   beginning of a new play with a different color. It should have
   a reckless curiosity, with great charm and sweetness. Hamlet
   has resolved all his problems. Otherwise, they'll think we're
   just killing time till the end.

As Osric entered the scene with his plumed hat, Gielgud
came up with the idea that it would be amusing if Osric put
the hat behind his back and then leaned forward to make himself look like an ostrich. At another point he had the feather
tickle Osric so that he turned around to see what it was and
then became embarrassed at discovering it was his own hat.
Sir John watched this twice, very amused and chuckling to himself. The third time through he decided to cut the business as
being "too elaborate and distracting."

In a blocking rearrangement of the scene, Gielgud placed
Osric center, between Hamlet and Horatio, so it became necessary to cut Horatio's aside to Hamlet, "his purse is empty already." "Do we need it?" asked Sir John. "Do you mind?"
Then, on the next restaging, which had Hamlet and Horatio
together at Osric's left, he put the line back in.

On the "fall of a sparrow" speech, Gielgud asked Burton to
give three distinct colors to the line. "If it be now, 'tis not to
come" (outward quality); "If it be not to come, it will be now"
(introspective); "if it be not now, yet it will come" (warmly
to Horatio).

It was announced that following lunch the entire play would
be run. At 2:30 the run began. Jean Rosenthal sat next to Sir

John, and he whispered lighting explanations to her during the run. The first act ran an hour and twenty-five minutes and was followed by a note session.

GIELGUD   A little bit crisper, Bernardo, on "the rivals of my watch." Much better, that whole scene—simpler. The first scene was very good. The opening of the court scene was very good. Alfred, you left out "We doubt it nothing, heartily farewell." And you put in a "Laertes" where it doesn't come.

Hamlet, when you say "Aye, madam, it is common," can you suspend the end of that line so that you not only echo her, but also give the impression that you have something more to say? "Aye, madam, it is common, *but*—." Anticipate something more. Your first speech was most beautiful, and the whole of your opening scene. The only thing I don't very much like, and it's my fault, is when you cross above Claudius on the "suits of woe." Would it be possible to move in front of him?

And I think, Harry, we should push all of the platforms upstage another foot. That affects Miss Rosenthal, and also Ben Edwards.

Hamlet, I thought it would be good if you looked around at the court and the King when he says "You are the most immediate to our throne," and they all bow; look as if you were to say "How dare you all bow to me in that sycophantic way when you didn't do anything for me when the election was made." When Horatio and the soldiers come in, you always say to them "I am very glad to see you." That's from another scene. It's "I am glad to see you well." And I don't feel that you're suddenly stung when Horatio says "My lord, I came to see your father's funeral," which is the one thing you don't want to talk about. It's the beginning of a terrible bitterness. You always make it too casual; I think you should wince. It's too early in the play not to show that it hurts you, especially from Horatio, who loved your father.

Linda, when you come on, just give one look after Hamlet. It's rather good, your overlapping. Then when Laertes says to you "My necessaries are embarked," give another look back to where Hamlet exited before you go into the scene.

Much better, John Cullum, that scene today. It's still a tiny bit casual on phrasing here and there. Have the coat over your arm when you come in, instead of wearing it. "Farewell, Ophelia"—I never hear that, or "Remember well what I have said to you." Otherwise, excellent. In the second platform scene, Richard, "The King doth wake tonight" was rather rushed, and I think it will be hard for the audience to catch it. I thought you recognized the Ghost too quickly; the effect was marvelous, but it was a bit prepared.

Beautiful, your performance, Marcellus, beautiful—very sensitive and lovely.

Richard, when the Ghost says "won to his shameful lust the will of my most seeming virtuous Queen," can you give a groan after? It needs a cry of some kind. And will you work with the recording several times so that the timing is correct? Then when the Ghost leaves, I think it might be better to start walking down the stairway as the cocks are crowing so that by the end you only have one step to fall down. To fall from the top is so terribly noisy when you hit the platform, and you're liable to tear your clothes. Contrive to get down earlier, and then fall. Then when you got up for the "O all you host of heaven," you stood very still and very strong. It seems to me it ought to go faster, both in speech and movement. You talk about your "distracted globe." You ought to be a whirling dervish moving around. Otherwise, that scene was beautiful, and you got all the changes so well.

The positions in the Reynaldo scene were off. Hume and Dillon, can you work that out? Hume, twice you got up and crossed center; that isn't good. Can't we contrive another move? Maybe cross to the other side of the table. Beautiful scene, though; you play it marvelously. It just wants another position.

Very good, Richard, the antic disposition. But try to find something fantastic for your entrance—hand over your head, or something strange. Then when you tear the page out of the book in the scene with Polonius, take a step back and do it a bit large so that in this enormous house we're sure to see what you're doing. Draw it out and spread it. "*Many* confines, wards, dungeons." You missed the "many" today.

The entrance of the Players was very good. Richard, be careful to keep your back straight when you're sitting on the stool listening to the First Player's speech. You crouched a bit and it looked old and tired; and I would like to see more of your face during all that. Let's have your eyes in our direction occasionally so the audience gets your reaction. Then when Polonius interrupts the Old Player, don't come in with "It shall to the barber's with your beard" too quickly. Give it a deadly pause and be more outraged, like Princess Margaret being interrupted. Give Polonius an icy stare.

George Voskovec, take your time. You rush the whole thing a bit. Take the pauses and the commas and the phrasing and make the whole thing a bit old-fashioned in manner. You play with great feeling and sensitivity, but there are great effects you can get.

In the "rogue and peasant slave," Richard, it's "*from* her working all his visage wanned." You always say "by her working." It doesn't seem to make sense to me. You always leave out "*property* and most dear life." And you always mix up "plucks off my beard, blows it in my face, tweaks me by the nose." I know it's a trifle, but it's only a question of looking at the script when you're at home. And also "remorseless, lecherous, treacherous, kindless." They're all so famous, you know; it'll be noticed at once. But you did the soliloquy marvelously. The exit was so wicked and sort of elfin. I loved it. And the speed at the beginning, marvelous! Much the best you've ever done it. Beautiful. And I liked the "to be or not to be" and the nunnery scene.

When you come on, King, after the "rogue and peasant slave," I think you should just glance after Hamlet. If you look too long, we believe you can still see him running up the corridor. Perhaps you should look after him at the end of your first speech. You mask Ophelia on her entrance there,

King. Could you be onstage a little bit further? She has an important entrance in that scene. I toyed with the idea of bringing her on from the opposite side, but that wouldn't be any good. She must come on where Polonius comes.

There were fewer notes for the second act:

GIELGUD Players, play the dumb show and the word play more for the King and Queen.

Richard, I think "Is this the prologue or the posy of a ring" is said to Ophelia, rather than to the Player. The exit of the court was very good. Richard, I think that after the "stricken deer" you should roar with laughter.

Now, something I don't like is the beginning of the recorder scene. It could be that I've arranged it badly, but Guildenstern rushes for that stool the moment the scene begins. Otherwise, it was very fine, that act. I have no more.

I do think it would be good if you looked at the sword, Richard, before you say "Up sword." It has more power if you look at the blade. It draws attention to it. In the closet scene you always leave out "You shall not budge," and it's "grace and *blush*." You always say "grace and—" something else.

That's all I have for this act. I was delighted with it. I think it was extremely good. Look at how there are less notes —only four pages for two acts today, compared to about six I had on Friday. Well, on, on. Five minutes for anyone who wants it.

After the break Act Three was begun. It ran smoothly up to the last scene, when the old problems in staging again began to plague Sir John—the long pauses while getting the cups back and forth between the King, Hamlet, and the Queen. Because it was 7:00 P.M. and all were tired, Gielgud ended the rehearsal.

GIELGUD We'll start with this scene at eleven o'clock tomorrow morning when we are all fresh.

CHAPTER IV

The Fourth Week of Rehearsals

WEDNESDAY, FEBRUARY 19

11:00 A.M.　Scene 16

2:30 P.M.　Scenes 14-16 (Act III)

WITH FOUR WORKING rehearsals remaining and opening night a week away, Gielgud began at 11:00 A.M. with a complete restaging of the troublesome final court scene. Obviously, he had been working on the solution the night before. He began by placing the Queen in the state chair at the beginning, instead of the King, keeping the King on his feet moving about. He also found that traffic problems were considerably simplified if Hamlet chose his foils first. A small table for the wine cups placed next to the state chair also helped matters.

GIELGUD　Can we cut all the King's lines about the trumpet and the cannon going off during the fight? I can't understand why Shakespeare wrote all that stuff just before Fortinbras comes on.

HERLIE　John, is what I'm doing all right after drinking the poison? I know Gertrude begins to feel a bit seedy, but I don't want to look drunk.

GIELGUD   No, you don't. It's fine.

The six Courtiers in the scene practiced lifting Hamlet to their shoulders to carry him out at the end. It took four trys to get everyone in step and lifting simultaneously.

After lunch Act Three was begun. Drake asked that some interplay between the King and Queen be inserted after Laertes demands to know how Polonius was killed.

DRAKE   The King is in a spot here. He knows that Hamlet is guilty and wants to appear to Gertrude to be protecting Hamlet; yet he also wants Laertes to get his vengeance by killing Hamlet.

Watching the scene from the side of the room, Burton suggested that Laertes, on his entrance, place his sword at the King's throat. This was tried and kept in.

The rest of the act was run to the grave scene, at which point Gielgud apologized to the company for stopping.

GIELGUD   Will you continue running this act on your own? I'll see the rest of it in the morning. I'm afraid I've got to go rest because of this awful cold I've got.

BURTON   John, why don't you stay in bed in the morning and then come at noon. Then we can run the act once again in the morning before you come to see it.

Gielgud thanked him and agreed, and the rehearsal progressed through the end of the act without the director. After the rehearsal Burton ran his first scene with Rosencrantz and Guildenstern, and after some discussion decided to eliminate the business of Guildenstern stealing a peek at Hamlet's book.

THURSDAY, FEBRUARY 20

10:30 A.M.   Run Act III; repeat last scene
12:00 NOON   Repeat Act III for Gielgud
2:30 P.M.   Work through scenes 1-5

AT 10:30 THE COMPANY ran the third act, repeating the last scene to clear up some uncertainties in movements. It was during this repeat that Burton asked Bob Milli (Horatio) to place a cloak over him after the death speech to hide Hamlet's panting.

At noon Gielgud came back feeling much better and the cast ran the third act for him. It ran fifty minutes and Sir John was pleased with it. He gave a new entrance position to the Queen and the Gentleman at the beginning of the act and decided to cut the Gentleman's re-entrance with Ophelia for the mad scene. He gave the following notes for the remainder of the act:

GIELGUD   George Rose [First Gravedigger], can you establish the grave once it is set by walking over and looking into it? Perhaps you could do it during the argument with the other Gravedigger.

Hamlet, I think I've got you too far away just before the Osric scene, when you're alone with Horatio. See if you can be down next to the footlights for "There's a divinity which shapes our ends."

DRAKE   John, in the last scene, would you mind if I cut the business of going over to Laertes and telling him to give Hamlet the fatal stab before they begin the last bout? I think that's something Laertes would have to decide for himself.

GIELGUD   Yes, we can do it that way, too. That's all right.

The afternoon session was devoted to the first act, which progressed as far as the Hamlet-Polonius book scene. Gielgud made these comments during the scenes:

GIELGUD Richard, don't play full front so much in the "too, too solid flesh" soliloquy. Give us your profile and use the stage more. That will bring it into the scene and relate it so that it's more natural and less like a speech. You've got to keep more excited when the soldiers tell you of the Ghost. It kills the tempo if you are down. Come right in with the lines. Don't hesitate at such moments as " 'Tis very strange."

The positions of Ophelia and Laertes in the farewell scene were altered so that they would resemble those of their reuniting in the mad scene.

In the second platform scene Burton reminded Horatio and Marcellus that once they got into the theatre the three of them had to agree on the positions where they would visualize the Ghost. Gielgud commented concerning the Ghost voice:

GIELGUD I think it's too loud now. I could record it over with more whispers, but I don't want it coming out like Dracula or Vincent Price. Can we try it at a lower volume level, or perhaps on some different speaker combinations? Richard, in the incantation when you first see the Ghost, be sure you emphasize the four "why's." And be even more demanding when you're alone with him, when you say "Wither wilt thou lead me?" Then when he says "Mark me," be terribly surprised and terrified when you answer "I will." It's the first time you hear this thing speak. Keep the drama of loving the old boy, yet at the same time be terrified of him.

GIELGUD BEGAN THIS morning where he had left off the previous afternoon, with the book scene between Hamlet and Polonius. Burton had an idea for the scene. He took his position at the top of the stairway and entered with his face buried in the book; he was wearing his coat over one arm so that it hung loosely at his side. When Polonius went to help him on with the other sleeve, the coat was found to be on the wrong arm so that Hamlet slipped into it backwards.

GIELGUD   Excellent! Keep that. And can you do some sort of wild laugh with it?

In the Rosencrantz-Guildenstern-Hamlet scene Gielgud asked why the business of Hamlet catching Guildenstern looking at the book had been cut. He insisted that it be put back in.

During the First Player's Pyrrhus speech this conversation occurred:

BURTON   John, how do you want me to say that line "Mobled Queen"?

GIELGUD   Well, I don't know. I used to play it as reminiscent, thinking of his mother.

BURTON   How about as if he's disgusted with such a bad line?

GIELGUD   Oh, that's wonderful! That'll make Polonius' following line, "Mobled Queen is good," twice as funny. But then I think we must see you get the idea of doing the play for

the King earlier. Perhaps on "the unnerved father falls."
That would be a good spot.

He gave notes following the afternoon run of the first act:

GIELGUD   I still don't get the feeling in the first scene that you
all sense the Ghost behind you when Marcellus says "Peace,
break thee off." You must immediately be aware of something when the bell strikes one. The hair stands up on the
back of your necks. Otherwise I thought that was very
smooth. How did you feel about the new things, Richard?
They seemed to go well, I thought.

BURTON   I wasn't strictly here, John.

GIELGUD   You were slow in the first scene. Hume, don't forget
to beckon to the ambassadors. Richard, why do you say "I
will speak to thee"? I think it's "I will *speak* to thee."

BURTON   I'm not sure, John. Something about previously having mentioned to Horatio that I'm going to speak to the
Ghost.

GIELGUD   I think you ought to fall to your knees *after* you say
"O, all you host of heaven." You always fall before. And you
left out "Fie, fie" before "hold, hold, my heart." I have very
little more. Dillon Evans, you make such a terrific move offstage on your Reynaldo exit, it takes you right out of the
scene; whereas if you're still hovering for your portfolio you
wouldn't get off so far. Otherwise that scene was good.
"Truly I do *fear* it," Ophelia. "Truly I do *fear* it. Truly I
do *fear* it." Polonius, I thought it might be good if you went
to the door and silenced the music the Players are making
before their entrance. Go to the door and signal and the
music will stop. Then it begins again without your permission
when they come on. Let's not have all of the Players ransack-
ing the cart for the script when Hamlet asks the Old Player
to do the speech about Priam's slaughter. You looked as if
you were Walt Disney's dwarfs digging for treasure. Two of

you will be enough. Richard, you got "remorseless, treacher-ous, lecherous" in the wrong order, but then you shouted loud enough on "O, vengeance!" to make up for it. The line is "You should *not* have believed me," Richard. You always say "You should not have *believed* me." That's all. I thought it was very smooth. You all seemed to know what you were about. It was four minutes longer than last time—but there wasn't much spirit in it before.

DRAKE   John, in the dumb show I should like to make a plea for the return of the poisoning business. Hamlet says "mich-ing mallecho" and "mischief" and we talk about all kinds of things, but nothing really happens.

GIELGUD   That's the fun of it. We don't really see.

DRAKE   This is just the Dover Wilson theory.

GIELGUD   Well, this was Voskovec's idea and I think it was brilliant of him—not to show the poisoning until the play-with-words begins. The first time he poisons him behind the scenes. I think the more vague it is, the better.

   Well, tomorrow we are ready to go with a run in costume at one o'clock. Let's try to really give a performance. So "screw your courage to the sticking point" and let's have a show tomorrow.

SATURDAY, FEBRUARY 22

12:00 NOON   Final run-through—entire play

AT 11:00 A.M. the cast began arriving to try on the clothes they would wear for performances. They paraded before Sir John, who either approved the clothes or suggested changes to costumer Jane Greenwood. At 12:00, when all were assembled and all the costumes had been reviewed, last-minute instructions were given for the afternoon run:

GIELGUD Let's really try to make today a performance. Now that you're leaving my hands—helping or otherwise—you've got to do it yourselves. What pleased me so is that during this last week your characterizations have begun to grow together. And I've got to let you go your own ways now. But now if you will only experience the play—let it *happen* to you. A great difficulty always with these famous, famous plays is that you get a performance which is good and sound, well rehearsed, but it just doesn't *live* because the actors all know that the audience knows perfectly well everything that's going to happen. That's the hardest thing about these plays of Shakespeare's. Therefore, if you will only *not* know that Claudius did the murder until it's revealed to you, and really believe that a Ghost has appeared on the battlements, it will be exciting. If we once feel that the play is pre-known it somehow becomes dead. If you can only make them believe it's really happening for the first time—that's the most difficult thing of all. But I think we will achieve this if you will empty yourselves of the impressions of the scenes themselves and all the work we've done on them and play as it goes. Find the *line* of the play and experience it as it develops. This will give the impression of real occurrence, and contemporary occurrence. But otherwise it's an old, stale play which we're playing in a stunty way.

But I think we have found a lot of new life in it through doing it in the rehearsal clothes. And we shall find more as we play it, I hope, if the audience accepts it, and I believe they will. But I can't do much more now. I can only correct a few technical mistakes and improve some of the grouping. And now I can't give you anything more. You all work marvelously together and I think you've found your characters very truly. Now if you'll only act it together as a team and let it occur. Let it happen before our eyes. Then it will be very exciting. Don't know it ever happened before, either at rehearsal, or on paper, or in Granville-Barker, or in essays, or in Dover Wilson, or in anything else. Try to forget it's a very famous classic and play as if it's a very exciting new play which the public has never seen before. And then I think you will get the excitement. So let's play through this afternoon really like a show, if you can. I won't stop anybody at all. I'll take notes, and we'll time it. And if things go wrong just go right ahead.

He gave these notes after the first act:

GIELGUD Very good! Wonderful, wonderful. I'd like to make just one bit of restaging. We've got to have Hamlet isolated from the others at the end of the second platform scene when he says "The time is out of joint." But instead of having him go upstage by himself as we've been doing, let's have you just stay in place, Richard, while Horatio and Marcellus start to leave and you stay behind. Now let me give these notes.

"Show of *violence*," Marcellus. You always say "*show* of violence." Don't pause after "the cock that is the trumpet to the morn." And can you lift the end of the scene a bit more in tone after the Ghost has gone? It's so exciting, the exit of the Ghost, that the last five speeches will be an anticlimax if we're not careful. Give it another pace. I want it to still be cold and frightened, but it must build in vocal interest to the coming of the dawn. Horatio, when you say "russet mantle clad," keep the inflection up on the end of that phrase because there's more to come.

Richard, I don't know whether you want to wear your wristwatch. You look splendid in that get-up. (Burton was wearing slacks and sweater.) I think the King's wristwatch is all right, but I don't think Horatio should wear his. Somehow it's very distracting. The King should look smart and worldly, and the watch seems to help that. I'm not even sure, Richard, that you shouldn't wear that ring.

BURTON Well, I've never been onstage without it.

GIELGUD 'Then you must wear it. I know how you feel; I have one that I'm the same way about. You played that act very beautifully.

BURTON I must say it's amazing, John, remembering the last Hamlet I did. In that production at the end of the first act I used to be dead tired. You've controlled me so well.

GIELGUD Well, the performance was very beautiful. You were so delicate. And it was marvelous what you did after your scene with the Ghost.

Bernardo, wear a sword in the second scene when you come in to Hamlet. "More in sorrow that in *anger*." You always say "More in *sorrow* than in anger."

I can't make up my mind, Hume, about how you should use Laertes' red raincoat lining when you say "rich, not gaudy." I don't know whether it's cleverer to see it when you first take it from him, as you are doing, or to keep the business of noticing it up your sleeve until you say the line. I think we'd best leave it as it is. Otherwise it may seem cute.

Ophelia, you will take your flower at your *waist*, won't you? And have it downstage so we see you take it out. It must be done exactly as you do it in the mad scene.

Very good, Laertes, you found it today. Very good!

Hume, I think when you say "Affection? Pooh" you should be more scornful. You make a short, comic, little "pooh!" (falsetto) and I think it should be "poooo!" (very bass). It's only a touch. You didn't show enough dumbfoundedness on seeing the Ghost for the first time. You should almost faint there, Richard. You go down on your knees too cutely.

BURTON I've always wanted to do a much slower reaction there.

GIELGUD Well then, do. It's far too set, though. It needs something very fearful. Really almost faint and then go down slowly.

BURTON   I once had a letter when I was doing Hamlet at the Old Vic from a man who said that while I was seeing the Ghost for the first time he went out, had a drink, and when he came back I still hadn't gotten over it.

GIELGUD   When you go off following the Ghost don't worry about moving slowly after him. Almost run off the stage. "Oh horrible, horrible, most horrible." Take much longer with that. Wonderful what you did on "O all you host of heaven," wonderful! The whole of that passage after the Ghost left was absolutely thrilling. And you did a marvelous effect when you sat there on the steps. I don't know whether you were aware of it. You were shivering, cold, emotionally exhausted, and everything else. Except you said "O, all you *host* of heaven," and it should be "O, all you host of *heaven*," to the stars. But do remember what you did in that scene. It was so exciting—different from anything you've ever done. And also the lightness, I love that too. But the scene before with the men was a bit slow. "Saw you not his face?" You shouldn't be light there. Couldn't you work that up? You were doing it before, but this time you didn't remember it until halfway through. Then it was marvelous. You didn't start quite warm enough with them, I don't think. And I thought you didn't give Horatio as warm a greeting as you gave later to Rosencrantz and Guildenstern. Horatio's the last person you expected to see. So it's "What in *faith* make *you* from Wittenberg?" "I'm so happy to see you!" And then do the scene lightly and deftly up to the mention of the Ghost.

In the swearing scene, you must make "you hear this fellow in the cellerage" a question. It isn't clear whether Horatio and Marcellus really hear the Ghost say "Swear, swear, swear." That scene was fine at the beginning and up through the Ghost, but the swearing didn't come off. It should be terrifying and awesome. It *is* fun and mad, but make it more eerie too. Really listen for the "swears!" and be more surprised when they come from different places. You don't play that up fully and it loses effect. Dillon, don't bow like Osric when you go off in the Reynaldo scene.* Just bow from the waist. And I think you should have a bowler or some other kind of hat. I think a bowler would be amusing. Don't wear it, just carry it. Otherwise, good scene. Beautiful, Hume, the whole thing.

Richard, your greeting to Rosencrantz and Guildenstern was a bit *too* happy. I don't think you're that mad about them.

BURTON What if I didn't quite remember their names?

GIELGUD No. I think it just needs a little less enthusiasm. It looked a bit naïve. "My thanks are *too* dear a ha'penny," I think it should be read.

BURTON Can I say "halfpenny"? Americans don't understand "ha'penny."

GIELGUD Yes, do. Certainly. . . . "We *were* sent for," Guildenstern. And I always feel that you crowd Hamlet when he sits on the stool for "man delights not me."

The business of Polonius stopping the music for the Players' entrance is no good. I'm sorry I suggested it. Throw it out. So sorry, it was stupid. Richard [Sterne], you weren't playing the pipe when you came on and you must when the recording you made starts. Play as you walk.

George [Voskovec], when you're in the great Pyrrhus speech I think it's a bit corny if you stop and wait for the Player to hand you the sword on "his antique sword, rebellious to his arm." Just put your hand out for it and they'll have it ready for you. As a good actor, you would go on with the words just the same. I think it will be more subtle.

When Hamlet says "It shall to the barber's with your beard," Rosencrantz and Guildenstern should be amused by that and grin at one another.

CRONYN John, while we're on this scene, I feel frightfully busy through all this. Are you sure it's all right?

* Dillon Evans doubled as Osric and Reynaldo in the production.

GIELGUD We'll try it for a night or two. The comedy in this play is so very valuable. They're going to adore all your stuff. It's very easy to take anything out that we decide is too much.

BURTON You should see what some Poloniuses get up to!

GIELGUD Oh, they're such bores! The first one I ever saw was a man called Olman Clark, who had a long white beard and a great staff. He played it to H. B. Irving's Hamlet [son of the great Irving]. And I remember even as a boy being frightfully bored with his whole performance. But since then I have played with several good ones. But no Polonius as good as yours, Hume. Richard, you said "In a dreeeam of passion." You rather imitated my habit of dragging out a word.

BURTON Well, I'm working with you, aren't I? (Burton gives an affectionate imitation of Gielgud.) "In a dreeeeam of passion."

GIELGUD (deliberately) "Plucks off my beard, and blows it in my face, tweaks me by the nose, and gives me. . . ."

BURTON Yes, luv. I was doing that at half past two this morning and I buggered it up again.

GIELGUD Nobody will notice except me. You entered a little fast before "To be or not to be." The speech itself was frightfully good, but I think you took it a little too slow. "The *law's* delay." Bring out "law."

BURTON The trouble with you, John, is that you know the damn thing so well you see many different readings. The last time you gave me "the law's *delay*," with "delay" as the important word. So maybe I dropped the "law" too much this time.

GIELGUD Yes, sorry. I think, Ophelia, you should cry when Hamlet seizes you by the wrist.

BURTON   John, Linda's doing something awfully good. She's
done it three times and still I'm so stupid that I haven't
seized hold of it. You know when I come back and say "I've
heard of your paintings too, well enough"? She reaches out
as if to touch me on the face. I don't know quite what for,
but as if to touch me—which is a marvelous opportunity for
me to grab her arm. Wouldn't it be better there than before?

GIELGUD   Yes. Let's do it then. And I think at the end of
the speech, the last time you say "To a nunnery, go," you
shouldn't be quite so brutal. More of a kind of despair. But
it was a marvelous performance of the whole act. If it is as
well played as that on Wednesday I shall sit in front and be
very, very happy. Everyone was playing and there was a real
liveliness to it. Didn't you all feel that it was lively and interesting? It really was. It was a beautiful performance. All
right, let's take ten minutes for a break.

Gielgud made some comments following the second-act run:

GIELGUD   I haven't any notes. That act dragged a bit. It wasn't
as well played as it was the other day. On the other hand,
the first act was so much better. I expect you're all very tired.
So just let's bat on and we'll start the last act at half past
four. Take ten minutes.

After the third act he went back and rearranged some of the
final court scene groupings. He also gave Ophelia some specific
cues for more vocal variety in the mad scene.

GIELGUD   All right, that's all we need to do for now. Thanks
very much. Have a good rest over the weekend. A thousand
thanks for all your hard work and labors. It's been very en-
joyable working with you, I can assure you. And let's hope
Monday night won't be too catastrophic when we get all
the lights and sound effects. I think it's in good shape, and
we won't have as many strange things to cope with as in
most productions. We've already had the platform and the

steps and most of the props, so it will be easier. The lights
and sound are the chief things to be added. It isn't like having all the terror of the scenery and costumes for the first
time. So I'll see you Monday night. Thank you so much.

SUNDAY, FEBRUARY 23

No rehearsal.   Technical set-up onstage

SHORTLY BEFORE MIDNIGHT Saturday the strike crew of
Little Me began removing their equipment and scenery. At
4:00 A.M. the *Hamlet* crew began setting up their lights, scenery, and sound equipment. The crews worked on through the
day and by midnight Sunday enough of the set was in place
for Jean Rosenthal to begin angling and focusing the lights.

MONDAY, FEBRUARY 24

8:00 P.M.   Technical run-through

MISS ROSENTHAL SPENT the entire day setting up light cues.
Meanwhile the actors began moving their make-up, costumes,
and personal belongings into the center's spacious and well-
equipped dressing rooms. When it was time for the run-through
to begin, the light cues had been set only as far as the end of
the second act. During the run, lights for the third act were
simply turned on for general illumination.

At 8:00 P.M. the technical run-through began. Gielgud anxiously watched from the auditorium as costumes, lights, sound, scenery, and actors were all brought together onstage for the first time. Sir John stopped the play twice to rerun sound cues, once to close the center doors, and once to change the position of the coatrack used to represent the arras in the nunnery and closet scenes. For the most part lights and sound were left to catch up with the action as the play continued. By 1:30 A.M. the entire play had been run. The company remained in position as Sir John came onstage with them.

GIELGUD It was really wonderful. It's remarkable how little went wrong, and I haven't any notes for you. All we must do tomorrow is bring it up to a certain pitch, which I'm sure you'll be able to do. Let's come tomorrow afternoon just for about two hours between two and four, and we can set the curtain calls and walk the last act for the light cues. I'm delighted with the performance. There is so much there. Now everybody go home and get a good night's sleep.

TUESDAY, FEBRUARY 25

8:00 P.M.   Preview performance—Benefit of the
Canadian National Ballet

DURING THE AFTERNOON rehearsal, the curtain call was rehearsed and set and the actors were then told not to exert themselves while walking through their positions for the lights in the final act. The principals were released from these maneuvers, with their understudies standing in for them.

A rather unreceptive audience filled the house for the preview. Seats had been sold at a premium for a benefit of the Canadian National Ballet and all of society turned out. After the performance Gielgud rushed on to the stage, holding everyone in place immediately after the final call.

GIELGUD   It went well. But I'm afraid I've made a terrible mistake. It all lacks color and majesty and it's my fault. Tomorrow night you'll all wear capes!

Not quite sure of having heard correctly, the bewildered cast wandered back to the dressing rooms, where a call came over the theatre squawk-boxes: "Entire company report to the Green Room tomorrow at one o'clock."

WEDNESDAY, FEBRUARY 26

1:00 P.M.   Notes in the Green Room

2:00 P.M.   Rehearsal for Act III light cues

8:00 P.M.   Toronto opening night

THE COMPANY ASSEMBLED at 1:00 P.M. in the Green Room Lounge for notes and discussion.

GIELGUD   Last night I didn't feel that the play gathered any momentum until after the third scene. After that, it began to go well, but the beginning was terribly "one toe in the water." It hadn't much confidence. I know there were mistakes in the lights and sound, and those will be right tonight. But it's essential that you really take the play by the neck in the first scene and *give* it to them. I have a feeling that excellent as everybody is—and you've really done beautiful teamwork—that there isn't enough power in the play yet. It isn't played with enough passion. And in the second scene everyone is a bit too amiable. I don't feel the wickedness yet. Alfred, you can use more low tones. It can afford more weight. And Eileen, I think I've given you too much nodding and beckoning in the beginning.

HERLIE   But so many of those Courtiers come up to me.

GIELGUD   Yes, but don't nod your head at them. Just smile and keep some mystery behind it all.

HERLIE   I'd rather they didn't all come trotting up, actually.

GIELGUD   Well, it's quite good, that, because it gives them movement. That's interesting. And for that very reason you can do less. I've asked Jane that you have a rich-colored stole over your arm in that scene.

But as I said, my feeling is that everybody is a bit too nice; Rosencrantz and Guildenstern, even you Hume, lovely as you were last night. Try to find, as it goes along, a certain malice and wickedness. They're bad, shallow people, the people in this play. All except Hamlet, Horatio, the Gravedigger, and the Player King. They all have a zestful superficiality which should create a feeling of corruption. I know it's easier to create that feeling in a costume production. But with the rehearsal clothes, and certainly in this enormous theatre, you've got to paint with very broad brush strokes, or else it's lost. You all started to find the space last night, but it will take a few more performances to master it.

Now in the play scenes, and I don't know whether we can do this without rehearsing it, I want the castle* folded up as everyone is rushing off. I tried scrapping the castle altogether, but that doesn't work. So when you run off with the lanterns and the stool, one of you take the bottom half of the castle and turn it upstage and we'll just see the back of the thing for the rest of the act. I tried it this morning and it looks very good.

Another thing that's frightfully important for anyone who uses the rostrum—you've got to use the whole width of it. From where I was sitting, people were continually masked.

* The twofold piece of scenery used by the Players in the *Murder of Gonzago* play.

You must play all the way to the side of the downstage platform, or we can't see people in the center doors.

And in the last scene, Kit Kulkin, do be careful. You're
awfully good as the Player Queen and I'm delighted with
you, but in the last scene when you're a Courtier don't stand
there listening to the King and Laertes as if you could hear
what they were saying when they have their asides. But there
is Richard Sterne over on the side. And is anybody else there
in that corner? No? Well, Kit, go over and talk to Richard
whenever you get a chance. Richard, call him over. Because
those asides of Laertes and the King must be clear and you
mustn't overhear them.

DRAKE What was so amusing last night about "It is the poisoned cup. It is too late"?

GIELGUD Well, they thought killing the King and killing Polonius were both funny.

HERLIE Oh, they thought the closet scene was hilarious.

GIELGUD And they will, you know, I think they will. My little
taxi driver was very amusing about it on the way down this
morning. I gave him tickets last night. He loved it—mad
about it. But he said it was so funny when the old man got
killed behind the clothesrack. And this is the modern world.
They think poisonings and killings are damned funny. It's
very extraordinary, isn't it?

Alfred, we're going to get you a red cape for tonight. Wear
it in the first scene and perhaps in the prayer scene. And if
you could also wear it at the end, you could muffle yourself
in it when Hamlet kills you and make a great red swirl when
you lie on the table. Do you mind? I think it will help you.
The brown suit doesn't look very good when you're thrown
on the table, and I think the red cape will look fine. And I
do beg you, Linda, in the mad scene, to wear your blouse
right open. Modesty aside! Don't tie it in front. I suppose it
would be too much for you not to have it at all, just to wear

the brassiere and the skirt. Do you think that would be too much? Would it embarrass you?

MARSH Yes.

GIELGUD It would. Well, perhaps it wouldn't be so good. You might look like the Playboy Bunny of Elsinore. And Rosencrantz, don't come on with that empty scabbard in the "Hide fox" scene. Leave it offstage. It looks most indecent, that white flexible scabbard hanging like that.

At the end of the mad scene, when Ophelia runs out for the last time and the Queen follows after her, I want the crowd to divide so that some go off to the right and some to the left. And take longer to do it. It looks silly if you all rush after the Queen. Let's just have John Hetherington follow her and the others can look at each other rather puzzled and then slowly disperse.

Linda, I feel I've not been very good with you in the mad scene, making you sit down on the floor so often. It seems as if you're always on the ground. Don't you feel that yourself?

MARSH No.

GIELGUD I didn't feel it at rehearsal, but I felt it last night. I thought "Oh, no, surely I'm not going to make her sit down on the floor again." It's wonderful when you first come on and do your little dance, but I wish you'd stay standing a little longer. Then when Laertes says "O Rose of May" you can look round at him as if to say "What are you talking about?" so we all think you're going to respond to that. And then swoop down the stairs for "They bore him barefaced on the bier." Then don't sit on the floor when you talk about the flowers. Walk over to the table and put the flowers on it and then pat the top of it as if it were a coffin lid. Do you know what I mean? And all the time I keep thinking of how to give you a different exit, because I've given you the same thing twice in a row in that scene. You must go out that way the first time and you've got to come back through the crowd by the same door. Perhaps the first time you could just creep out. Get into the doorway and look back on "Good night, ladies," and when you turn to the men in the doorway, they'll draw back in horror and you can slyly slip out between them. Then after the scene with Laertes you can rush out. That would be better. As it is, both exits seem a little bit the same. It's awful for me to ask you to do something new tonight, but we'll go up on the stage in a few minutes and try these things. And I missed a lot of the scene, Linda, because you kept your back to the audience so much. We need to have your eyes and they should look very extraordinary. Before you come on frighten yourself to death in the dressing room. Well, we'll work with it. I know you'll have more confidence tonight, darling. Just let it rip and don't be afraid.

CRONYN John, excuse me, one little bit with Linda. After I've said "You're not to see Hamlet any more," then I turn and say "Come your ways," and she is looking off after Hamlet—which I'm sure is right. Would it be possible for her to say "I will obey, my lord" a little bit sooner? Otherwise I start to go, and by the time she answers I'm off in the next county. And yet I don't want to linger for it because that would detract from her attention on Hamlet.

GIELGUD So you want her to turn quicker and say it to you?

CRONYN She doesn't have to turn to me. Just so she speaks sooner.

GIELGUD Yes. Try to remember that, Linda.
    Now it's quite obvious that in spite of all my devices and designs they are going to applaud the play at a number of places. When that happens, I think we can afford to delay, but not too much. Go on with some action or movement, so they won't clap for ten minutes. Let them see that the play's continuing.
    Then I have a plan which Alex Cohen likes very much. I want to try the play with only *one* intermission. Hamlet still

gets a rest and the second interval as it is now makes it awfully difficult for Linda in the mad scene. So perhaps on Saturday we can come for ten minutes and practice going from the Fortinbras scene directly into the Queen's entrance with the Gentleman for the mad scene. I'm sure it will be an enormous help. I thought of it immediately last night. Then each part will be an hour and a half.

BURTON   John, you're absolutely right about cutting the interval. Do you think we ought to do it for tonight? Because I know when I came on for the grave scene there was great difficulty for George [Rose]. George is the best actor in the world, but he wasn't going over. And I'm sure it was because the second interval made the show that much longer and they were tired.

GIELGUD   Well, I'm all for it. Let's do it tonight, then. We can go up and try it after we finish here. I'll work with the lights this afternoon, and we can put a note in the program that there will be only one intermission.

But you see, our actual playing time was only three hours and five minutes. That's all. I was jolly proud of it. It wasn't long or boring for a single moment. But I didn't feel you really had the audience in the first scene, Richard.

BURTON   No. I knew I didn't. I felt they were with me up to my first line. Then I knew they weren't there. We were losing them somehow. Maybe I was too subdued. I was very nervous, of course.

GIELGUD   I thought you were too gentle. That scene needed more weight and more projection. We've got to get the play under way. I know it's difficult. But after the first three scenes it was amazing. They were attentive. I was watching. They hadn't really come to see the play at all, and that's why I was so delighted that they stayed it out. They'd only come to look at each other's frocks—shouting and screaming and admiring Elizabeth, instead of watching *Hamlet*.

BURTON Well, it was a good thing we experimented with them. Elizabeth can't sit out in the audience any more. She put eighteen minutes on the play! I don't think that last night's audience had much interest in the play.

GIELGUD Well, the first scene didn't really work. I'm sure it disappointed them. And then in the second scene they were staggered by the clothes.

BURTON Well, we suspected it would take them time to get used to the clothes, but last night's audience was particularly unsophisticated.

GIELGUD Or oversophisticated.

BURTON Or over-dull. They didn't know *Hamlet* at all. Elizabeth told me some of the comments she heard about the play and they're extraordinary! Like the old lady who said "Isn't it full of quotations?"

GIELGUD But because of the rehearsal clothes we must be more definite. You've got to hit the nail on the head with the words. But we were hampered last night. The minute the curtain went up I knew the first scene was going to fail because there were lights all over the stage where they shouldn't have been and the light for the Ghost wasn't there, the footsteps didn't come, the cock didn't crow—which is absolutely vital to that first scene. And consequently it all went wrong.

A lot of Alex's friends who said they missed the plumes in the first act came round to it visually by the end of the second act because finally they got the idea that they had to imagine the costumes themselves. It's so funny. But it does show that there has to be a certain panache to the opening which perhaps we haven't found yet.

BURTON John, I felt yesterday when I watched the court scene before I came on that there ought to be a splash of color.

GIELGUD Well, there will be tonight. Jane's getting the capes, so don't be surprised. Perhaps, Eileen, you could have a gold regency scarf over your shoulders and hanging from your elbows—one like they wore in the Jane Austen period. I'd wear it in the first scene—a thing like we used to put on the piano. George [Rose], I don't think your cap is a good plan.

ROSE Not at all?

GIELGUD Well, take it off very early. It seemed to squash you down. And I don't much like the boots.

ROSE I'm not mad about them.

GIELGUD Well, then, cut them.

ROSE Should I wear an old pair of shoes?

GIELGUD Yes. Do whatever you feel about the clothes. I had a feeling you were not absolutely at ease with your clothes and with your performance last night as I know you can be.

ROSE And we cut some lines, too.

GIELGUD Yes, Richard cut "did these bones cost no more the breeding." I nearly shouted out, but I decided not to. Now will you all remember in the first court scene to be more cruel and sinister. You know, you're all a bit young. (He laughs to himself.) I suddenly remembered that I'd written in a book thirty years ago that if I ever did this play again I would have a lot of *old* Courtiers who belonged to the old King— old ladies and gentlemen. And we haven't any in this company. So if they're young they've got to be vicious and cruel, so that we feel this court is corrupt.

That's one of the disadvantages of the rehearsal clothes. Rosencrantz and Guildenstern are so much more real than they usually are; but Guildenstern should not be just a booby —he should be a *cunning* booby. And Rosencrantz, be a little sharper and more rapier-like—a fine foil for Hamlet. But they need more power, especially in this big theatre. You need to spread it in this theatre—then when I come to see you in Boston I can tell you you're all acting your heads off and hamming it up terribly and we can make it less again.

But last night I didn't hear "To be or not to be" or "Where's your father?" at all. I was sitting in a very bad seat and I didn't hear a lot, but I wrote those down because (he laughs) they're two lines that people might miss, you know.

Somebody suggested something to me last night for the Fortinbras scene and I cursed myself for not having thought of it before. We'll have the marching and the whistling begin loud and then fade away and then fade up again, so that it sounds as if each regiment goes by and then disappears. I think it'll be much more convincing. I'm going to do all the sound effects again this afternoon.

Richard, I did long for you to have a scarf and gloves in that scene—and a hat in your hand. If you don't want the hat it doesn't matter. But somehow it does need something a little bit more. I tell you what it looks like. It gives the funny effect that you're in evening dress and have been arrested and taken to the police station in your motoring coat. It was the effect of the black trousers and the white shirt with that brown coat. It looks just like somebody who's been arrested for driving badly on the way to a nightclub. If you can use the scarf you wear in the graveyard scene it would look very nice. And at the end of the scene, could you exit through the center doors rather than walking across the stage? Because you don't go off after Fortinbras' army. I think it would be a better exit to turn on your heel and walk straight out through the doors at the back.

BURTON Well, in that case, Rosey and Gildey will have to go out that way before I do.

GIELGUD I think it would be better. Then they won't have to come all the way across the stage for their exit. It's good for the Captain and Fortinbras to pass across. I don't feel that any of you place the army, any more than you place the Ghost. It would be much more convincing if you could agree exactly where you see them. And if you could really imagine during that Fortinbras scene that you are watching people passing . . . people passing . . . people passing. It's some-thing which I think you can devise as you go on playing it. It applies to the Captain too.

PHILIP COOLIDGE (the Captain) Where would you like the army to be? About tenth-row aisle?

GIELGUD No. I think it should be in the wings. Harry [stage manager] is the army. Somebody told me, and I don't know what you think, Richard, that it's impossible to behead some-body by swinging the sword like a saber, that you really ought to hold it straight up and down as if you were going to plunge it into the King's back. It's an effective movement that you do, but I daresay it would be impossible, unless you were a professional executioner, to behead somebody with a sword.

BURTON I'm not going to behead him. I'm going to brain him! Bring the sword right down across his skull.

GIELGUD Oh, is that what you're going to do? I see. I've always had the feeling you were trying to behead him. But, anyhow, it's all right.

BURTON He would certainly feel it—at least a nasty pain be-tween the eyes.

GIELGUD I think the shouts should carry on longer after you all rush out from the play scene. It would be wonderful if the shouts could stop on "Thus runs the world away." Carry them into the wings a bit longer. Even go out through the doors and up to your dressing rooms. It seems unnatural if the noise stops so quickly.

Richard, I still felt you needed much more of a stagger when you saw the Ghost. Do a terrific pantomime of recogni-tion. When you kneel right down deliberately it looks too calm. It needs a totter, and then a gasp, and then a fall. You can do something very, very . . . pictorial there. You might think it's quite exaggerated, but it will hold for this house.

DRAKE   John, would it be all right in the play scene on "The King rises" if in rising I shove the throne back? The exit around it is so awkward.

GIELGUD   You could even be so bewildered that you run down the steps and then realize you're on the stage and then turn and fly up the stairs. I think that might be very effective. You could be in such a state that you wouldn't know you were down in the middle of it all; then suddenly realize it and make a thrilling exit.

DRAKE   I'll be in Hamlet's lap. That's the only trouble there.

GIELGUD   Well, he'll back off away from you. Then on "Frighted with false fire?" he can come back to you and then you run up the stairs. I think that might be rather good.

BURTON   John, it was very distracting last night the way the lights kept changing all the time. Was that because they were still experimenting?

GIELGUD   There are a number of long fades and they also have a follow spot on you which they lost once or twice and it got onto the scenery. I noticed that.

   I've made the "Hide fox" scene much darker. Don't be put out by that tonight. There will be follow spots so you won't be lost, but the stage itself will be very dark for that scene and also the prayer scene.

BURTON   A number of people said they didn't believe the foot-steps of the Ghost. I don't know what we can do about it.

GIELGUD   Do we dare cut them? If they sound right they're effective. I'll work on them this afternoon. They still sound too much like a railway train. It's terribly hard to get the sound of footsteps on stone. Larry [Olivier] invented the famous effect of the heart beating which he used in the film. Some sound is needed, definitely.

BURTON   Why not make it a completely artificial sound, John? Make it a drum.

GIELGUD That might be good. What about the drums we use at the end of the play? Let's try them tonight. I quite agree with you. It's the attempt at being realistic that isn't working.

Laertes, I think we must cut that business of your holding the sword at the King's throat. It looks a bit absurd. But all the things before that were very good.

BURTON John, you know what you were saying about not being able to hear "Where's your father?" Do you think if instead of turning and looking at Ophelia it would be effective if I looked straight out front?

GIELGUD Might be.

BURTON It has to be soft. That way they'd hear me.

GIELGUD All right, try it.

BURTON (to Linda Marsh) So we'll try that tonight, sweetheart.

CRONYN Was the movement of the clothing rack just before "Where's your father?" all right?

GIELGUD I was sitting on the wrong side of the house, so I couldn't see it.

CRONYN Could you see my hand, Richard?

BURTON Ah, well, no. But I don't need to. All I need to see is the clothes moving.

GIELGUD There was something I .wanted to say. . . . I thought the play-within-the-play was terribly effective. Very good. It all came together and had some wonderful excitement. But that wasn't what I wanted to. . . . Oh, I know! Philip Coolidge [the Captain], you do look rather ineffective in the Fortinbras scene. There's no feeling of the outdoors. Wear a hat.

And the Ambassador needs something in the last scene because there's old Fortinbras all got up with a helmet under his arm and his overcoat round his shoulders, and you look as if you just came out of a dime store. It doesn't work. Ask Jane if you can't have something a little more important for that last scene. Wear an overcoat over your shoulders if you've got one. Are there any other questions?

ROSE   John, is it all right if we lighten the skull?

GIELGUD   Is the skull too heavy?

ROSE   No. Too dark.

GIELGUD   Oh, well, tell them, tell them. Of course.

ROSE   It should look ivory-colored with mud on it.

GIELGUD   Yes, it should, it should. Alfred, I always feel that "not that I think you do not love your father" is superfluous. Would you like to cut it?

DRAKE   I'd rather cut another one. Could we cut the five lines before the offstage shouts so that my speech ends with "infect his ear with pestilent speeches of his father's death"?

GIELGUD   Just as you like. That affects the crowd noises, then, so be sure they know. In the first court scene I think it would be better if Hamlet sat on the stool by the rostrum instead of at the end of the table. With Hamlet in the center nobody listens to a word because they are wondering why he doesn't speak. It seems to me so important that the King must have the stage. I always found the same difficulty when I played it. I used to put myself behind chairs and pillars. Richard, let's have you sit on the stool tonight.

The lines "Drink off this potion. Is thy union here? Follow my Mother" are always a bit funny. I think you must do it quite cold-bloodedly and quite slowly. The moment you do it in a hustle on the table, it somehow looks as if you're rolling the King up in a blanket. It's a bit ridiculous. But Alfred's going to wear a red cape. After you stab him he can throw it open. Then you take him by the throat and press him back on the table with the cup. Force him back and *slowly* pour the thing down his throat. I still wish you could get the cup onto the table, Richard, after you have forced him to drink it. It seems stupid if you hold on to it. I used to have the same difficulty. You hold it there just asking for Horatio to take it. So if you can, when you get it, just shove it onto the table.

Well, that's all I have. I thought it looked immensely promising. It was a marvelous piece of teamwork above all, which was what pleased me so much. The only thing is that you're all a bit too fond of one another—this may not last, of course! There is an affectionate feeling which is marvelous, but not cruel and sinister enough for this play. We knew it wouldn't all be there last night. It couldn't have been. This is such a great play you must go on working at it and making it richer.

I'm hoping to get away for a few days so that I can leave you to your own devices and then come back to it with a fresher eye. Right now I'm hanging on every word and I'm not really fair to the performance. I'm sure I'll see it better if I take a break. Now we'll go onstage and try some of these things.

For the next hour the cast walked through the major blocking changes. Sir John then dismissed the company with instructions to "take a little rest." He himself stayed on through the afternoon checking light and sound cues.

Meanwhile an urgent trip was made to the Canadian Shakespeare Festival, ninety miles away at Stratford, from whence two dozen capes were borrowed and rushed back to Toronto.

A half hour before the curtain the capes were distributed with instructions on how to wear them given by Miss Greenwood. There was just time for the actors to make a few practice crosses on the set before beginning the performance.

‡   ‡   ‡

There was great excitement for the performance. Critics had come from Canada, the United States, and England. Many celebrities were present. With the exception of a few uneasy moments in the final duel, the show ran smoothly and was much applauded at the final curtain.

Mr. Cohen gave a party for the company following the performance in the lobby of the theatre. Several members of the cast stayed up to read the local reviews. There was little agreement in them, as the following excerpts illustrate:

BURTON—THE COMPLETE HAMLET

Rockets return from space burning white-hot. Richard Burton, orbiting out among the celluloid stars for almost ten years, plunged back on to the stage last night burning just as brightly. It was a magnificent re-entry to the theatre for the wayward Welshman in Sir John Gielgud's streamlined *Hamlet*. . . .

Burton's performance is a masterpiece. He is the closest we shall come in this generation to the complete Hamlet. . . . Above all he is triumphantly articulate. Burton's voice is a supremely tuned instrument that can thunder like drums and ring like swords. . . .

Sir John has dared parade upon the O'Keefe Centre a naked *Hamlet* bared down to the taut skin of the text. And how that skin shines, once it's out from under its usual muffling trappings. On a scant but solid, partially un-painted scaffold of platform and stairs, the players pass in rough rehearsal clothes. . . . There is no pageantry about this production. . . . Groupings are blunt and basic, external movements pared to a minimum to reveal the swift thrust and eddy of action and idea within. It is as if the soul body of the play was sliced open to disclose the heart clenching spasmodically, nerves twitching and writhing. . . .

Things lag only when Burton is out of sight. And that is because he is surrounded by such a startlingly weak company. Hume Cronyn is an exception. His Polonius is superbly shaped. . . .

Sir John intervenes in his own production only once as the ghost of the elder Hamlet and only here does a disturbing note of gimmickry intrude. . . . The only indication of his spectre's arrival is the opening and closing of the huge doors at the rear, which seems a rather clumsy way for a spirit to get about. (Ron Evans—*The Toronto Telegram*)

BURTON DISAPPOINTING

There is no doubt at any time that Richard Burton is an actor big enough to undertake the role, a fact not always true of modern Hamlets. He has great personal magnetism, a superb voice and a fund of wit as well as intelligence. Given all these attributes one is still aware that last night's was a disappointing performance.

Burton's Hamlet has gusts of greatness, flashes of intensity, touches of humanity and occasional depths of thought. But there were other passages that seemed loosely related to a central concept. . . .

The great soliloquies are spoken with imagination and intelligence, never as set pieces marking the progress of an actor, yet they do not strike deep into our hearts.

. . . the quality of speech that made Gielgud a great Hamlet served this production notably as the late King Hamlet. The device of a disembodied voice is impressive, but a speechless invisible Ghost proved hard to accept at first.

The absent Gielgud was one of three memorable performances. The other two were from Hume Cronyn as Polonius and George Rose as the Gravedigger. . . . The other major roles perhaps suffered in relationship with Burton's Hamlet. . . .

Ben Edwards' backstage setting supplies much of the evening's beauty, coupled with the sparse, always expressive groupings of the Gielgud direction. The bare platforms are immensely useful in shape, and the high brick backing—centered on two towering scene-doors—achieves lofty beauty in Jean Rosenthal's fitful lighting. Jane Greenwood's choice of modern rehearsal wear is tasteful and subtle. In fact, one is put off rather by the touches of costume than by the absence of it in a production which principally demonstrates that a well-understood play needs no frills, but that a great Hamlet demands great playing from even the best of actors. (Herbert Whittaker—*The Globe and Mail*)

HAMLET UNDONE

Any discussion of Sir John Gielgud's production of *Hamlet* must start with the bold fact that as of its pre-Broadway opening last night at the O'Keefe Centre it is an unmitigated disaster. . . .

Certainly as Richard Burton is handling Hamlet at the moment . . . he has no substantial or living quality. There Mr. Burton is on the stage, a performer of the most unmistakable physical and vocal power, but his movements have an inner slackness and his hands carry on private conversations. . . . The voice is diminished in its effectiveness by a persistent rasp. His is a performance, right now, without a controlling point of view to the extent that he has any identity at all. . . .

Most of the other performers are manifestly his inferior. . . . George Rose displays a mild competence in the actor-proof part of the First Gravedigger, and Hume Cronyn is singular in the cast in evincing some idea of the point of his character.

. . . if there is one thing the show doesn't have it is any sense of actors working towards a common purpose. However close they are to one another on the center stage, each performer in *Hamlet* occupies a self-contained unrelated world.

The list of short-comings extends much further, however. The stage is formless—an assortment of turbulent and familiar effects floating about at random. The set is an eyesore. The costuming makes no sense. The performance throughout is a parade of artistic horrors. Its main redeeming feature, and that will not do, is that it is well meant. (Nathan Cohen—*The Toronto Star*)

CHAPTER V

Toronto, Boston, and New York

THURSDAY, FEBRUARY 27

THE NEGATIVE REVIEWS created unrest among the company and rumors of replacements, restaging, and new costuming began to be spread. It was even rumored that the play was being done over as a costume production with full sets. Half an hour before the second performance the company was called into the Green Room, where these anxieties were subsequently dispelled.

Mr. Cohen spoke to the cast first, assuring them that he was not worried about the notices, that when the production was undertaken controversy was predicted and even welcomed. He further added that no major changes were being planned.

Sir John then told the actors not to be disheartened, that he felt everyone had played well.

GIELGUD There are a few things I think we can improve, but now I must let you alone for a few days until you've had a chance to feel out the performances. Then I'll come back next week and fix the few things which may need attention.

Gielgud did not stay for the performance that evening, but left immediately for New York, his destination on several plane flights during the next three weeks; he was engaged in a special "Homage to Shakespeare" presentation at Lincoln Center.

Following the evening performance, morale was greatly boosted by an onstage birthday party for Elizabeth Taylor. Miss Taylor up to this time had spent most of her days in her hotel room, confined there by the crowds. She appeared at only two of the rehearsals and observed quietly from the rear of the hall. Once the show was into performances she was a backstage visitor almost nightly, watching from the wings and helping Burton and the other actors with make-up. A lovely and gracious person, she became fast friends with the actors and stagehands.

The company presented her with a large, flower-decorated cake inscribed with the words "To our Mascot and Den Mother —Love and Happy Birthday—The Company." Miss Taylor, wearing a black V-neck sweater and black slacks, ran to the prop table and returned with Hamlet's sword. Giving a perfect imitation of Burton's reading of "Now might I do it pat, now he is a-praying—and now I'll do't," she swung the sword in an arc behind her head and brought it down on the cake, masterfully hacking it in two.

TUESDAY, MARCH 3

12:00 noon   Rehearse Act I

UNKNOWN TO THE COMPANY, Gielgud had returned to Toronto to watch the previous evening's performance. He called a noon rehearsal to make some adjustments in the first act.

For the first entrance of the court, the King, the Queen, and

Hamlet were redirected to enter together with the court. The new position for Hamlet at the side of the stage opposite the council table necessitated the elimination of the business in which Hamlet had dropped his medallion noisily on the table when the King said "thinking by our late dear brother's death."

For the beginning of the Laertes farewell scene Linda Marsh showed Gielgud a new entrance she wanted to try. She entered down the stairway and met Laertes at the bottom, jumping into his arms. Gielgud permitted the change but cautioned Miss Marsh that Ophelia should be "thoughtful and remote; not frisky." In the same scene, Gielgud asked that the business of Polonius seeing Laertes' red coat lining on the line "rich, not gaudy" be cut.

CRONYN   I'm awfully fond of that, John. I wish you wouldn't cut it.

GIELGUD   But the coat lining is such a great red flag in that scene. Perhaps we can cut it down so that it's just a strip beneath Laertes' collar. As it is now, that's all we look at in that scene.

At the end of the Reynaldo scene, Gielgud cut the gag of Reynaldo forgetting his briefcase and Polonius calling him back for it. In the "rogue and peasant slave" soliloquy Gielgud suggested that Burton alter his reading of "O vengeance!" Burton had been reading it with a long wail on the final syllable of "vengeance" and Gielgud recommended putting the energy into the first syllable of the word: "O *ven*geance!" (Note: Burton first hit upon the idea for his celebrated reading of the line— a long, sustained, descending glissando on "O" followed by a tearful and almost inaudible "vengeance"—during his opening-night performance in New York.)

Gielgud watched the show again that evening. Immediately after the curtain call he held the cast in place for some notes.

GIELGUD   I think the new things are much better. Courtiers, do be careful in that first court scene that you aren't all folding your arms. At one point the King folded his and I looked round the stage and everybody in the scene was doing the same thing. And I think we have too many capes in that scene. Will two or three of you leave them off? Also, I want to cut Fortinbras' helmet and overcoat. Let's take the dragon off Fortinbras' banner so that it's just a plain white one. At the beginning of the mad scene I want the Queen and the Gentleman to enter down the stairway instead of coming up the ramp.

Hamlet, somehow we've got to get you to force the King to watch the play-with-words since he pays so little attention to the dumb show. That's all I have. I'll watch again tomorrow night. Thank you all.

THURSDAY, MARCH 5

1:00 P.M.

GIELGUD REHEARSED ALL of the scenes in which Bernardo appears, with Robert Burr going in as the replacement for Bernardo. After watching the evening show, Gielgud called a rehearsal for the next afternoon.

FRIDAY, MARCH 6

1:00 P.M.　　Company meets in Green Room for notes

GIELGUD　Very good last night, Bernardo. "Keep you in the *rear* of your affection," Laertes. Philip, have more importance as the Ambassador. We've understated the political theme of the play with the cuts, so you need to be stronger and more imposing. Not too much laughing, Rosencrantz and Guildenstern, in your first scene with Hamlet. It's getting too much. And let's cut your comic bow. (They had bowed simultaneously on their first greeting to Hamlet.) Slow down for weeping in the Hecuba speech, George Voskovec. You should be almost overcome when you get up. You recover too quickly.

Some lunatic rang me up from the University yesterday with a lot of idiotic ideas. He said the songs in the mad scene should be "hot-cha-cha." But that got me to thinking that they could be much coarser and more jolly, Linda, so that we get the feeling of a bawdy song you might have heard some drunken men sing in the street. You didn't really understand it then, and up till this scene you've repressed it, but now it comes out. It might be frightening.

Could one of the two court ladies do her hair differently? You both are wearing it the same way. And pick up your skirts by the middle, not the sides.

In the prayer scene, Richard, the gesture with the sword is terribly effective, but I never quite believe you really mean to kill the King with it. It's a tremendous theatrical effect, but it doesn't give the intention of killing. I don't know what it is. Could it be more impulsive?

BURTON When I do it properly I can hear the audience gasp.

GIELGUD Perhaps it's just too slow. But find it your own way. Let's cut the Queen's jewelry box in the closet scene. I thought "How is it with you lady" was too flip. They almost laughed. Use a dead voice for that, Richard. And I think "O throw away the worser part of it" needs to be more glorious. It's a very mellow couplet. When you say "I must to England," prepare us for the irony of that. I thought you were too mournful on that. Be thinking of the "adders fanged" when you say that. "Good night, Mother" seemed a bit too curt. There are many ways of doing that line, but try to find a different color for it. George Rose, you got very odd last night and gave another new performance. The Gravediggers were very unhappy last night. I couldn't bear you laughing at your own jokes. Both of you were working too hard, and it began to look like musical comedy. I'm sure, George, you must just sit back on the scene, and although it's very late in the evening, enjoy it your own way and be leisurely. You rushed last night because you thought they were bored with it, and it got too jolly. I'm going to try having the Courtiers set the props for you before you come on. I think having you do it yourself is too distracting. But try not to play too hard. Richard, I always feel there can be a pause before "How long will a man lie in the earth." It marks a new section. And I think you should stay standing for the Alexander speech. The skull is too yellow. It looks like a pumpkin. Make it much more white. And when you jowl it to the ground it makes too much noise when it hits the floor. See if you can throw it down on your knapsack.

Osric was too belligerent last night, Dillon. Play a little lighter. In the last scene there was too much red on the foil tip. I could see it from the tenth row. Richard, let's try it with a capsule in your hand. I also want to cut that cloak Horatio's been covering you with when you die. I don't think the breathing will be visible. And there are still too many capes in the court scene. I want to cut some of them, too.

Alex Cohen had an idea which I like very much and which we'll try tonight. We're going to leave the curtain up while the audience is arriving. Then about five minutes before we start, the Courtiers will place the furniture for the first act. Then we'll lower the curtain just before we begin. Let's go up on the stage now and work that out.

After arranging the new opening, Gielgud spent half an hour reworking the final court scene. He changed the way in which Hamlet poisoned the King so that Hamlet forced him down to the floor on one knee, rather than pressing him onto the table. He also changed the method of carrying Hamlet's body off at the end. Instead of having four men carry him off at waist height, six men lifted the body up to their shoulders and carried him off. While this was being practiced, Burton's understudy, Robert Burr, stood in for him.

After the rehearsal Gielgud left Toronto for ten days.

SUNDAY, MARCH 15

BURTON AND ELIZABETH TAYLOR were married in Montreal. They returned to Toronto to find a dressing room full of wedding gifts from the company—an assortment of pots and pans and other useful kitchen wares, including an onion chopper, a mousetrap, and two rolling pins.

MONDAY, MARCH 16

GIELGUD RETURNED to Toronto and spent part of the afternoon at a recording studio making a new tape for the Ghost scenes. Burton accompanied him to the session so that the timing of the pauses for Hamlet's interjections would be accurate. The new tape had more full voice and less whispering than the previous one. It was played at the evening performance.

There was also a new effect for the Ghost itself. The moving light and sound of footsteps were replaced by a huge shadow projection on the rear wall of a figure in a cloak and helmet. An actor standing in the wings in front of a spotlight behind the stage-left tormentor created the shadow which moved as the Ghost spoke. The stereophonic effect of the moving voice was cut in favor of a single speaker for the whole speech.

Just before the performance, Gielgud went around to the dressing rooms to greet everyone. He suggested to Alfred Drake that the King be drunk during the play scene. He told Burton to try a new move for the death speech. Instead of falling back into the chair on the line "Oh, I die, Horatio," he should remain standing until the very last, collapsing into Horatio's arms on "The rest is silence."

After the performance Burton gave a curtain speech to the audience in which he presented his wife "for the first time on any stage." When the new Mrs. Burton joined him center stage, he cited a line from the play in honor of the occasion—Hamlet's line to Ophelia in the nunnery scene, "I say we will have no more marriages!"

TUESDAY, MARCH 17

1:00 P.M.   Rehearsal on stage. Scenes 1, 2, 3, 4, and 7

SELECTED SCENES WERE run in the short afternoon rehearsal with the main intent of adjusting the time intervals for scene transitions. In most instances the length of these transitions was extended. One of the few interruptions was made in the Ghost swearing scene for the following comment:

GIELGUD There must be a crazy effect on the "Hillo ho ho" cries of the falconer, followed by the strangeness of seeing human beings of the real world after the Ghost has vanished. Then the men must be awed with terror when the Ghost is in the cellar. The audience will laugh in this scene and you must let them. "Well said, old mole" and "Hic et ubique" are laugh lines. Then hold for all laughing to cease after Horatio says "O, day and night, but this is wonderous strange," so that the audience comes back to seriousness for "And therefore as a stranger give it welcome."

Just before the evening performance Sir John sent a message around to the actors in the platform scenes not to wear their overcoats. At the end of the show he held everyone for comments:

GIELGUD Much better without the overcoats! Let's cut all of them, as well as the capes. They only seem to confuse people who don't realize that you use them in rehearsals without the rest of the costumes. I think, Richard, we should keep you in the black sweater through the whole play.* I think it's best not to have any changes of clothes, except for Osric and the Second Gravedigger, who are doubling. The Players should still wear their coats when they first come on. By that time people have gotten used to the clothes, but let's cut all the other coats, hats, capes, and what have you.

Richard, I think you ought to cut the mimicking of Guildenstern in the recorder scene. It's become too elaborate and we don't listen to the lines. That's all. I want to make one other change tomorrow. I've decided to cut Horatio's letter scene; so if Laertes, Claudius, and Gertrude could come just a half hour before the matinée tomorrow we can work that out. Thank you, everyone. Very good work.

* This eliminated the need for using fake blood on Laertes' foil during the duel.

WEDNESDAY, MARCH 18

1:00 P.M.   Half-hour rehearsal combining scenes
14 and 14A (14X cut)

To SAVE TIME and avoid repetition Gielgud cut the scene in
which Horatio reads Hamlet's letter. By a slight alteration of
lines he then combined the mad scene, which preceded the
letter-reading sections, with the Laertes-King plotting scene
which followed. After the matinée, Gielgud left Toronto and
rejoined the company the following Tuesday in Boston.

SATURDAY, MARCH 21

Toronto closing night

‡   ‡   ‡

SUNDAY, MARCH 22

THE ENTIRE COMPANY flew to Boston on a chartered plane.
Lunching on filet mignon en route, several actors speculated
that crowds in Boston would diminish, Bostonians being noted
for their sophistication.

When the plane landed a horde of three thousand sophisticates broke through the terminal gates and descended onto the landing field. Leaving the plane was delayed more than an hour until the plane could taxi into a hanger where the company was transferred to police-escorted limousines.

The Burtons faced another aggressive throng in the lobby of their hotel. Pushed and shoved, their clothes and hair torn at, they barely escaped serious injury in getting to their suite.

TUESDAY, MARCH 24

Boston opening night, Shubert Theatre

GIELGUD RETURNED TO watch the performance among an extremely enthusiastic group of first-nighters. He made several notes as he watched. After the show he started backstage but ran into an enormous crowd outside the theatre. Pushing his way to the stage door he was told sharply by the police to move along! "But I'm the director," he protested. "Sorry buddy, no one gets in that door." In desperation he returned to his hotel and wrote a note to the stage manager calling a rehearsal for noon on Thursday. (He could not rehearse on Wednesday because union rules prohibit rehearsals on matinée days.)

Notices for the show were impressive, as the following quotations demonstrate:

HAIL HAMLET! BRAVO BURTON!

Now there is the Burton Hamlet. It's a great Hamlet, this one, that takes its place in the long line now legendary—the Booth Hamlet, the Barrymore, the Olivier, the Gielgud. . . .

It takes a great Hamlet to work in plain black trousers and jumper, white T shirt showing at the chest, suavely tailored as the outfit may be, and make an audience see the noble prince. . . .

But this is no traditional portrayal. There is no peevish

brooding nor whining. This Burton Hamlet is a sarcastic, slashing, bitter one, the seething fires inside barely controlled. . . . His beautifully disciplined voice brings out the sense of each word, of each line. His lithe body moves only a minimum. In his face "all the stops" are shown. . . .

John Gielgud deserves great credit for the spareness of his direction, for the eloquence of the production, for the sense of newness which must be felt in Shakespeare. It is a *Hamlet* to thrill an audience, to bring unexpected laughs along with the smiles of recognition, to remain in the memory as a remarkable experience in the theatre. (Alta Maloney—*Boston Traveler*)

BURTON WITH BRILLIANT SUPPORT GIVES HAMLET PASSION, WARMTH

[Richard Burton] has poetry and passion in his bones and in his voice; only once or twice did he rush his speeches so that he was hard to understand. For the most part he gave us the music, the meaning and the passion of this extraordinary role. Humor was there too, and warmth and the pride of a man born for great things.

John Gielgud, whose own unforgettable Hamlet was seen here 28 years ago, conceived the idea of presenting "Hamlet" in rehearsal clothes with props and lights, and only the suggestion of scenery. . . . Sir John is an artist of the first rank and his speaking of the Ghost's lines was a fine contribution to the performance, but the drabness of those rehearsal clothes was depressing and monotonous. . . .

This production of "Hamlet" will be here for two weeks. It is an experience you should not miss. (Elinor Hughes—*Boston Herald*)

RICHARD BURTON BRILLIANT IN UNCONVENTIONAL "HAMLET"

Although it has come-as-you-are costumes, no scenery and few props, "Hamlet" at the Shubert has a genuine tragic hero in Richard Burton. Here, for once, is no niddling neurasthenic posing after ghosts and hanging himself on vowels, but a roaring, rasping, anguished and querulous human being in torment, a man bent on revenge and desperately in search of his soul. Unfortunately, the production is also on a kind of a search and I'm not sure where its honesty lies.

Guided by a concept of director John Gielgud, this "Hamlet"

is starkly unconventional. . . . It is Gielgud's idea that the illusion is nearly all in Shakespeare's language, and without the trappings to trick the eye, the audience is asked to pay attention, to listen, to intellectualize. The concept sounds plausible, looks practical, but it seems to me, in actual performance, peculiarly pretentious. . . .

Burton's brilliance blinds most of the supporting cast, not many of whom can stand the shine of his presence nor the glaring, penetrating clarity of the Gielgud concept. . . .

The costumes are motley, rather as though the actors were on their way to rehearse some other show. . . . The overall effect, I think, is far more distracting than the traditional Elizabethan costumes Gielgud was trying to escape.

And so, an unconventional "Hamlet," but one in which we have, at least, a significant hero, Mr. Burton. The rest should be silenced. (Kevin Kelly—*Boston Globe*)

BURTON "HAMLET" FAULTY, EXCITING

Although it is notably imperfect at this moment, Sir John Gielgud's production of "Hamlet," which stars Richard Burton at the Shubert, is a theatrical experience of much power and excitement, frequently tender, sometimes deeply moving, often wildly and honestly passionate.

Presented on platforms on a bare stage, in contemporary costumes that are sometimes intrusive, sometimes apt, it lacks the grandeur and the grace of the conventional "Hamlet" and —largely because Mr. Burton's voice is not musical—it hasn't the poetic beauty which the greatest productions have had. . . .

The burden of proof falls largely on Richard Burton, as it always must on the star of every "Hamlet," however conceived. He is up to it in most ways and he has moments of greatness.

He begins dubiously. . . . Perhaps because he is trying too hard to seem cute, he is uneasily cute in his first scene. . . .

As he proceeds, he gains strength. . . . He is not afraid to howl out his hero's woes at the top of his lungs as he does with magnificent effect in the "rogue and peasant slave" soliloquy. . . . He is heartbreaking as he moans at the ghost's accusation against his mother, terrifying and at the same time terribly touching in the wild, whirling words of the passage that follows the departure of the ghost. With Ophelia, he is gentle and tender till he decides her father is eavesdropping, then his rage is frightening—and moving. He never sacrifices the humanity of Hamlet to the young man's fury. . . .

His major weakness becomes apparent when the ghost, represented in this production only by a great moving shadow on the stage wall, begins to speak. The voice of the ghost is the voice of John Gielgud, and in it is all the passion and meaning which Burton commands and—at the same time—a melodious "poetic" quality which Richard Burton lacks. If he had that, this might be a great "Hamlet." (Elliot Norton—*The Record American*)

THURSDAY, MARCH 26

　　12:00 noon　Restaging of scene 8 (play scene)
　　2:30 P.M.　Work on scenes 10, 13, 15, and 16

BEFORE THE REHEARSAL BEGAN, Gielgud again asked Cronyn to cut the coat lining business; once more Cronyn made a plea for keeping it in because it helped him "to relate to something physical in the scene so that it's not just a list of platitudes." The lining stayed, but was cut down to a still smaller size.

The Captain and Osric were added to the group of Courtiers in the play scene. There were many significant changes and additions made in this scene. To begin with, the advice to the players speech began almost at the rise of the curtain, with Hamlet hurrying onto the platform to give it; the Players were grouped around him, helping each other into costumes, setting the chairs for the court, and looking over some lines at the last minute. Thus Gielgud eliminated the elaborate previous business in which the Players took two or three minutes setting up their scenery, lighting the lantern footlights, and putting on their costumes and make-up.

Gielgud made some comments on the scene:

GIELGUD　I want everyone in this court to be very jolly. They have had a good dinner and are slightly high—especially the

King. Ophelia, remain cool and try not to look at Hamlet when he embarrasses you. You can feel all of the eyes of the court on you, so you fan yourself. Everybody is conoodling with everybody in this court; the King with the Queen, the Courtiers with ladies. But they begin to get a bit uneasy when Hamlet says "my father died within two hours." Ophelia is at the breaking point—nervous, brokenhearted, dismayed, terrified, and ashamed. Remember that the next time we see her is in the mad scene, and the audience should see that coming.

Then, at the end of the dumb show, let's have Hamlet take Ophelia's fan away from her. Richard, be sure you emphasize the alliteration in "Be not you ashamed to show," so that the line sounds very bitter and bawdy. The court is shocked, but let's have one lady laugh lewdly at that. Hamlet is trying to see how Claudius and Gertrude will react to the way he treats Ophelia. He tries to use her in the way he knows Claudius is using Gertrude. He tries to shame them, yet not absolutely to expose them because he can't arouse too much suspicion at this point.

Since the King paid so little attention to the dumb show, you've got to force him to watch the play-with-words. Take him by the wrist, as if telling him it's rude not to listen.

BURTON   Suppose, John, I took his cup away from him.

GIELGUD   Yes, excellent! Only do it after you say "wormwood, wormwood." That's when the tension begins to mount. The King does not understand at first what's going on. He'd stop the play if he figured it out. Little by little the suspense is wound up and the King watches the play intently.

After a half-hour break, work resumed on the closet scene and the Fortinbras scene. In the latter, business of Fortinbras giving the Captain a letter to deliver was added on the line "Go, Captain." For the line "This is the imposthume of much wealth," Gielgud told Burton to let the thought come suddenly, "like an abscess breaking, which can kill someone." He also pointed out that the line "Am I a coward" from the "rogue and peasant slave" soliloquy is recalled in the Fortinbras soliloquy when Hamlet says "one part wisdom, and ever three parts coward."

In the graveyard scene Gielgud asked Burton for a "lighter, more quizzical feeling to show that he's revived, not down; all is resolved and he's glad to be back." The Osric scene was re-blocked with Hamlet placed nearer to Horatio to establish a closeness between the two. After restaging the Laertes-King plotting scene and polishing the end of the grave scene, Gielgud held a two-hour session alone with Linda Marsh, working on the mad scene. These were some of his comments to her:

GIELGUD Give an imperious command to your first line, "Where is the beauteous majesty of Denmark?" Everyone tries to avoid a mad person. When they speak, the voice comes out of nowhere and there is nothing behind what they say. The songs come from nothing, the voice doesn't belong to the head. . . . The entrance must be striking. Put in sudden stops and abrupt changes of mood throughout the scene. Not sad and sentimental. Many of the movements should be awkward, uncontrolled, and unladylike. Be open and nod like a child when you sing "at his heels a stone," and then be cross and furious when you say "Pray you, mark!" Ophelia is all alone in her own world. Give a tragic overtone to "Lord we know what we are," then suddenly come back to yourself on "we know not what we may be." It all has an illogicality. There is no justification for what she blurts out, and it comes in a stream like a drunken person. . . . When Laertes comes in, look at him blankly. Nothing interests you. Nothing has love or charm. Nothing matters or is worth living for. Show us a hollowness—a hopelessness. She has no wishes by the end of the scene. Perhaps she had some on her first entrance, but by the second entrance, none.

FRIDAY, MARCH 27

1:00 P.M.   Restage final court scene

GIELGUD AGAIN REARRANGED the end of the final scene so that Hamlet now forced Claudius over the arm of the chair of state while pouring the poison down his throat, so that the King died slumped over the arm of the chair. He added the business of Hamlet throwing the King out of the chair onto the floor just after he wrested the poisoned cup from Horatio's grasp. Finally he inserted the ironic touch of Hamlet seeing the King dead at his feet and giving a faint smile before collapsing into his rightful throne on "The rest is silence."

A new carry was worked out, in which the Courtiers lifted Hamlet first to their shoulders and then hoisted him to arms' length above their heads while marching out in step to the funeral drum.

TUESDAY, MARCH 31

1:00 P.M.   Scenes 2 and 7

AT THIS, THE LAST REHEARSAL, general notes were given first.

GIELGUD   This play is a poem, full of poetry, color, and mystery. Those that play it as such go over one hundred percent. Last night I couldn't hear the first scene. You all were whispering. It needs crisp, forceful diction. Use the old trick of working on the lines with a pencil between your teeth. Make the

Courtiers much happier. They're rich and warm and they've just had a big meal, and into this comes the only bad news of the scene, the Prince. The scene with Hamlet, Horatio, Marcellus, and Bernardo after the court scene was too fast. Don't anticipate the lines before they are spoken. You can get pace by vocal contrast as well as speed. It looks too re- hearsed now. When you get a fresh thought it's like turning the pages of a book. Do something different and change the tone.

Rosencrantz and Guildenstern need to be more charming and natural. They were Hamlet's friends, not thugs.

After the King has watched Hamlet and Ophelia in the nunnery scene he's afraid of what Hamlet knows. There's a change in him when he comes back. Now he's tense. He looks at Ophelia with disgust, as if to say she wasn't much good. He then suddenly gets the idea to send Hamlet away to England—which in those days was like Timbuktu.

The beginning of the closet scene was too fast. It has a slow crescendo up to the killing of Polonius. Then all of the scenes after that, up to the Fortinbras soliloquy, must be played allegro. Remember, acting is not natural—though it must seem so. It is selective. Think of a great space around yourselves with the need to focus the eye of the audience on specific things you want them to see.

After the note session Gielgud changed Hamlet's first entrance so that the King and Queen came on together and Hamlet followed them a little behind, interrupting the King just as he was about to begin speaking. There was also a change at the end of the nunnery scene, just before the first-act curtain. The previous ending had the King and Polonius exit together, leav- ing Ophelia softly crying on the steps of the platform as the curtain fell. This was changed so that Ophelia was given a tearful exit after Polonius tells her "We heard it all." The King then exited up the stairway at the end of his speech, leaving Polonius alone onstage to give a bewildered look after Ophelia as the curtain falls.

SATURDAY, APRIL 4

Boston closing night

‡ ‡ ‡

MONDAY, APRIL 6

New York, Lunt-Fontanne Theatre—first preview

GIELGUD GAVE THESE notes onstage after the performance:

GIELGUD All open-air scenes must be cleaner and grander to give the out-of-doors sense. Keep the night scenes high and frosty. Make the Courtiers more smug and well fed. Captain, be a bit more robust and jolly. Ophelia, take a moment of recognition when Laertes comes back. Just a flash. Delight more in the poisoning plot, Alfred. That's all. See you tomorrow night.

TUESDAY, APRIL 7
Second preview

GIELGUD GAVE BURTON the following letter on arriving at the theatre:

Dear Richard,

Your opening scenes were splendid last night. Simple and true. You can still be a bit *wilder* in the scene of swearing with Horatio and Marcellus. But *don't* be put off by the King in your first scene—just hate him! I have asked him to be more urbane, expansive, and confident.

Opening of nunnery scene *very* good. But after "Where's your father?" don't be so sure of your speeches and movements. It should seem as if you are caught in a trap and don't know whether to attack, retreat, burst into tears, or rush out of the room—confused hysteria, almost not knowing what you are doing. Be happier and more relaxed when you hear the Players are coming. Let us see the *connection* between the speech about pretending to be mad (in the platform scene) and your entrance to Polonius. *Underneath* the antics and points of humor with Polonius and Ros and Guild, I still do not feel that you are bitterly resentful at *having* to play the fool to deceive them. He longs to trust them, dreads seeing the King and Queen for fear they will guess the truth, yet longs to find a way to prove their guilt. "Something like the murder of my father" should surely have a kind of *horror* in it also. Don't lose pace toward the end of that soliloquy. Sudenly see the King coming, and swiftly move toward the exit. "Am I a coward?" etc.—good, but not *too* loud and violent, as that is apt to spoil the big climax of "O vengeance"—now *very* good.

In the second act. be a bit more fascinated by the *art* of the actors—hence the advice, intellectual and practical detailed advice, showing he loved the theatre as a princely amateur before all this trouble came to him. The nervousness and anxiety are good, but don't do so much of it that it blurs the detail of the prose and the good sense of the remarks about acting. Then a complete change with Horatio—a sudden relief at being able to talk (again) about personal feelings and a desire to unburden himself to somebody just before the crisis. "Now Mother, what's the matter." Stronger—was not heard last night. The same *confused* wildness that I spoke of in the platform and nunnery, differently used, of course, should propel you in the recorder's scene—pace, pace—and in the "Safely stowed" and "Politic worms." "I'm getting out of this hellish prison at last. I don't care who knows what I know! Somehow I'll get him in the end."

Fortinbras scene—more *athletic* voice—open air—a new attitude on getting out of doors. Men marching, banners flying, feet tramping. The soldier in Hamlet (his father, remember) —a more strong, determined conviction that he will *succeed* in taking action—contemplative mood starting to dispel—he'll fight the pirates, return, and complete his destiny.

Graveyard scene good, but resist a tendency to be too thoughtful—the philosophy—Yorick speech—must be in a higher, more fascinated vein. Hamlet thinks and talks of death yet no longer fears to take action, even if it brings him to risk dying because of it.

Osric scene—start with almost unnatural vividness, interest the audience at all costs, let them see a new *intention*, even though the cuts make the text difficult for you. The feeling of certainty about death coming must not lead you to self-pity or sadness at all—be more amused (and fascinated in a way) by Osric—like a curious visitor coming to see one in a nursing home, and suddenly diverting one unreasonably—a heightened awareness of everything, *curiosity*—what is to become of me? I must achieve the King's death before I go.

More real *strength* in your *intention* in the last scene. Take in what Laertes says, pinpoint the King, be determined not to let Horatio drink, look for the people you speak to, find them. Fight the poison as it spreads through your body; very important to insist about Fortinbras and the succession. Suddenly free yourself from doubts, responsibilities, but leave things as tidy as possible; a prince must die worthily, an example. Only a last tenderness for Mum and Horatio. Hope this makes sense— or some of it—

Love,
John

After the performance Gielgud again spoke to the cast onstage:

GIELGUD Marvelous, everyone. I have no notes. Play it that well on Thursday. Try to relax tomorrow and come back refreshed for opening night. I've loved working with you and I think we've got on very well. Have a brilliant performance.

WEDNESDAY, APRIL 8

1:00 P.M.   Understudies rehearse second act

‡   ‡   ‡

THURSDAY, APRIL 9

New York opening night

A RECORD CROWD, large even by New York standards, completely filled the Forty-sixth Street block in front of the Lunt-Fontanne theatre, overflowing into Broadway at one end and into Eighth Avenue at the other. First-nighters had to show their tickets to get through police lines in front of the theatre.

Gielgud saw the production for the last time. He soon left for Russia to tour *Ages of Man*, his one-man recital of Shakespeare.

Following the performance Mr. Cohen gave a $10,000 cast party in the Rainbow Room on the sixty-sixth floor of Rockefeller Center.

Most critics agreed that the show was an experience not to be missed, though they differed as to what they felt were the

merits of the production. The following are some highlights
from the reviews:

RICHARD BURTON SCORES AS HAMLET

The fact to be stated at once is that Richard Burton is a very
fine Hamlet, indeed. His Prince of Denmark is forceful, direct,
unpretentiously eloquent, more thoughtfully introspective than
darkly melancholy with the glint of ironic humor, and decid-
edly a man of action and feeling. And John Gielgud's production of Shakespeare's towering masterpiece, which had its
eagerly-awaited opening at the Lunt-Fontanne Theatre last
night, is stirring and skillful, with Hume Cronyn presenting a
memorable characterization of the blundering old Polonius.

If there was any worry over the idea of acting "Hamlet" in
rehearsal clothes, it can be dropped immediately. The plan
worked just as Mr. Gielgud predicted it would, destroying the
possibility of an ostentation of trappings and enabling the production to concentrate on the action, in addition to allowing
time for using more of the play's text than is usually to be
found. Mr. Gielgud's other contribution to the evening, his
voice over a microphone for the lines of the ghost, also worked
out with impressive effectiveness. . . . (Richard Watts, Jr.—
New York Post)

RICHARD BURTON AS HAMLET

The first and most important thing to be said about the "Hamlet" that opened last night at the Lunt-Fontanne Theater is
that it is Shakespeare, not a self-indulgent holiday for a star.
Richard Burton dominates the drama, as Hamlet should. For
his is a performance of electrical power and sweeping virility.
But it does not burst the bounds of the framework set for it by
John Gielgud's staging. . . .

Mr. Gielgud has pitched the performance to match Mr. Burton's range and intensity. The company for the most part has
been well-chosen, though it is not and cannot be expected
everywhere to approach the crispness of Hamlet's attack, the
scope of his voice, the peaks of his fury and remorse.

Mr. Gielgud's own Hamlet years ago was much different—
more sinuous and refined. It is his merit that he has found a
new way to look at the play in keeping with Mr. Burton's style
and view of the role. . . .

As one sits through a long evening that seems all too short, one is humbled afresh by the surge of Shakespeare's poetry, by his tenderness and by his disillusioned awareness of man and his ways. It is the grandeur of "Hamlet" not of the actor or director that prevails. (Howard Taubman—*New York Times*)

BURTON'S HAMLET

Richard Burton is one of the most magnificently equipped actors living. . . . He places on open display not only all of his own reverberating resources . . . but also all of the myriad qualities which the man Hamlet requires. All except one. Mr. Burton is without feeling. . . . The absence of genuinely felt heat—the kind of heat that will actually inform a raging soliloquy instead of reporting it at an adopted pitch—splits the performance, and perhaps even the production, in two. The wit is there, the intelligence stands clear. . . . But when mind is not enough, when passion must clamor up through mind and burst it asunder, Mr. Burton does no more than open another organ-stop and shift speeds: faster, faster. . . .

I am forced to conclude that it is this missing factor in the central role—an absence of personal intensity and personal intimacy—that leaves Hamlet without any directly sensed relationship . . . that has left an exceptionally distinguished company hovering in very little distinction on the sidelines. . . . With the exception of Mr. Cronyn, director Gielgud's ideal choices are to be found breathless in the effort to grasp what seems ungraspable. . . .

Has Mr. Gielgud, who has himself been a brilliant Hamlet, simply lost the impulse that once made him define the play? Has he been hesitant about helping Mr. Burton to find that seething first step that eventually turns over an embattled cosmos? I would say that the production—bearing with it so much that is potentially good—should be seen if for no other reason than to create the discussion that will help resolve what is at the moment a baffling situation. (Walter Kerr—*New York Herald Tribune*)

FORTHRIGHT PRINCE

Richard Burton depicts the Danish prince as a man cold, bold and ironic. He makes no attempt to demonstrate any of the customary Freudian conclusions about the character, and the question here is not *whether* Hamlet will revenge himself upon the king who murdered his father but *when*. . . . Mr. Burton delivers the Shakespearean verses effectively and without any

unnecessary flourishes. In this presentation, the members of the
cast wear rehearsal clothes and run through their paces on a
practically bare stage, which is a trifle disconcerting at first but
after a while seems natural enough. . . . I was somewhat disappointed by certain scenes—particularly those involving Hamlet and Queen Gertrude . . . but I found most of the production compelling. . . . I can't imagine how anyone could
improve upon Hume Cronyn's portrayal of that boring old
quidnunc, Polonius, and the rest of the cast—especially George
Rose, as the First Gravedigger—does well by the Bard. (*The
New Yorker*)

CROWNING IRONY

Burton offers an unprecedented Hamlet—a fusion of the grand
manner of the role's great nineteenth-century interpreters with
the most contemporary width and indirection. Cutting through
all the sanctified recent conceptions of the part, from the pallid
intellectual to the neurotic son, he plays Hamlet to the full, as
the complex, tortured but infinitely conscious and, above all,
animate figure of the text.

His timing is flawless, his range immense; he is fully up to
great diapasons of passion and despair. But what lifts his performance above that of any Hamlet in memory is his reinter-
pretation of the familiar. Time and again he takes a speech or
an action we had thought fixed forever in an unshakable conception, and daringly hurls it into new life.

He is humorous when we expect solemnity and withdrawn
when we anticipate aggression. . . . The entire performance is
overwhelming, a revelation of what Shakespeare can be like, a
monument to the actor's art, and a new base from which our
imaginations can recover from their sleep. (*Newsweek*)

PRINCE OF THOUGHT

Richard Burton plays Hamlet as Hamlet would like to have
been. He may be self-critical, but he is never self-doubting. He
is whole of soul, single of mind, undivided of purpose. If the
text will not permit him to sweep to his revenge, there is never
any question that he is speeding towards it with unblunted zeal.
Burton's Hamlet is master of the stage, master of Elsinore,
and master of himself. And there's the rub. A masterful Hamlet
is more heroic than tragic, and can scarcely evoke the torment
of a man who is to be overmastered by fortune and by fate. . . .

Burton and Director John Gielgud have made intelligence

the touchstone of the play. This is a thinking man's *Hamlet*, the kind G. B. Shaw might have written, and it is cool, clever, lucid, fresh, contemporary and vivid, but seldom emotionally affecting. What Burton does best is to turn sensibility into sense, modulate a phrase so that it rings with present meaning rather than bygone eloquence. He has put his passion into Hamlet's language rather than his character. He banishes the staling curse of familiarity from the soliloquies. . . .

As acting, Richard Burton's performance is a technician's marvel. His voice has gem-cutting precision and he can outroar Times Square traffic, though he lacks the liquid melody that Gielgud supplies as the voice of Hamlet's father's unseen ghost. His hands punctuate the speeches with percussive rhythm and instinctive grace. He is virile, yet mannerly, as sweet of temper as he is quick to anger, and his wary eyes dart from foe to friend with the swiftness of thought. . . .

The rehearsal clothes in which this *Hamlet* is performed tend to reduce the actors to the unregality of their garb. But Shakespeare's kingliest crown is English, and as this 400th anniversary year begins, Richard Burton's lips are brushing it with glory. (*Time*)

SUNDAY, APRIL 19

THE ENTIRE PRODUCTION was recorded at an all-day session in the studios of Columbia Records.

TUESDAY, JUNE 30
WEDNESDAY, JULY 1

Production filmed during three successive stage performances by Electronovision, Inc.

‡   ‡   ‡

SATURDAY, AUGUST 8

The production closed after 138 performances, setting records as the longest-running *Hamlet* ever to play New York (Gielgud had set the previous record of 132 performances in 1936), and the most profitable presentation of the play in stage history (grossing an estimated $1,250,000 during the eighteen-week run in New York).

A telegram arrived at the theatre for Richard Burton:

ALL CONGRATULATIONS. THINKING OF YOU FONDLY TO-NIGHT AS ALWAYS. PLEASE GIVE MY LOVE TO THE COM-PANY. WISH I COULD HAVE BEEN WITH YOU ONCE MORE.

JOHN GIELGUD

John Gielgud Directs Richard Burton in **HAMLET**

Photographs by courtesy of Friedman-Abeles

The Gravedigger (George Rose) and Hamlet become fast friends by discussing death, which unites all men.

Polonius hides behind a clothes rack (the "arras")
before Hamlet kills him in the closet scene.

The Courtiers express a feeling of uneasiness as
Hamlet tells Ophelia "Look you how cheerfully
my mother looks...and my father died within
two hours."

Hamlet pours the poison down Claudius'
throat—here on the table; later the action was
restaged so that Claudius was poisoned over
the arm of the chair.

The Courtiers watch the stylized dumb show
with bewildered amusement.

Gielgud restages the duel with Laertes,
clearing up the "traffic" problems.

Gielgud describes the mood of the "rogue and peasant slave" soliloquy to Burton.

Burton's "antic disposition",—his hair mussed and his jacket reversed—puzzles the snooping Polonius (Hume Cronyn).

While he was watching the play, Gielgud was
also acting all the parts with the actors, reflecting
the emotions in his facial expressions.

At the first read-through of the script, Gielgud
describes the Queen's willow speech to Eileen

The problem in the troublesome final court scene was how to get the poisoned cup to Hamlet and Horatio at the end. Richard Sterne (center) makes a mental note of the solution.

Burton and Gielgud think about possible solutions to the problems that have arisen during the day's rehearsal.

PART TWO

John Gielgud's Production
of

HAMLET

PRINCE OF DENMARK

by William Shakespeare

The Prompt-Script

‡   ‡   ‡

A Note on the Prompt-Script

THE FOLLOWING is the text of the play as performed in production, into which I have inserted descriptions of the stage action and have attempted to give some indication of how the actors read their lines. These notations were made after observing the show first hand in some one hundred and seventy performances.

A stage production changes continually, though often imperceptibly, but Burton, in keeping with the rehearsal format of the show, varied his performance considerably from night to night. In an interview he once gave to a group of students, he described Hamlet as "the Renaissance counterpart of a manic-depressive." In his delineation of that particular psychological characteristic, Burton frequently interchanged moments of high excitement and deep depression. Thus in Burton's performance a line read with high ecstasy one night might be delivered in tearful despondency the next. In most of these instances I have attempted to describe what Burton did most frequently, though in cases where the actor indicated no favoritism, the choice of descriptive phrases is my own (based on what seemed most effective).

A word on the cutting: The full standard text of *Hamlet*, compiled from both First Folio and Second Quarto editions, contains 3,927 lines. In the script Gielgud provided for the actors at the first rehearsal he had deleted 508 lines of this full text. During the course of rehearsals Gielgud cut another 197 lines and restored 52 of the lines he had originally cut. Thus the final version that reached Broadway was a total of 3,274 lines in length.*

Capitalized words in the dialogue indicate spoken emphasis; a series of dots (. . .) signify a short pause between words; longer pauses are indicated by the word "pause"; a dash at the end of a line indicates that the speech was interrupted by loss of thought, change in mind, or speaking by the next character; the accent mark (ˎ) indicates a pronounced syllabic ending. In general, punctuation adheres to recitation rather than syntax.

‡　　　‡　　　‡

The reader might find it interesting to follow this prompt-script while listening to the complete recording of the show (Columbia Record Album DOL-302). The recorded and the stage versions compare closely, though not exactly, the differences between the two media necessitating some changes.

R.L.S.

* It is interesting to note that by the Brubaker formula of $S = L/1000$ (playing time in hours of any given Shakespearean play equals the number of lines in the play divided by 1000), the production adhered almost exactly, with a running time of three hours and twelve minutes.

‡ ‡ ‡

SHAKESPEARE wrote his words specifically for actors and for the interpretation and embellishment which only actors can give; and his words demand this interpretation and embellishment before they surrender their full content or disclose their ultimate potency. No commentary on Hamlet, of all the countless hundreds that have been written, would be a more useful aid to a larger understanding of his character than a detailed record of the readings, the gestures, the business employed in the successive performances of the part by Burbage, by Betterton, by Garrick, by Kemble, by Macready, by Forrest, by Booth and by Irving. They have been compelled by their professional training to acquire an insight into this character—an insight to be obtained only in the theatre itself and hopelessly unattainable in the library, even by the most scholarly.

Brander Mathews

John Gielgud's production of HAMLET

*was presented by Alexander H. Cohen on April 9, 1964,
at the Lunt-Fontanne Theatre in New York City with
the following cast:*

CLAUDIUS, King of Denmark, brother of the late King	Alfred Drake
HAMLET, son of the late King, nephew to the present King	Richard Burton
POLONIUS, Lord Chamberlain	Hume Cronyn
HORATIO, friend to Hamlet	Robert Milli
LAERTES, son to Polonius	John Cullum
VOLTIMAND	Philip Coolidge
CORNELIUS	Hugh Alexander
ROSENCRANTZ } Courtiers	Clement Fowler
GUILDENSTERN	William Redfield
OSRIC	Dillon Evans
A GENTLEMAN	Richard Sterne
A PRIEST	Barnard Hughes
MARCELLUS } Officers	Barnard Hughes
BERNARDO	Robert Burr
FRANCISCO, a soldier	Michael Ebert
REYNALDO, servant to Polonius	Dillon Evans
FIRST PLAYER KING	George Voskovec
PLAYER QUEEN	Cristopher Culkin
PLAYER LUCIANUS } Group of traveling actors	Geoff Garland
PLAYER PROLOGUE	John Hetherington
PLAYER MUSICIAN	Richard Sterne
FIRST GRAVEDIGGER	George Rose
SECOND GRAVEDIGGER	Hugh Alexander

FORTINBRAS, Prince of Norway	Michael Ebert
A CAPTAIN	Philip Coolidge
ENGLISH AMBASSADOR	Hugh Alexander
GERTRUDE, Queen of Denmark, mother of Hamlet	Eileen Herlie
OPHELIA, daughter to Polonius	Linda Marsh
GHOST OF HAMLET'S FATHER	Voice of John Gielgud

LORDS, LADIES, OFFICERS,
MESSENGERS, ATTENDANTS
>Robert Burr, Cristopher Culkin,
>Michael Ebert, Dillon Evans, Geoff Garland,
>Alex Giannini, Claude Harz, John Hetherington,
>Gerome Ragni, Linda Seff, Richard Sterne,
>Carol Teitel, Frederick Young

Designed by Ben Edwards

Lighting by Jean Rosenthal

Clothes by Jane Greenwood

PROGRAM NOTE

THIS is a *Hamlet* acted in rehearsal clothes, stripped of
all extraneous trappings, so the beauty of the language
and imagery may shine through unencumbered by an
elaborate reconstruction of any particular historical period. This performance is conceived as a final run-
through, as actors call it. When a play has been thoroughly prepared, there is always a full final rehearsal of
the text and action played straight through, without interruption from the director. Properties or substitutes
are provided for the actors, but the costumes, scenery,
and lighting are yet to be added. It often happens, however, that these final adjuncts, however beautiful, may
cramp the players' imagination and detract from the poetic imagery of Shakespeare's text.

John Gielgud

SCENE DESIGNATIONS

* This second intermission was eliminated after the preview performance in Toronto on February 25; Act Two and Act Three were combined.

ACT THREE

14	Ophelia's first mad scene; Laertes' riot; Ophelia's second mad scene	IV,v
14X†	Horatio's letter scene	IV,vi
14A	Laertes-King plotting scene	IV,vii
15	Graveyard scene	V,i
16	Hamlet-Horatio-Osric scene; final court scene; duel	V,ii

† Scene 14X was cut in Toronto on March 18; scenes 14 and 14A were fused into one long scene.

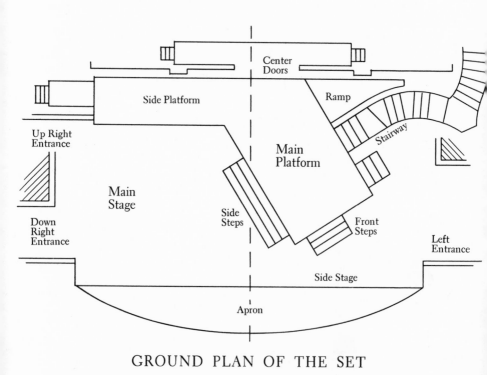

GROUND PLAN OF THE SET

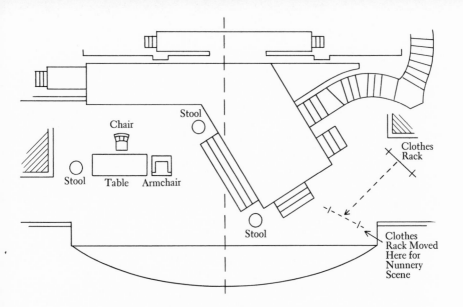

SETTING: Scenes 1-7

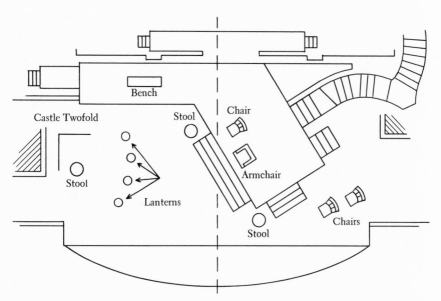

SETTING: Scene 8—The Play Scene

ACT ONE

As the audience enter the theatre they are confronted by what appears to be the gray brick wall of the rear of the stage, against which have been placed several unpainted platforms, some step units, and the scaffolding of a grand circular stairway. At the center of the rear wall is a pair of high, counterweighted, loading-dock doors. A clothing rack full of capes and robes is just visible in the stage-left wings.

A few minutes before the play begins, four actors who will appear as COURTIERS carry on the properties used for the first act. These include a long wooden table with folding legs, which is placed just right of center on the main stage, parallel to the front of the stage; a large, padded blue armchair, which represents the chair of state, placed in the center of the stage, just right of the table; a wooden straight-backed chair, centered behind the table; and three small, round wooden stools, one placed at the right end of the table, the other two placed at either end of the wide steps in front of the platform. This furniture arrangement remains fixed throughout the first act.

After the properties have been set, the curtain is lowered; the houselights dim to half and then go out.

SCENE 1

As the curtain rises, a pale blue light on the platform area reveals the figure of FRANCISCO on guard at his post. He carries a long pike as he paces back and forth with a heavy tread, shivering in the cold.

BERNARDO (Suddenly appears on the side platform. He sees FRANCISCO and for a moment thinks he may be the GHOST *he has seen before. He lowers the pike he is carrying to guard position and cries out suddenly and forcefully, like a pistol shot)* Who's there?

FRANCISCO   *(Startled, he turns, lowers his pike, and shouts back)* Nay, answer ME. Stand and unfold yourself.

BERNARDO   *(Giving the password)* Long live the King.

FRANCISCO   *(Relieved, recognizing his voice)* Bernardo!

BERNARDO   *(Approaching him)* He.

FRANCISCO   You come most carefully upon your hour.

BERNARDO   'Tis now struck twelve. Get thee to bed, Francisco.

FRANCISCO   For this relief much thanks. 'Tis bitter cold,
And I am sick at heart. *(He could say more, but he avoids it)*

BERNARDO *(Nervously)*   Have you had QUIET guard?

FRANCISCO   Not a MOUSE stirring.

BERNARDO   Well, good night. *(He takes his post on the main platform. FRANCISCO starts off toward the side platform).* *(BERNARDO calls after FRANCISCO)*
If you do meet Horatio and Marcellus,
The rivals of my watch, bid them make haste.

   (Footsteps and voices are heard offstage)

FRANCISCO *(On edge, he levels his pike)*   I think I hear them. *(Calling)* Stand ho! Who is there?

HORATIO *(Entering from the side platform)*   FRIENDS to this ground!

MARCELLUS *(Following him onstage with a lantern and wearing a sword)*   And liegemen to the Dane.

FRANCISCO *(To BERNARDO)*   Give you good night. *(He starts to go)*

MARCELLUS (*Passing him*) O farewell, honest soldier. (*Seeing the figure of* BERNARDO *downstage*) Who hath relieved you?

FRANCISCO Bernardo hath my place. (*To* HORATIO) Give you good night. (*He exits right of the side platform*)

MARCELLUS Holla, Bernardo?

BERNARDO (*Trying to see in the dark*) Say— What, is Horatio there?

HORATIO (*Good naturedly*) A piece of him. (*He comes down on the main platform*)

BERNARDO Welcome, Horatio. Welcome, good Marcellus.

MARCELLUS (*Holding his lantern out over the edge of the platform, peering into the distance. He speaks with embarrassed fear*) What, has this THING appeared again tonight?

BERNARDO I have seen nothing.

MARCELLUS Horatio say 'tis but our fantasy, (HORATIO *laughs*)
And will not let belief take hold of him
Touching this dreaded sight twice seen of us.
Therefore I have entreated him along,
With us to watch the minutes of this night,
That if again this apparition come,
He may approve our eyes and speak to it.

HORATIO (*Skeptically*) Tush, tush! 'Twill not appear.

BERNARDO Sit down awhile,
And let us once again assail your ears
That are so fortified AGAINST our story
What we have two nights SEEN!

HORATIO Well, sit we down,
And let us hear Bernardo speak of this.

(*He sits at the top of the front steps, right of the platform*)

BERNARDO (*Kneeling next to* HORATIO *on the platform*)
Last night of all,   (*Points up at the sky*)
When yond same star that's westward from the pole
Had made his course to illume that part of heaven
Where now it burns, Marcellus and myself—
   (*A distant bell chimes once.* BERNARDO *is terrified*)
The bell THEN beating one—

   (*The huge shadow of an armoured figure appears on the back wall*)

MARCELLUS   Peace! Break thee off! Look where it comes again!

   (*They all see the* GHOST *in front of the stage; the shadow of it appears behind them.* BERNARDO *backs up to the stairway,* HORATIO *retreats to the center doors,* MARCELLUS *backs down the side steps and draws his sword*)

BERNARDO   In the same figure, like the king that's dead.

MARCELLUS   Thou art a scholar; speak to it, Horatio.

BERNARDO (*With much emotion*)   Looks it not like the KING?
Mark it, Horatio.

HORATIO (*Dumbfounded*)   Most like! It harrows me with fear
and wonder!

BERNARDO   It would be spoke to.

MARCELLUS   Question it, Horatio.

HORATIO (*Awesomely*)   What art thou, that usurp'st this time
of night,
Together with that fair and warlike form
In which the majesty of buried Denmark
Did sometimes march? By heaven, I charge thee, SPEAK!

   (*The shadow enlarges, as if it were stalking back*)

MARCELLUS   It is offended!

BERNARDO   See, it stalks away.

HORATIO   (*Following the shadow to the front of the platform*)
Stay! Speak, speak, I charge thee, SPEAK!

> (*The shadow gets larger until it completely blackens the rear wall and disappears*)

MARCELLUS   'Tis gone, and will not answer.

> (HORATIO *shudders and collapses on the front steps*)

BERNARDO   How now, Horatio? You tremble and look pale.
Is not this something more than fantasy?
What think you on't?

HORATIO   (*Shaken*)   Before my God, I might not this believe
Without the sensible and true avouch
Of mine own eyes.

MARCELLUS   Is it not like the King?

HORATIO   (*Recalling with dismay*)   As thou art to thyself.
Such was the very ARMOUR he had on
When he the ambitious Norway combated.
So frowned he once, when in an angry parle
He smote the sleddèd Polacks on the ice.
(*Softly*)   'Tis strange.

MARCELLUS   Thus twice before, and jump at this dead hour,
With martial stalk hath he gone by our watch.

HORATIO   In what particular thought to work, I know not.
But in the gross and scope of my opinion,
This bodes some strange eruption to our state.
> (*Musing to himself, as he recalls his history studies*)
In the most high and palmy state of Rome,
A little ere the mightiest Julius fell,
The graves stood tenantless, and the sheeted dead
Did squeak and gibber in the Roman streets.
> (*The shadow reappears suddenly*)
But soft! Behold! Lo, where it comes again!

(MARCELLUS *and* BERNARDO *retreat.* HORATIO *stands his ground*) I'll cross it though it blast me! (*Shouts*) Stay, . . . illusion!
If thou hast any sound or use of voice,
Speak to me! (*The shadow advances one step.* HORATIO *falls back a step*)
If there be any good thing to be done
That may to thee do ease, and grace to me,
Speak to me! (*Another advance, another retreat*)
If thou art privy to thy country's fate
Which happily foreknowing may avoid, (*The shadow reaches huge proportions*)
Speak of it! Stay and speak! (*A cock crows and the shadow turns and falters*) Stop it, Marcellus!

BERNARDO (*Raising his pike*) Shall I strike at it with my partisan?

HORATIO Do, if it will not stand.

BERNARDO (*Crashing the pike down on the platform in an attempt to hit the* GHOST) 'Tis here!

HORATIO (*Lunges forward and tries to grab it*) 'Tis HERE!

(*The shadow vanishes*)

MARCELLUS 'Tis gone. (*Pause.* MARCELLUS *speaks nobly, solemnly*) We do it wrong, being so majestical,
To offer it this show of violence;
For it is, as the air, invulnerable (*He picks up his lantern*)
And our vain blows malicious mockery.

BERNARDO (*Looking to* HORATIO *for approval*) It was ABOUT to speak, when the cock crew.

HORATIO And then it started like a guilty thing
Upon a fearful summons. I have heard
The cock, that is the trumpet to the morn,
Doth with his lofty and shrill-sounding throat
Awake the god of day. (*Coming onto the front steps, look-*

ing out after the spirit)   And at his warning,
Whether in sea or fire, in earth or air,
The extravagant and erring spirit hies
To his confine.

    (*The lights slowly begin to change to a warm amber*)

MARCELLUS   It faded on the crowing of the cock.
    (*Religiously, as a benediction*)   Some say that ever 'gainst
      that season comes
Wherein our Saviour's birth is celebrated,
The bird of dawning singeth all night long.
.And then they say no spirit dare stir abroad;
The nights are wholesome; then no planets strike,
No fairy takes, nor witch hath power to charm,
So hallowed and so gracious is that time.

HORATIO (*Facing upstage to* MARCELLUS)
So have I heard and do in part believe it.   (*Feeling the
warmth of the sun on the back of his neck, he turns and faces
out*)
But look! The morn in russet mantle clad
Walks o'er the dew of yon high eastern hill.
Break we our watch up; (MARCELLUS *blows out his lantern*)
    and by my advice
Let us impart what we have seen tonight
Unto young Hamlet. For upon my life,
This spirit dumb to us, will speak to him.

    (*They nod in agreement and all hurry off down left*)

SCENE 2

*The lights rise fully on the entire stage. The court enters
immediately, talking loudly.* POLONIUS *and* LAERTES *are the first*

*to enter, coming down the stairway. The old man uses a thin
straight cane to support his lame right leg and carries a portfolio
under his left arm. As they reach the platform, two attendants
come up the ramp and take their places at either side of the center doors. They are followed up the ramp by the Ambassadors,*
CORNELIUS *and* VOLTIMAND, *who stand at the center of the platform.* POLONIUS *crosses to his place behind the right of the table
while* LAERTES *remains at the left side of the platform. By this
time, six additional* COURTIERS *have entered and placed themselves around the periphery of the setting. All members of the
court greet one another and engage in a moment of idle chatter
until* CLAUDIUS *and* GERTRUDE *enter through the center doors. All
bow and kneel.* CLAUDIUS *escorts* GERTRUDE *on his left arm down
to the armchair where he seats her. He then takes his place behind
the center of the table. He is just about to begin speaking when*
HAMLET *enters tardily through the center doors. The* COURTIERS
*all bow to him, but he keeps his head low and does not ac-
knowledge them. He comes down the steps and sits on the stool
below the front corner of the platform.*

CLAUDIUS (*Trying not to let* HAMLET's *behavior affect him, he
speaks affably, grandly, with great tact, not wanting anyone
to think he is not sorry over* THE ELDER Hamlet's *death*)
Though yet of Hamlet our dear brother's death
The memory be green, and that it us befitted
To bear our hearts in grief, and our whole kingdom
To be contracted in one brow of woe,
Yet so far hath discretion fought with nature
That we with wisest sorrow think on him,
Together with remembrance of ourselves.
    (*Taking* GERTRUDE's *hand, he speaks more brightly*)
Therefore our sometime sister, now our Queen,
The imperial jointress of this warlike state
    (*Crossing behind her to center stage*)
Have we, as 'twere with a DEFEATED joy,
With one auspicious and one dropping eye,

(*He glances at* HAMLET, *who has been staring straight
ahead through all this*)
With mirth in funeral, and with dirge in marriage,
In equal scale weighing delight and dole,
Taken to wife. Nor have we herein barred
Your better wisdoms, which have freely gone
With this affair along. For all, our thanks.
    (*All bow.* CLAUDIUS *crosses back to his place behind the
table and picks up a schedule which* POLONIUS *has
placed in front of him*) Now follows that you know.
(POLONIUS *beckons the Ambassadors forward.* CORNELIUS *and*
VOLTIMAND *come down the steps to center stage,* CORNELIUS
glancing at HAMLET *as he passes behind him.* CLAUDIUS *sits in a
chair behind the table*)
Young Fortinbras,
Holding a weak supposal of our worth,
Or thinking by our late dear brother's death*
Our state to be disjoint and out of frame,
Colleaguèd with this dream of his advantage,
He hath not failed to pester us with message
Importing the surrender of those lands
Lost by his father, with all bonds of law,
To our most valiant brother.   (*He picks up a letter*)
We have here writ
To Norway, uncle of young Fortinbras,
Who, (*With a slight chuckle*) impotent and bed-rid, scarcely
   hears
Of this his nephew's purpose, to suppress
His further gait herein; (*He folds the letter and hands it to*
POLONIUS)
And we here dispatch
You, good Cornelius, and you, Voltimand,

---

* It was at this point that Hamlet originally dropped a medallion on the
table, interrupting the King. This business was eliminated in the second
week of performances in Toronto when Hamlet was placed on the opposite side of the stage.

For bearers of this greeting to old Norway.
> (POLONIUS *crosses behind* CLAUDIUS *and gives the letter to* VOLTIMAND)

Farewell! And let your haste commend your duty.

VOLTIMAND (*Taking the letter*)   In that and all things will we show our duty.

CLAUDIUS   We doubt it nothing. Heartily farewell.
> (VOLTIMAND *and* CORNELIUS *bow and exit by the ramp.* POLONIUS *beckons* LAERTES *forward to the right of the platform. He then whispers in* CLAUDIUS' *ear.* CLAUDIUS *nods and smiles. He rises and crosses up the steps to* LAERTES. CLAUDIUS *speaks warmly*) And now, Laertes, what's the news with YOU?

You told us of some suit. What is't, Laertes?
You cannot speak of reason to the Dane
> (*He gives another look to* HAMLET, *who still faces front, motionless*)

And lose your voice. What would'st thou beg, Laertes,
That shall not be my offer, not thy asking?
The head is not more native to the heart,
The hand more instrumental to the mouth,
Than is the throne of Denmark to thy father.
What would'st thou have, Laertes?

LAERTES (*Kneeling before him*)   My dread lord,
Your leave and favour to return to France,
From whence though willingly I CAME to Denmark
To show my duty in your coronation,
Yet now I must confess, that duty done,
My thoughts and wishes bend again toward France,
And bow them to your gracious leave and pardon.

CLAUDIUS   Have you your FATHER's leave? What says Polonius?

POLONIUS (*Crossing center stage, he speaks proudly and dotingly*)   He hath, my lord, wrung from me my slow leave
By laboursome petition. And, at last,

Upon his will I sealed my hard consent.
I do beseech you, give him leave to go.

CLAUDIUS   Take thy fair hour, Laertes, time be thine.
>   (LAERTES *kisses the ring on* CLAUDIUS' *extended hand and*
>   *rises, about to leave.* CLAUDIUS *grasps his shoulder and,*
>   *knowing the way of young men in Paris, adds good-*
>   *humoredly*)
And thy best graces spend it at thy will! (LAERTES *smiles and*
exits left down the ramp. There is a pause. Realizing that the
court is very much aware of HAMLET'S *recalcitrance,* CLAUDIUS
looks at him a moment, trying to decide what to do. He
comes part way down the steps behind HAMLET *and speaks*
gently)   But now, my cousin Hamlet, and my son—

HAMLET (*Immobile, looking straight ahead, he says softly to*
himself)   A little more than kin, and less than kind.

>   (POLONIUS *looks to see if* CLAUDIUS *heard* HAMLET *speak*)

CLAUDIUS (*Aware that* HAMLET *has said something, but not*
knowing precisely what)
How is it that the clouds still hang on you?

HAMLET (*Aloud, still facing front, without emotion*)
Not so, my lord. I am too much in the sun.

>   (CLAUDIUS *looks to* GERTRUDE *for help*)

GERTRUDE (*With much concern*)   Good Hamlet, cast thy
    nighted colour off,
And let thine eye look like a friend on Denmark.
Do not for ever with thy vailèd lids
Seek for thy noble father in the dust.
Thou know'st 'tis common, all that lives must die,
Passing through nature to eternity.

HAMLET (*Flatly*)   Aye, madam, it is common.

GERTRUDE   If it be,
Why seems it so particular with THEE?

HAMLET (*Showing slight affront, he turns toward her*)
"SEEMS," madam? Nay, it IS. I know not "SEEMS."
'Tis not alone my inky cloak, good mother,
Nor customary suits of solemn black,
Nor windy suspiration of forced breath,
No, nor the fruitful river in the eye,
Nor the dejected haviour of the visage,
Together with all forms, modes, shapes of grief
That can denote me truly. These indeed "SEEM,"
For they are actions that a man might . . . (*He glances at*
CLAUDIUS) play.
But I have that within which passeth show—
These (*indicating his clothes*) but the trappings and the suits
of woe.

(GERTRUDE *looks helplessly to* CLAUDIUS)

CLAUDIUS (*Stepping up on the platform directly above* HAMLET)
'Tis sweet and commendable in your nature, Hamlet,
To give these mourning duties to your father.
But you must know, your father lost a father;
That father lost, lost his; and the survivor bound
In filial obligation for some term
To do obsequious sorrow. (*He looks to the nearby* COURTIERS,
who smile and nod their approval) But to persever
In OBSTINATE condolement is a course
Of impious stubbornness. 'Tis UNMANLY grief.
    (HAMLET *raises his head almost imperceptibly, tighten-
    ing with resentment*)
It shows a will most incorrect to heaven,
A heart unfortified, a mind impatient,
An understanding simple and unschooled.
For what we know must be and IS as (*Picking up* HAMLET's
word) "common"
As any the most vulgar thing to sense. (CLAUDIUS *crosses right
to the front of the table.* GERTRUDE *reaches out as he passes her,*

entreating leniency with HAMLET, *but her gesture goes un-
noticed*) Why should we in our peevish opposition
Take it to heart? (*He turns and faces* HAMLET) Fie, 'tis a
    fault to heaven,
A fault against the dead, a fault to nature.
        (*Crossing center toward* HAMLET, *appealingly*)
We pray you, throw to earth
This unprevailing woe, and think of US
As of a father. For let the world take note;
YOU are the most immediate to our throne;
        (COURTIERS *all bow to* HAMLET; POLONIUS *does so a bit
        reluctantly*)
And with no less nobility of love
Than that which dearest father bears his son
Do I impart toward you. (*With a touch of mustard*) For
    your intent
In going back to school in Wittenberg,
It is most retrograde to our desire,
And we beseech you, (*With a threatening smile*) BEND you,
    to remain
Here in the cheer and comfort of our eye,
Our chiefest courtier, cousin, and our son.

GERTRUDE (*Crossing to* HAMLET, *who stands in her presence*)
Let not thy mother lose her prayers, Hamlet.
I pray thee, stay with us. Go not to Wittenberg.

        (*She goes to caress his cheek with her hand*)

HAMLET (*Moving away to avoid her touch*)
I shall in all my best obey you, madam.

        (GERTRUDE *searches his face questioningly*)

CLAUDIUS (*Atoning for* HAMLET's *reaction*)
Why, 'tis a loving and a fair reply.
        (*He crosses to* GERTRUDE, *puts his hands on her shoul-
        ders, and caresses them*)
Be as OURSELF in Denmark.

(*Offering her his hand*) Madam, come.
This gentle and forced accord of Hamlet
Sits smiling to my heart; (*He escorts her up the steps to the
front of the center doors*) in grace whereof,
No jocund health that Denmark drinks today,
But the great cannon to the clouds shall tell;
And the King's rouse, the heaven shall bruit again,
Re-speaking earthly thunder. Come, away!

> (*The* COURTIERS *all bow to* CLAUDIUS *and* GERTRUDE, *who
> exit through the center doors.* COURTIERS *then bow to*
> HAMLET, *who does not acknowledge them.* COURTIERS
> *exit.* HAMLET *begins to follow off after* CLAUDIUS *and*
> GERTRUDE, *but stops center stage, unable to follow; he
> turns away and supports his weight on the back of the
> armchair*)

HAMLET (*Sadly, with intense despair*)
O, that this too too solid flesh would melt,
Thaw and resolve itself into a dew.
Or that the Everlasting had not fixed
His canon 'gainst self-slaughter. O God! God,
How weary, stale, flat, and unprofitable
Seem to me all the uses of this world!
(*Vehemently*) Fie on't, ah fie! 'Tis an unweeded garden
That grows to seed. Things rank and gross in nature
Possess it merely. (*Pointing to the armchair*) That it should
    come to THIS!
But two months dead— nay not so much, not two—
So EXCELLENT a King, that was, to this,
Hyperion to a satyr. So loving to my mother,
That he might not beteem the winds of heaven
Visit her face too roughly. (*He sits in the armchair*) Heaven
    and earth,
Must I remember? Why, she would hang on him
As if increase of appetite had grown
By what it fed on. And yet within a month—
Let me not think on't. (*With bitter anger*) Frailty, thy

NAME is WOMAN.
(*Incredulously*)A little month; (*He jumps up and paces about
anxiously and uneasily*) or e're those SHOES were old
With which she followed my poor father's body
Like Niobe, all tears; why she, even she—
(*Anguished*) O God, a beast that wants discourse of reason
Would have mourned longer— married with my uncle,
(*Slowly, with emphasis*) My father's brother, but no more
  like my father
Than I to Hercules. (*Tumultuously*) Within a month!
Ere yet the salt of most unrighteous tears
Had left the flushing in her gallèd eyes,
She MARRIED! O most wicked speed, to post
With such dexterity to incestuous sheets.
(*He comes back to the chair and sits in it wearily. He speaks
softly, hopelessly*) It is not, nor it cannot come to good.
(*Tearfully*) But break, my heart, for I must hold my tongue.

  (HORATIO, MARCELLUS, *and* BERNARDO *come hurrying up
  the ramp*)

HORATIO (*Tentatively, as if afraid of intruding*)   Hail to your
  lordship.

HAMLET (*Not looking at him, he gets up and starts to go; then
  he says mechanically*) I am glad to see you well. (*Suddenly
  recognizing him*)   Horatio! Or I do forget MYSELF!

HORATIO (*Meeting him center stage, he shakes* HAMLET's *hand*)
  The same, my lord, and your poor servant ever.

HAMLET   Sir, my good friend, I'll CHANGE that name with
  you.
  And what make you from Wittenberg, Horatio? (*Seeing the
  others*) Marcellus?

MARCELLUS   My good lord.

HAMLET   I am very glad to see you. (*To* BERNARDO, *politely,
  unable to recall his name*) Good even . . . sir.
  (*Pressing*) But what, in faith, make you from Wittenberg?

HORATIO (*Jesting, not quite knowing how to tell him what has happened*) A truant disposition, good my lord.

HAMLET (*With a little laugh*) Ha, ha. I would not hear your enemy say so!
(*Crossing to the table*) Nor shall you do my ear that violence
To make it truster of your own report
AGAINST yourself. I know you are no truant. (*He sits at the edge of the table*)
But what is your affair in Elsinore?
We'll teach you to drink DEEP ere you depart.

HORATIO My lord, I came to see your father's funeral

HAMLET (*Sadly, with a touch of bitterness*)
I pray thee do not mock me, fellow student,
I think it was to see my mother's wedding.

HORATIO Indeed, my lord, it followed hard upon.

HAMLET (*Sardonically*) Thrift! Thrift, Horatio! The funeral baked meats
Did coldly furnish forth the marriage tables!
(*Despondently*) Would I had met my dearest foe in heaven
Or ever I had seen that day, Horatio.
(*Staring fixedly ahead*) My father— me thinks I see my father.

HORATIO (*Alarmed, he,* MARCELLUS, *and* BERNARDO *exchange a look*) Where, my lord?

HAMLET (*Puzzled over his alarm, he answers matter-of-factly*)
In my mind's eye, Horatio.

HORATIO I saw him once, he was a goodly King.

HAMLET (*Majestically*) He was a MAN. (*Pause*) Take him for all in all,
I shall not look upon his like again.

HORATIO My lord, I think I saw him yesternight.

HAMLET (*Not comprehending*) Saw . . . (*Suddenly he stands horrified*) WHO!

HORATIO My lord, the King your father.

HAMLET (*Astounded*) The King, my father!

HORATIO Season your admiration for a while
With an attent ear, till I may deliver
Upon the witness of these gentlemen
This marvel to you.

      (MARCELLUS *and* BERNARDO *come forward in affirmation*)

HAMLET For God's love, let me hear.

HORATIO Two nights together had these gentlemen,
Marcellus and Bernardo, on their watch
In the dead vast and middle of the night
Been thus encountered: A figure, like your father,
Armed at point exactly, (*Indicating his body*) cap-a-pe,
Appears before them, and with solemn march
Goes slow and stately by them. THRICE he walked
By their oppressed and fear-surprisèd eyes
Within his truncheon's length, whilst they, distilled
Almost to jelly with the act of fear,
Stand dumb, and speak not to him. This to me
In dreadful secrecy impart they did,
And I with them the third night kept the watch,
Where, as they had delivered, both in time,
Form of the thing, each word made true and good,
The apparition comes!
(HAMLET *paces toward stage center*) I KNEW your father;
These hands are not more like.

HAMLET (*He halts and questions* MARCELLUS) But where was
this?

MARCELLUS My lord, upon the platform where we watched.

HAMLET (*Turns excitedly to* HORATIO)   Did you not speak to
   it?

HORATIO   My lord, I DID,
   But answer made it none. Yet once methought
   It lifted up its head and did address
   Itself to motion, like as it would speak;
   But even then the morning cock crew loud,
   And at the sound it shrunk in haste away
   And vanished from our sight.

HAMLET (*Incredulously*)   'Tis very strange.

HORATIO   As I do live, my honoured lord, 'tis true!
   And we did think it writ down in our duty
   To let you know of it.

HAMLET   Indeed, indeed, sirs, but this troubles me.
   (*A thought strikes him*) Hold you the watch tonight?

BERNARDO   We do, my lord.

HAMLET (*Anxiously*)   ARMED, say you!

MARCELLUS   Armed, my lord.

HAMLET (*Accelerating the dialogue*)   From top to toe?

BERNARDO   My lord, from head to foot.

HAMLET (*Testing them*)   Then saw you not his FACE?

HORATIO   Oh yes, my lord, he wore his beaver up.

HAMLET   What looked he, (*Fearfully*) frowningly?

HORATIO   A countenance more in SORROW than in anger.

HAMLET (*Rapidly*)   Pale, or red?

HORATIO   Nay, very pale.

HAMLET (*Racing the words*)   And fixed his eyes upon you?

HORATIO   Most constantly.

HAMLET (*Intensely*)   I would I had been there!

HORATIO   It would have much amazed you.

HAMLET (*Impatiently*)   Very like, very like. (*Persisting*) Stayed it long?

HORATIO   While one with moderate haste might tell a hundred.

BERNARDO   Longer.

HORATIO   Not when *I* saw it.

HAMLET (*Pressing*)   His beard was grizzled, no?

HORATIO (*Concurring*)   It was as I have seen it in his life,
A sable silvered. (*Pause*)

HAMLET (*Paces and looks to each of them. Finally, he speaks
with resolution*)   I will watch tonight.
Perchance 'twill walk again.

HORATIO   I warrant it will.

HAMLET   If it assume my noble father's person,
I'll speak to it, though hell itself should gape
And bid me hold my peace. (*He checks to see that no one
has overheard, then beckons them close to him*) I pray you
all,
If you have hitherto concealed this sight,
Let it be tenable in your silence still.
And whatsoever else shall hap tonight,
Give it an understanding, but (*He puts his finger to his lips*)
no tongue.
I will requite your loves. (*Shaking hands with* BERNARDO *and*
MARCELLUS) So, fare you well.
Upon the platform 'twixt eleven and twelve
I'll visit you.

BERNARDO   Our duty to your honour.

HAMLET   Your loves, as mine to you. (BERNARDO *and* MARCEL-
LUS *start off toward the ramp.* HORATIO *is about to leave with*

them when HAMLET *catches him by the hand and says to him warmly*) Farewell. (*Left alone, he comes forward to the apron in agitation and says softly to himself*)
My father's spirit, in arms! All is not well.
I doubt some foul play. (*Looking up uneasily*) Would the
    night were come!
Til then sit still, my soul. (OPHELIA *enters and watches* HAMLET
from the top of the stairway) Foul deeds will rise,
Though all the earth o'erwhelm them to men's eyes.

(*He exits down right, unaware of* OPHELIA'S *presence*)

SCENE 3

OPHELIA *comes down the stairway, confused, watching after*
HAMLET.

LAERTES (*Enters down left with a coat on his arm. He crosses
up onto the platform and confronts her. His jubilant manner
diverts her presentiments*)
My necessaries are embarked. Farewell.
And, sister, (*He picks her up off the stairway and swings her
around onto the platform*) as the winds give benefit
And convoy is assistant, do not sleep,
But let me hear from you.

OPHELIA (*Laughing*)   Do you doubt that?

LAERTES (*Suddenly becoming serious and worldly wise*)
For Hamlet, (*She looks off right again*) and the trifling of
    his favour,
Hold it a fashion, and a toy in blood;
(*He puts his arm around her, walking her forward to the side
steps*)
A violet in the youth of primy nature,

Forward, not PERMANENT, sweet, not LASTING,
The perfume and suppliance of a minute,
No more.

OPHELIA   No more but so?

LAERTES (*Firmly*) Think it no more. (*He takes her by the
hand and, dropping his coat on the downstage corner of the
platform, he sits with her on the steps*)
Perhaps he loves you NOW,
And now no soil nor cautel doth besmirch
The virtue of his will, but you must FEAR.
His greatness weighed, his will is not his own;
For he himself is subject to his birth.
He may not, as UNVALUED persons do,
Carve for HIMSELF, for on his choice depends
The safety and the health of this whole state.
Then weigh what loss your honour may sustain
If with too credent ear you LIST his songs,
Or lose your heart, or your chaste treasure open
To his unmastered importunity. (*She gets up impatiently
and stands on the platform; he stands and turns to her, taking
her hand imploringly*)
Fear it, Ophelia. Fear it, my dear sister,
And keep you in the REAR of your affection,
Out of the shot and danger of desire.
The chariest maid is prodigal enough
If she unmask her beauty to the MOON!

OPHELIA (*Taking him by the arm down the front steps to the
side stage*)
I shall the effect of this good lesson keep
As watchman to my heart. (*Humorously, she lectures him
back*) But, good my brother,
Do not as some ungracious pastors do,
Show me the steep and thorny way to heaven,
Whiles like a puffed and reckless libertine,
HIMSELF the primrose path of dalliance treads

And recks not his own rede. (*She takes him in her arms as if she wanted to stay forever*)

LAERTES (*Laughing*) O fear ME not. (He taps her on the nose)
I stay too long— (*He starts for his coat but sees* POLONIUS *coming down the stairway; he says softly to her*) but here my
father comes
(*Then aloud to* POLONIUS *with an embarrassed grin*)
A double blessing is a double grace!
Occasion smiles upon a SECOND leave.

POLONIUS (*Surprised to see him still in the house, he says somewhat sternly and with fluster*) Yet here, Laertes? (*Shooing him*) Aboard, aboard, for shame!
The wind sits in the shoulder of your sail,
And you are stayed for! (LAERTES *picks up his coat from the platform and is about to go when* POLONIUS *stops him with a gesture and motions him back to the front steps*) There—
my blessing with thee!
(*He takes the coat from* LAERTES *and kisses him on the cheek.* LAERTES *turns his back to him; he holds out his arms, waiting to be helped into the coat. Changing his mind,* POLONIUS *puts the coat over his own arm and starts to lecture*)
And these few precepts in thy memory
Look thou character. (LAERTES *faces him*) Give thy thoughts
no tongue,
Nor any unproportioned thought his act.
Be thou familiar, but by no means vulgar. (*Coming down the side steps*)
Those friends thou HAST, and their adoption tried,
Grapple them unto thy soul with hoops of steel; (*He sits on a stool in front of the platform*)
But do not dull thy palm with entertainment
Of each new-hatched, unfledged comrade (*He looks to* OPHELIA *to be sure she also is paying attention*) Beware
Of entrance to a quarrel, but being in,
Bear it that the opposèd may beware of THEE.

Give every man thy ear, but few thy voice.
Take each man's censure, but reserve THY judgment.
Costly thy habit as thy purse can buy,
But not expressed in fancy; rich, (*Holding up the red lining
of* LAERTES' *coat*) not GAUDY!
For the apparel oft proclaims the man,
And they in France of the best rank and station
Are of a most select and generous chief in that.
  (OPHELIA *comes to* POLONIUS' *right shoulder and puts her
  arm around him lovingly.* POLONIUS *puts his hand on hers,
  addressing both children*)
Neither a borrower nor a lender be,
For loan oft loses both itself and friend,
And borrowing dulls the edge of husbandry. (*He rises, crosses
to* LAERTES, *places his hand on his shoulder, and says warmly
and sincerely*)
This above all: To thine own self be true,
And it must follow as the night the day
Thou canst not then be false to any man. (*He slaps* LAERTES'
cheek affectionately)
Farewell! (*He hands him the coat*) My blessing season this
  in thee.

LAERTES Most humbly do I take my leave, my lord.

POLONIUS (*Stepping up on the platform*)
  The time invites you.
  (*Pointing off right with his cane*) Go, your servants tend.

LAERTES (*Crossing to* OPHELIA) Farewell, Ophelia.
  (*Seriously*) And remember well
  What I have said to you.

OPHELIA (*Taking a red rose from her waist, she puts it in his
  buttonhole*) 'Tis in my memory locked,
  And you yourself shall keep the key of it.

LAERTES (*He kisses her*) Farewell. (*He gives a wave back to
  POLONIUS as he hurries off down right*)

POLONIUS (*Waves; he and* OPHELIA *stand for a brief moment watching after* LAERTES. *Then, after reflecting a moment, he says firmly*)
What is't, Ophelia, he hath said to you?

OPHELIA (*Turning to him, she says shyly and sweetly*)
So please you, something touching the Lord Hamlet.

POLONIUS   Marry, well bethought.
Tis told me he hath very oft of late
Given PRIVATE time to you, and you yourself
Have of your audience been most free and bounteous.
If it be so, as so 'tis put on ME—
And that in way of caution— I must tell you,
You do not understand yourself so clearly
As it behoves my daughter, and your honour. (*She is puzzled*)
What is between you? Give me up the truth!

OPHELIA   He hath, my lord, of late made many tenders
Of his affection to me.

POLONIUS (*Scornfully*)   Affection? (*Falsetto*) POOH! You speak
like a green girl
Unsifted in such perilous circumstance.
Do you believe his "tenders," as you call them?

OPHELIA   I do not know, my lord, what I should THINK.

POLONIUS (*Coming down the front steps*)   Marry, I'll teach
you. Think yourself a BABY.
That you have ta'en these "tenders" for true pay
Which are not sterling. "Tender" yourself more dearly,
Or—not to crack the wind of a poor phrase,
Running it thus—you'll "tender" me a fool.

OPHELIA (*Protesting gently*)   My lord, he hath importuned me
with love
In honourable fashion.

POLONIUS   Aye, fashion you may CALL it (*He sits on the stool and says disgustedly, pushing the air with his palm*) Go to, go to.

OPHELIA (*Kneeling on the steps at his right*)
And hath given countenance to his speech, my lord,
With almost all the holy vows of heaven.

POLONIUS   Aye, springes to catch woodcocks. I do know
When the blood burns how prodigal the soul
Lends the tongue vows. These blazes, daughter,
Giving more light than heat, extinct in both,
You must not take for fire. From this time
Be something SCANTER of your maiden presence. (*She stands*)
Set your entreatments at a higher rate
Than a command to parley. (*He rises*) For Lord Hamlet,
(*Going up the front steps*)
Believe so much in him that he is young,
And with a larger tether may he walk
Than may be given you. In few, Ophelia,
Do not believe his vows. (*He pauses to see if this has taken effect, then adds firmly, by way of summary*) This is for all!
I would not in plain terms from this time forth
Have you so slander any moment's leisure
As to give words or talk with the Lord Hamlet. (*She looks off right*)
Look to it, I charge you! (*He starts off, then turns back, feeling he may have been too harsh; he says to her in a warmer tone, extending his hand*) Come your ways. (*He exits from the ramp*)

OPHELIA   I shall obey, my lord. (*She follows after POLONIUS*)

SCENE 4

The lights fade to a dim blue on the platform area. HAMLET *enters right of the side platform, followed closely by* HORATIO *and* MARCELLUS. *They come downstage to the main platform and look out over the edge as if they are high up on a large wall.*

HAMLET (*Trying to be calm, but terribly anxious*)
The air bites shrewdly, it is very cold.

HORATIO   It is a nipping and an eager air.

HAMLET   What hour now?

HORATIO   I think it lacks of twelve.

MARCELLUS   No, it is struck.

HORATIO   Indeed? I heard it not. It then draws near the season
Wherein the spirit held his wont to walk.
(*A distant cannon shot is heard, followed by cheering and carousing voices*)
What doth THIS mean, my lord?

HAMLET (*He walks away disgusted and says sarcastically*)
The King doth wake tonight and takes his rouse,
Keeps wassail, and the swaggering upspring reels;
(*There is another shot and a cheer*)
And as he drains his draughts of Rhenish down,
The kettle-drum and trumpet thus bray out
The triumph of his pledge.

HORATIO   Is it a custom?

HAMLET   Aye, marry is't,
But to my mind, though I am native here
And to the manner born, it is a custom

More honoured in the BREACH than the observance.
(*Another shot, this the loudest yet, is followed by cheer-ing which fades out, as if a party were breaking up.* HAMLET *turns upstage between* HORATIO *and* MARCELLUS, *facing them*)
This heavy-headed revel east and west
Makes us traduced, and taxed of other nations.
They clepe us drunkards, a . . . (*He stops, seeing the look of horror in* HORATIO's *face*)

HORATIO   Look, my lord. It comes!

HAMLET (*He turns, gives a cry of anguish, falls to his knees, and crosses himself*)
Angels and ministers of grace, defend us.
Be thou a spirit of health, or goblin damned?
Bring with thee airs from heaven, or blasts from hell?
Be thy intents wicked or charitable?
Thou comst in such a questionable shape
That I WILL speak to thee. (*He stands*) I'll call thee Hamlet!
King? Father? ROYAL DANE! (*He pauses for the* GHOST *to reply; then pleading*) O, answer me!
Let me not burst in ignorance, but tell
Why thy canonized bones, hearsèd in death,
Have burst their cerements? Why the sepulchre,
Wherein we saw thee quietly inurned,
Hath oped his ponderous and marble jaws
To cast thee up again? What may this mean,
That thou, dead corse, again in complete steel
Revisits thus the glimpses of the moon,
Making night hideous, and we fools of nature
So horridly to shake our disposition
With thoughts beyond the reaches of our souls?
(*He whispers*) Say, why is this? Wherefore?
(*Crying out*) What should we DO?

(*A huge cloaked arm waves in front of the shadow*)

HORATIO   It beckons you to go away with it,
As if it some impartment did desire
To you alone.

(*There is another wave of the shadow's arm*)

MARCELLUS   Look with what courteous action
It waves you to a more removèd ground.
(HAMLET *takes a step toward it.* MARCELLUS *restrains him by
the left arm*) But do not go with it!

HORATIO (*Grasping* HAMLET's *right arm*) No, by no means!

HAMLET   It will not speak; then will I follow it.

HORATIO   Do not, my Lord.

HAMLET (*Struggling fiercely between them*) Why, what should
    be the fear?
I do not set my life at a pin's fee,
And for my soul, what can it do to that,
Being a thing immortal as itself? (*The* GHOST *beckons again*)
It waves me forth again. I'll follow it.

> (HAMLET *has forced his way to the first step in front of the
> platform.* HORATIO *and* MARCELLUS *stand above him on
> the platform, still restraining him*)

HORATIO   What if it tempt you toward the flood, my lord,
Or to the dreadful summit of the cliff
That beetles o'er his base into the sea,
And there assume some other horrible form
Which might deprive your sovereignty of reason,
And draw you into madness?

(*The* GHOST *beckons*)

HAMLET   It waves me still.
Go on, I'll follow thee.

MARCELLUS   You shall not go, my lord.

HAMLET   Hold off your hands!

HORATIO   Be ruled, you shall not go.

HAMLET   (*Twisting furiously between them*)   My fate cries out!
And makes each petty artery in this body
As hardy as the Nemean lion's nerve. (*The* GHOST *beckons*)
Still am I called. Unhand me, gentlemen (*He breaks from
their hold*)
By heaven, I'll make a ghost of him that lets me.
> (HORATIO *takes a step toward him;* HAMLET *pulls* MAR-
> CELLUS' *sword from its scabbard and holds* HORATIO *off
> with it*)

I say, away! (*He turns toward the* GHOST, *holds the hilt of
the sword before him as a cross*) Go on, I'll follow thee.

> (*The shadow enlarges until it fills the rear wall.* HAMLET
> *follows the* GHOST *off down left. The following lines
> come rapidly, almost on top of one another*)

HORATIO   He waxes desperate with imagination.

MARCELLUS   Let's follow; 'tis not fit thus to obey him.

HORATIO   Have after. To what issue will this come?

MARCELLUS   Something is rotten in the state of Denmark.

HORATIO   Heaven will direct it.

MARCELLUS   Nay, let's follow him.

> (*They run off left. For a moment the stage is empty. The
> rear doors open just a crack and* HAMLET *squeezes through,
> the hilt of the sword still before him. The shadow of the
> GHOST materializes into view on the rear wall*)

HAMLET   (*Demanding*)   Whither wilt thou lead me? (*He waits
for a reply, then comes forward to the center of the platform*)
Speak! I'll go no further!

GHOST   (*Ashen voiced*)   Mark me.

HAMLET (*Awed*)   I will.

GHOST   My hour is almost come
When I to sulphurous and tormenting FLAMES
Must render up myself.

HAMLET   Alas, poor ghost.

GHOST   PITY me not, but lend thy serious hearing
To what I shall unfold.

HAMLET   Speak! I am BOUND to hear.

GHOST (*Tremulously*)   So art thou to REVENGE, when thou
shalt hear.

HAMLET   What?

GHOST (*The head of the shadow nods slightly as it speaks*)
I AM thy father's spirit,
DOOMED for a certain term to walk the night,
And for the day confined to fast in fires,
Till the foul crimes done in my days of nature
Are burnt and purged away.
(HAMLET *crosses himself*) But that I am forbid
To tell the secrets of my prison-house,
I could a tale unfold whose lightest word
Would harrow up thy soul, freeze thy young blood,
Make thy two eyes like stars start from their spheres,
Thy knotted and combinèd locks to part,
And each particular hair to stand an end,
Like quills upon the fretful porpentine.
But this eternal blazon must not be
To ears of flesh and blood. List. List. O List!
If thou didst ever thy dear father love—

HAMLET (*About to break*)   O God!

GHOST   Revenge his foul and most unnatural MURDER!

HAMLET   MURDER!

GHOST   Murder most foul, as in the best it is,
  But this most foul, strange and unnatural.

HAMLET   Haste me to know it, that I, with wings as swift
  As meditation or the thoughts of love,
  May SWEEP to my revenge.

GHOST   I find thee apt.
  And duller shouldst thou be than the fat weed
  That roots itself in ease on Lethe wharf,
  Wouldst thou NOT stir in this. Now, Hamlet, hear:
  (*Quickly, directly*) 'Tis given out that sleeping in my
    orchard
  A serpent stung me. So the whole ear of Denmark
  Is by a forgèd process of my death
  Rankly abused. (*Aspirate*) But know, thou noble youth,
  The serpent that did sting thy father's life
  NOW WEARS HIS CROWN!

HAMLET (*Ecstatically*)   O my prophetic soul,
  My uncle!

GHOST (*Whispers*)   Ay! That incestuous, that adulterate beast,
  With witchcraft of his wit, with traitorous gifts—
  O wicked wit and gifts that have the power
  So to seduce—won to his shameful lust
  The will of my most seeming virtuous Queen!
      (HAMLET *gives an anguished cry*)
  But soft! (*The head of the shadow looks to the side*) Me-
    thinks I scent the morning air.
  Brief let me be. (*The lights begin coming up*) Sleeping within
    mine orchard,
  My custom always of the afternoon,
  Upon my secure hour, thy uncle stole
  With juice of cursèd hebenon in a vial (HAMLET *cringes*)
  And in the porches of mine ears did pour
  The leperous distilment; (HAMLET *writhes, cupping his hand
  over his ear, reliving the murder*) whose effect

Holds such an enmity with blood of man,
That swift as quicksilver it courses through
The natural gates and alleys of the body.
Thus was I, sleeping, by a brother's hand
Of life, of crown, of Queen, at once dispatched;
Cut off even in the blossoms of my sin,
Unhousel'd, disappointed, unaneled,
No reckoning made, but sent to my account
With all my imperfections on my head.

HAMLET (*Each repetition is more painful*)   O horrible, o horrible, most horrible!

GHOST (*Firmly*)   If thou hast nature in thee, bear it not.
Let not the royal bed of Denmark be
A couch for luxury and damned incest.
(HAMLET *straightens and emits an animal-like noise signifying*
"No!" The GHOST *speaks sadly*)
But howsoever thou pursuest this act,
Taint not thy mind, nor let thy soul contrive
Against thy mother aught. Leave her to heaven
And to those thorns that in her bosom lodge
To prick and sting her. (A *distant cock crows and throughout*
the rest of the GHOST's *speech the call is echoed by cocks all*
over the countryside) Fare thee well at once.
The glow-worm shows the matin to be near,
And 'gins to PALE his uneffectual fire.
Adieu, adieu. (*The voice and shadow fade*) Hamlet, remember me.

(*The doors close. Amber lights go up full on the platform*)

HAMLET (*Looking up*)   Oh, all you host of HEAVEN. (*He falls
to the platform, dropping his sword*) Oh earth! What else?
And shall I couple hell? Hold, hold, my heart.
And you, my sinews, grow not instant old,
(*With great summoning of all his strength*)
But bear me stiffly (*Rises*) UP. REMEMBER thee?

Aye, thou poor ghost, (*He puts his hands to his head*) whiles
    memory holds a seat
In this distracted globe. Remember THEE?
        (*The words race out now*)
Yea, from the table of my memory
I'll wipe away all trivial fond records,
All saws of books, all forms, all pressures past
That youth and observation copied there,
And thy commandment ALL ALONE shall live
Within the book and volume of my brain,
Unmixed with baser matter—yes, by heaven! (*He pauses,
then speaks woefully*) O most pernicious woman!
(*Insidiously*) O villain, villain! Smiling, damnéd VILLAIN.
My tables—(*He sits on top of the front steps, takes a pencil
and a small tablet* from his pants pocket and begins to scrib-
ble rapidly on it*) meet it is I set it down,
That one may smile and smile, and be a villain;
At least I'm sure it may be so in Denmark.
So, uncle—(*With a large finishing flourish to the writing, he
claps the tablet shut and holds it high above his head*) there
you are. (*Putting the tablet in his pocket*) Now to my word;
It is "adieu, adieu, remember me."
I have sworn't.

        (*There is a pause*)

HORATIO (*Off in the distance*)   My lord, my lord! (*Pause*)

MARCELLUS (*Off*)   Lord Hamlet!

HORATIO (*Getting closer*)   Heaven secure him.

HAMLET (*Softly, sadly, to himself*)   So be it.

MARCELLUS (*Giving a falconer's cry*)   Illo-ho-ho, my lord!

HAMLET (*Imitating* MARCELLUS)   "Illo-ho-ho, boy" Come bird,
    come!

---

* Burton actually held nothing, but pantomimed the business.

(*There is the sound of footsteps rushing on the outer platform.* HORATIO *forces the center doors open. He and* MARCELLUS *come through and rush down to* HAMLET)

MARCELLUS   How is't, my noble lord?

HORATIO   What news, my lord?

HAMLET (*He stands and says gleefully*)   O wonderful.

HORATIO   Good my lord, tell it.

HAMLET (*Flippantly*)   No. You will reveal it.

HORATIO   Not I, my lord, by heaven.

MARCELLUS   Nor I, my lord.

HAMLET (*He steps up on the platform, between them*)
How say you then—would heart of man once think it—
But you'll be secret?

HORATIO   Aye, by heaven, my lord.

HAMLET (*Deliberately baiting them*)
There's ne'er a villain dwelling in all Denmark
But he's an arrant knave.
          (*He starts to go up center*)

HORATIO (*Stopping him*)   There needs no ghost, my lord, come
     from the grave
To tell us this.

HAMLET (*Turning back to him with a forced smile and feigned ease*)
Why, right. You are in the right!
And so without more circumstance at all
I hold it fit that we shake hands and part;
You as your business and desire shall point you—
For every man hath business and desire,
(*Fearfully*) Such as it is—and for my own poor part,
Look you, I will go pray.
          (*He starts to leave again*)

HORATIO (*Protesting*)   These are but wild and whirling words,
   my lord.

HAMLET (*Tearfully*)   I'm sorry they offend you, heartily.
   (*Softly*) Yes, faith, heartily.

HORATIO   There's no offence, my lord.

HAMLET (*Grabbing* HORATIO *by the arm, he says furiously*)
   Yes, by Saint Patrick, but there is, Horatio,
   And much offence too. Touching this vision here—
      (*He almost tells him, but then breaks off, remembering
      that* MARCELLUS *is listening. He gives a little laugh and
      smiles*)
   It is an honest ghost, that let me tell you.
   For your desire to know what is between us,
   O'ermaster it as you may. And now, good friends,
   As you ARE friends, (*Pointing to* HORATIO) scholars, (*Point-
   ing to* MARCELLUS) soldiers,
   Give me one poor request.

HORATIO   What is't, my lord? We will.

HAMLET   Never make known what you have seen tonight.

HORATIO   My lord, we will not.

HAMLET   Nay, but swear it.

HORATIO   In faith,
   My lord, not I.

MARCELLUS   Nor I, my lord, in faith

HAMLET (*He sees the sword he has dropped and picks it up*)
   Upon my sword.

MARCELLUS   We have sworn, my lord, already.

HAMLET (*Insisting*)   Indeed, upon my sword, INDEED!

GHOST (*The voice coming from underneath the platform*)
   SWEAR!

(HORATIO *and* MARCELLUS *jump back*)

HAMLET (*Shouts down at the platform, laughing*)
Ali, ha, boy. Sayst thou so? Art thou THERE, truepenny?
(*He looks to* HORATIO *and* MARCELLUS *to check that they
have heard it*)
Come on! You hear this fellow in the cellarage?
Consent to swear.

HORATIO (*Shaken*)   Propose the oath, my lord.

HAMLET   Never to speak of this that you have seen,
Swear by my sword.

GHOST   SWEAR!

HAMLET (*He laughs hysterically, then scurries downstage to the
front steps*)
Hic et ubique? Then we'll shift our ground (*He motions
them downstage to him*)   Come hither, gentlemen,
And lay your hands again upon my sword.
Never to speak of this that you have heard,
Swear by my sword.

GHOST   Swear by his sword!

HAMLET (*Another wild laugh*)
Well said, old mole! Canst work i' the earth so fast?
A worthy pioneer. Once more remove, good friends.

(*He vaults to the left side of the platform*)

HORATIO (*To* MARCELLUS)   O day and night, but this is won-
drous strange.

HAMLET (*Sadly*)   And therefore as a stranger give it welcome;
There are more things in heaven and earth, Horatio,
Than are DREAMT of in your philosophy.
(*Spritely, fiendish*) But come!
Here, as before. Never, so help you mercy,
How strange or odd so e'er I bear myself—

As I perchance hereafter shall think meet
To put an ANTIC DISPOSITION on—
> (*He demonstrates this by mussing his hair, then pauses to see that they understand*)

That you at such times seeing me never shall,
(*He folds his arms*) With arms encumbered thus, or this head-shake,
Or by pronouncing of some doubtful phrase,
As (*Gabbling idiotically*) "well, well, we know"—or "we could and if we would"—
Or "if we list to speak"—or "there be an if they might"—
(*Sharply*) Or such ambiguous giving out—to note
That you know aught of me, this NOT to do,
So grace and mercy at your most need help you,
SWEAR!

> (HORATIO *and* MARCELLUS *kneel and place their hands on the hilt of the sword*)

GHOST   SWEAR!

HAMLET (*Kissing his fingers and touching them to the ground*)
Rest, rest, perturbed spirit. (*He stands wearily*) So, gentlemen,
With all my love I do commend me to you,
> (*He shivers.* HORATIO *puts his scarf around* HAMLET'S *neck*)

And what so poor a man as Hamlet is
May do to express his love and friending to you,
God willing, shall not lack. Let us go in together,
And still your fingers on your lips, I pray.
> (HORATIO *and* MARCELLUS *go up to the center doors. Downstage alone,* HAMLET *turns, looks out front, and speaks despondently to himself*)

The time is out of joint. O cursèd spite
That ever I was born to set it right.
> (*He turns back, crosses up to them, putting an arm around each*)

Nay, come—let's go together.
  (*They exit center*)

SCENE 5

During the first few lines of this scene, two COURTIERS *move the clothing rack down left on the side stage in position for the nunnery scene. The lights go up full.* REYNALDO *enters up right carrying a portfolio. He is followed by* POLONIUS, *who carries a cash box and a packet of notes.* REYNALDO *comes above the table,* POLONIUS *below it. They meet in front.*

POLONIUS (*Places the cash box on the table. He removes a bag of money from it and hands it to* REYNALDO *together with the packet of notes; he then says imperatively*)
Give him this money, and these notes, Reynaldo.

REYNALDO (*Weighing the moneybag*)   I will, my lord.

POLONIUS (*Slyly*)   You shall do marvellous wisely, good Reynaldo,
Before you visit him, to make inquire
Of his behaviour. (*He takes the portfolio from him, puts the notes into it, and places it on the table with his cane*)

REYNALDO (*Indulgently*)   My lord, I did INTEND it.

POLONIUS   Marry, well said. Very well said! Look you, sir,
      (*He indicates for* REYNALDO *to sit in the armchair*)
Inquire me first what Danskers are in Paris, (*He crosses to the left of the armchair*)
What company they keep, and finding
That they do know my son,
Take you as 'twere some DISTANT knowledge of him,

As thus; "I know his father and his friends,
And in part him—(REYNALDO *starts to rise, but* POLONIUS *stops him*) but," you may say, "not well.
But if't be he I mean, he's very wild,
Addicted—" so and so— (*He crosses behind the chair to above the table*) and there put on him
What forgeries you please. Marry, none so rank
As may dishonour him—take heed of that!

REYNALDO (*Suggesting*)   As gaming, my lord?

POLONIUS   Aye, Or drinking, fencing, swearing,
Quarreling, . . . (*He hesitates, then adds delicately*) DRAB-BING—you may go so far.

> (*He sits in the chair behind the table and flips the cash box shut*)

REYNALDO (*Stands, starts putting on his gloves, and asks, bewildered*)   But, my good lord—

POLONIUS   Wherefore should you do this?
Marry, sir, here's my drift.
Your party in converse, him you would sound.
He closes with you in this consequence:
"Good sir," or so, or "friend," or "gentleman,"
According to the phrase or the addition
Of man and country.

REYNALDO (*Giving a final tug on his gloves, hoping to end the conversation*)   Very good, my lord.

POLONIUS   And then sir does he this;
> (*Pause.* POLONIUS *looks blankly ahead*)
What was I about to say?
> (*Coming around in front of the table*)
By the mass I was about to say SOMETHING!
Where did I leave?

REYNALDO   At "closes in the consequence?"

POLONIUS (*Confused*)   At "closes in the conse—?" (*Suddenly
remembering, he pounces back to his thought gleefully*) Aye!
 Marry,
He closes with you thus: "I know the gentleman,
I saw him yesterday," or "t'other day,"
Or then, or then, with such or such; "AND," as you say,
"There was a-gaming, there o'ertook in's rouse,
There falling out at tennis," or perchance,
"I saw him enter such a house of sale—" (REYNALDO *looks
puzzled*)
Videlicet a BROTHEL, or so forth.
(REYNALDO *nods*) See you now, (*Grabbing* REYNALDO *firmly
by the right arm, he leads him three paces left*)
Your bait of falsehood takes this carp of truth.
     (*Crossing left of* REYNALDO, *he adds sagely*)
And thus do we of wisdom and of reach,
With windlasses, and with assays of bias,
By indirections find directions out. (*Turns to him*)
So by my former lecture and advice
Shall you, my son. (*Pause*) You have me, have you not?

REYNALDO (*Long-suffering*)   My lord, I have.

POLONIUS   God be wi' ye. Fare ye well.

REYNALDO (*He nods to him*)   Good my lord.
     (*He picks up the portfolio and crosses below the table
     around to the up right exit*)

POLONIUS (*Stopping him in his tracks*)   Observe his inclination
in YOURSELF.

REYNALDO (*Turns back and says with finality*)   I SHALL, my
lord. (*He goes out of the doorway completely*)

POLONIUS (*Calling after him*)   And . . . (REYNALDO *sticks his
head back in*) let him ply his music.

REYNALDO   Well, my lord! (*He whisks out*)
Polonius, farewell!

(OPHELIA *appears at the top of the stairway, out of breath and sobbing. She runs down the stairway, almost tripping over her skirt; she stops at the bottom, turns and looks back up, frightened*)

POLONIUS (*Holding the thigh of his game right leg, he hurries up the steps to the center of the platform*)
How, now, Ophelia! What's the matter?

OPHELIA (*Coming to him*) My lord, my lord, I have been so affrighted.

POLONIUS (*Taking her hands*) With what, in the same of God?

OPHELIA My lord, as I was sewing in my closet,
(*Giving a look back up the stairway*)
Lord Hamlet, with his doublet all unbraced,
No hat upon his head, his stockings fouled,
Ungartered, and down-gyvèd to his ankle,
Pale as his shirt, his knees knocking each other,
And with a look so piteous in purport
As if he had been loosèd out of hell
To speak of horrors—he comes before me.

POLONIUS (*Seizing her by the arms*) Mad for thy love?

OPHELIA (*Frightened*) My lord, I do not know,
But truly I do FEAR it. (*She moves away from him and crosses down the front steps*)

POLONIUS (*Crossing down side steps, following her intently*)
What SAID he?

OPHELIA (*Holding her wrist*)
He took me by the wrist, and held me HARD;
Then goes he to the length of all his arm,
And with his other hand thus o'er his brow,
He falls to such perusal of my face
As he would draw it. Long stayed he so. (*Crosses slowly to the right of the side stage*)

At last, a little shaking of mine arm,
And thrice his head thus waving up and down, (*She gives
another look up the stairway*)
He raised a sigh so piteous and profound
As it did seem to shatter all his bulk,
And end his being. (*Sits on the stool in front of the platform*)
That done, he lets me go,
And with his head over his shoulder turned,
He seemed to find his way without his eyes,
For out o' doors he went without their helps,
And to the last bended their light on me.

POLONIUS (*Makes a sudden start for the stairway as if to go after
HAMLET, then changes his mind as he announces*)
Come, go with me. I will go seek the KING.
This is the very ECSTASY of love! (*Picking up his cane from
the table, he turns back to her and says suddenly*)
What, have you given him any hard word of late?

OPHELIA (*Sadly reproachful, yet dignified*)   No, my good lord.
But as YOU did command,
I did repel his letters and denied
His access to me. (*She looks up the stairway*)

POLONIUS (*Absolutely certain*)   THAT hath made him mad!
    (*She looks at him in horror, as if to say "Not mad"*)
I am sorry that with better heed and judgment
I had not quoted him. I feared he did but trifle,
And meant to wreck thee. But beshrew my jealousy!
By heaven, it is as proper to our age
To cast beyond ourselves in our opinions,
As it is common for the younger sort
To lack discretion. (*Ordering her to him*) Come! Go we to
the King. (*He picks up the cash box from the table*) This
must be known. Come!

    (*He exits down right. OPHELIA follows him off*)

SCENE 6

ROSENCRANTZ *and* GUILDENSTERN *enter down left. They are escorted to the center of the platform by two Attendants, one of whom remains down left; the other takes his position left of the center doors.*

CLAUDIUS (*Enters by the stairway with* GERTRUDE. *They come to the bottom stair*)
    Welcome, dear Rosencrantz and Guildenstern. (*They bow*)
    Moreover, that we much did long to see you,
    The need we have to use you did provoke
    Our hasty sending. Something have you heard
    Of Hamlet's transformation. What it should be,
    More than his father's death, that thus hath put him
    So much from the understanding of himself,
    I cannot dream of. I entreat you both,
    That, being of so young days brought up with him,
    And since so neighbored to his youth and haviour,
    That you vouchsafe your rest here in our court
    Some little time. (GERTRUDE *crosses to the armchair,* CLAUDIUS *to center stage*) So by YOUR companies
    To draw him on to pleasures, and to gather
    So much as from occasion you may glean,
    Whether aught to us UNKNOWN afflicts him thus
    That opened lies within our remedy.
        (*He crosses behind the armchair*)

GERTRUDE (*Magnanimously*) Good gentlemen, he hath much
    talked of you, (*Sits in the armchair*)
    And sure I am two men there are not living
    To whom he more adheres. If it will please you
    To show us so much gentry and good will,
    As to expend your time with us awhile,

For the supply and profit of our hope,
Your visitation shall receive such thanks
As fits a King's remembrance.

ROSENCRANTZ (*Stepping forward, smilingly*)
Both your Majesties
Might by the sovereign power you have of us
Put your dread pleasures more into COMMAND
Than to entreaty. (*He looks at* GUILDENSTERN, *cueing him to speak*)

GUILDENSTERN (*Steps forward, fawningly*)   But we both obey,
And here give up ourselves in the full bent
To lay our service freely at your feet,
To be commanded.

CLAUDIUS (*Crossing center stage*)   Thanks Rosencrantz, and
gentle Guildenstern.

GERTRUDE (*Not wishing to slight either*)   Thanks Guildenstern,
and gentle Rosencrantz.
(*They nod*) And I beseech you instantly to visit
My too much changèd son. Go, one of you,
And bring these gentlemen where Hamlet is.

GUILDENSTERN   Heavens make our presence and our practices
Pleasant and helpful to him.

GERTRUDE   Aye, amen. (*They bow and exit, following the attendant off down left*)

POLONIUS (*Enters from the side platform, bustling with cheer*)
M'lord!
The ambassadors from Norway, my good lord,
Are joyfully returned.

CLAUDIUS   Thou still hast been the father of good news.

POLONIUS (*Crossing over the main platform to the side steps*)
Have I, my lord? I assure you, my good liege,
I hold my duty as I hold my soul,

Both to my God, and to my gracious King.
(*Confidentially*) And I do think—(*Looks around, spots the
Attendant left of the center doors.* CLAUDIUS *motions him off*)
  or else this brain of mine
Hunts not the trail of policy so sure
As it hath used to do—that I have found
The very cause of Hamlet's lunacy.

CLAUDIUS O speak of that. That I do LONG to hear.

POLONIUS Give first admittance to the ambassadors.
My news shall be the FRUIT to that great feast.

CLAUDIUS (*Putting a hand on* POLONIUS' *shoulder*)
Thyself do grace to them, and bring them in.
      (POLONIUS *bows, goes up on the platform, motions to an
      Attendant off right.* CLAUDIUS *goes to* GERTRUDE, *takes
      her by the hand below the table to down right. He says
      in his best comforting bedside manner*)
He tells me, my dear Gertrude, he hath found
The head and source of all your son's distemper.

GERTRUDE (*Troubled*) I doubt it is no other but the main;
His father's death, and our o'erhasty marriage.

CLAUDIUS (*Reassuringly*) Well, we shall sift him.
      (VOLTIMAND *and* CORNELIUS *enter right of the side plat-
      form, following an Attendant who stations himself right
      of the center doors. They cross to the center of the main
      platform*)
Welcome, my good friends! (*They bow*)
Say, Voltimand, what from our brother Norway?

VOLTIMAND (*Coming forward to the side steps*)
Most fair return of greetings and desires.
Young Fortinbras
Receives rebuke from Norway, and in fine,
Makes vow before his uncle never more
To give the assay of arms against your Majesty.

*(CLAUDIUS gives an approving look to GERTRUDE, who
smiles and sits on the stool to the right of the table)*
Whereon old Norway, overcome with joy,
Gives him commission to employ those soldiers,
So levied as before, against the Polack; *(CORNELIUS hands
him a document)*
With an entreaty herein further shown,
That it might please you to give quiet pass
Through your dominions for this enterprise.

CLAUDIUS *(Crossing center, he takes the document)*
It likes us well;
And at our more considered time
We'll think upon an answer to this business.
Meantime, we thank you for your well-took labour.
Go to your rest. At night we'll feast together.
Most welcome home.

> *(VOLTIMAND and CORNELIUS exit by the stairway. CLAU-
> DIUS crosses to the armchair, sits, and peruses the docu-
> ment)*

POLONIUS *(Waves the Attendant off right with his cane, and
speaks while coming forward to the front steps)*   This busi-
ness is well ended. *(Relishing his own dialectic)*
My liege, and madam; to expostulate
What majesty should BE, and what duty IS,
Why day is day, night night, and time is time,
Were nothing other but to waste night, day, and time.
Therefore, since brevity is the soul of wit,
And tediousness the limbs and outward flourishes,
I will be brief! *(He steps down onto the main stage)* Your
   noble son is mad. *(GERTRUDE rises)*
Mad CALL I it, for to define true madness,
What is it but to be nothing else but mad?
(Firmly) But let that go.

GERTRUDE *(Protesting)*   More matter with less art.

POLONIUS (*Offended*)   Madam, I swear I use no art at all.
  (*Crossing behind the armchair to the center of the table*)
  That he is mad, 'tis true. 'Tis true 'tis pity.
  And pity 'tis 'tis true—(GERTRUDE *starts to interpose but he*
  prevents her) a foolish figure,
  But farewell it, for I will use no art. (GERTRUDE *sits*)
  Mad let us grant him, then. And now remains
  That we find out the CAUSE of this effect;
  Or rather say, the cause of this DEFECT,
  For this effect-defective comes by cause.
  Thus it remains, and the remainder thus.
  Perpend; (*He takes a letter from his vest;* CLAUDIUS *motions*
  him to sit. POLONIUS *smiles, first unfolds the letter and puts*
  on the pair of Benjamin Franklin half-glasses that have been
  hanging on a chain around his neck)
  I have a daughter—have while she is mine—
        (CLAUDIUS *gives* GERTRUDE *a hopeless shrug*)
  Who in her duty and obedience, mark,
  Hath given me this. (*He sits on a chair in the center of the*
  table) Now gather and surmise:
  (*He reads*) "To the celestial and my soul's idol, the most
    beautified Ophelia."
  (*Glancing over to* GERTRUDE) That's an ill phrase, a vile
  phrase; beautified is a vile phrase! (GERTRUDE *points to the*
  letter, annoyed)
  But you shall hear—(*He mumbles his way over the first part*
  of the letter and the phrase) "Thus in her excellent white
    bosom these—"

GERTRUDE (*Incredulously*)   Came this from Hamlet to her?

POLONIUS (*He looks up, pauses, then turns to her and smiles*)
  Good madam, stay awhile; I will be faithful.
        (*He squints at the letter, mumbles through a few lines*
        of it until he again finds his place. He continues reading)
  "Doubt thou the stars are fire,

Doubt that the sun doth move,
Doubt truth to be a liar,
But, (*Emphasizing each word for* CLAUDIUS) NEVER DOUBT
I LOVE!" (*He gives a look to* CLAUDIUS *as if to say "Didn't I
tell you?"* GERTRUDE *is about to speak, but he continues
reading*) "O dear Ophelia, I am ill at these numbers.
(POLONIUS *nods in agreement*) I have not art to reckon my
groans, but that I love thee BEST (*He has trouble making
out some of the words*) O, MOST best, believe it. Adieu.
(*Holding the letter in front of* GERTRUDE *so that she may see
the handwriting*) Thine evermore, most dear lady, whilst
this machine is to him, HAMLET." (GERTRUDE *takes the letter and studies it.* POLONIUS *speaks to* CLAUDIUS)
This in obedience hath my daughter shown me,
And more above, hath his solicitings
As they fell out by time, by means, and place,
All given to mine ear.

CLAUDIUS   But how hath she
Received his love?

POLONIUS (*He starts to speak, then stands up impressively, takes
off his glasses, says with propriety*)   What do you think of
ME?

CLAUDIUS (*Thinks for a second as to whether he should really
tell him, then says tactfully*)   As of a man faithful and
honourable

POLONIUS   I would fain PROVE SO. But what MIGHT you think,
(*Pointing at the letter*)
When I had seen this hot love on the wing,
As I perceived it, I must tell you that,
BEFORE my daughter told me, what might you,
(*Turning to* GERTRUDE) Or my dear Majesty, your Queen
here, think, (*She hands the letter back to him*)
If I had played the desk, or table-book,
(*Turns to* CLAUDIUS) Or given my heart a winking, mute and
dumb, (*Holding out the letter*)

Or looked upon this love with IDLE sight;
WHAT might you think? No! I went round to work! (*Puts the letter back in his coat*)
And my young mistress thus I did bespeak:
"Lord Hamlet is a Prince out of thy star.
This must not be." And then I prescripts gave her
That she should lock herself from his resort,
Admit no messengers, receive no tokens.
This done, she took the fruits of my advice;
And he, repulsèd, a short tale to make,
Fell into a sadness, then into a fast, (*Crossing behind the armchair to center stage as he enumerates rapidly*)
Thence to a watch, thence into a weakness,
Thence to a lightness, and by this declension,
Into the MADNESS wherein now he raves;
(*Gravely, as an afterthought*) And all we mourn for.

CLAUDIUS (*Seriously, to* GERTRUDE)   Do YOU think 'tis this?

GERTRUDE   It may be, very like.

POLONIUS (*Indignantly*)   Hath there been such a time—I would
    fain know that—
That I have positively said 'tis so,
When it proved OTHERWISE?

CLAUDIUS   Not that I know.

POLONIUS (*Pointing to his head and shoulder*)
    Take THIS, from THIS, if THIS be otherwise.
    If circumstances lead me, I will find
    Where truth is hid, though it were hid indeed
    Within the CENTER.

CLAUDIUS   How may we try it further?

POLONIUS (*Crosses back to the center of the table, says con-fidentially, full of schemes*)
    You know sometimes he walks for hours together
    Here in the lobby.

GERTRUDE   So he does indeed.

POLONIUS   At such a time, I'LL LOOSE my daughter to him.
(TO CLAUDIUS) Be you and I behind an arras then,
Mark the encounter. (*Leaning on the table confidently*) If
he love her not,
And be not from his reason fall'n thereon,
Let me be no assistant for a state, (*Laughs*)
But keep a farm, and carters.

CLAUDIUS   We will try it.

GERTRUDE (*Stands and points to the stairway*)
But look where sadly the poor wretch comes reading.

POLONIUS (*Shooing* GERTRUDE *and* CLAUDIUS *off hurriedly down
right, sotto voce*)
Away, I do beseech you both, away!
I'll board him presently.
   (HAMLET *enters from the stairway, his hair mussed, his
   coat half on, an open book held in front of his face. As
   he reaches the platform,* POLONIUS *crosses up to him, and
   offering to help him on with his coat, he says obsequi-
   ously*) O, give me leave.
   (HAMLET, *his nose in the book, sticks out his right arm
   with the coat sleeve drooping over it. As* POLONIUS *pulls
   the sleeve up he realizes* HAMLET *is wearing the coat
   backwards.* HAMLET *gives him a silly grin.* POLONIUS,
   fearful of his derangement, asks with grave concern)
How does my good Lord Hamlet?

HAMLET (*Clipping his words*)   Well! God-a-mercy.
   (*He lifts his right leg high and swings it stiffly in a toy
   soldier fashion, doing an about-face. With his nose still
   in the book, he walks upstage on the platform, marching
   like an automaton*)

POLONIUS (*Following, unconsciously in step with him*)   Do
you know me, my lord?

HAMLET (*Stops*) Excellent well! (*With another stilted about-turn, he begins walking downstage, with* POLONIUS *still following*) You are a fishmonger!

POLONIUS (*Breaks his step and stops*) Not I, my lord,

HAMLET (*Tiring of the game*) Then I would you were so HONEST (*He speaks the word forcefully in* POLONIUS' *face*) a man.

POLONIUS Honest, my lord?

HAMLET (*Crossing to the right corner of the platform*) Aye, sire, to be honest, as this world goes, is to be one man picked out of ten thousand.

POLONIUS (*Crossing down to* HAMLET'S *left*) That's very true, my lord.

HAMLET (*Angrily*) For if the sun breed maggots in a dead dog, being a (*Points to the sky*) GOD . . . (*Points to the horizon*) KISSING . . . (*Points to the ground*) CARRION— (*Turning on him suddenly, he says quizzically*) Have you a daughter?

POLONIUS (*Still humoring him, says agreeably*) I have, my lord.

HAMLET Let her not walk in the sun. Conception is a blessing, but not as YOUR daughter may conceive. Friend . . . (*Shakes a finger at him*) look to't.
  (*He turns upstage and reads*)

POLONIUS (*Crossing down to the front of the platform, muttering to himself*) How say you by that? STILL harping on my daughter. Yet he knew me not at first. He said I was a fishmonger. (*Looks back at him, shakes his head hopelessly*) He is far gone, FAR GONE. And truly in MY youth, I suffered much extremity for love, very near this. I'll speak to him again. (*Crossing up behind him, he says aloud*) What do you read, my lord?

HAMLET   Words. (POLONIUS *starts to speak, but* HAMLET *cuts him off by repeating more sharply*) Words! (POLONIUS *again tries to explain, pointing at the book and taking a step toward him*) WORDS!

POLONIUS (*Loudly, as though speaking to a deaf person*)   What is the MATTER, my lord?

HAMLET (*Looking around, innocently*)   Between who?

POLONIUS (*His patience wearing thin*)   I mean the matter that you READ, my lord.

HAMLET (*With facetious dismay*)   Slanders, sir! (*Pointing into the book*) For the satirical rogue says here (*He begins forcing* POLONIUS *back toward the right edge of the platform*) that old men have grey beards, that their faces are wrinkled, their eyes purging thick amber and plum-tree gum, and that they have a plentiful lack of wit, together with MOST WEAK (*Swatting* POLONIUS' *behind*) HAMS. All which, sir, though I most powerfully and potently believe, yet I hold it not honest to have it thus set down; (*He tears a page from the book and hands it to* POLONIUS) for yourself, sir, should be as old as I am, if, (*Walking backward to the stairway*) like a crab, you could go backward.
      (*He sits on the stairway and reads*)

POLONIUS (*Looking at the torn page, he muses to himself*) Though this be madness, yet there is method in it. (*Going to him*) Will you walk out of the air, my lord?

HAMLET   Into my grave?

POLONIUS (*Laughs*)   Indeed, that IS out of the air. (*He turns away from him, laughing, shaking his head, his lips silently saying "how about that?" Then suddenly becoming serious, he ruminates to himself*) How pregnant sometimes his replies are; a happiness that madness often hits on, which reason and sanity could not so prosperously be delivered of. (*Venom-*

ously) I'll leave him, and suddenly contrive the means of meeting between HIM AND MY DAUGHTER. (*Turns to him decorously*) My honourable lord—(HAMLET *does not respond;* POLONIUS *speaks much louder*) I WILL MOST HUMBLY TAKE MY LEAVE OF YOU!

HAMLET (*Without looking up, he says offhandedly*)   You cannot, sir, take from me anything that I will more willingly part withal—(*Rises and says casually*) except my life . . . (*Sharply in* POLONIUS' *face*) EXCEPT MY LIFE . . . (*Crossing down the side steps onto the main stage, says sadly and introspectively*) except my life.

POLONIUS   Fare you well, my lord.
(*He starts for the ramp.* ROSENCRANTZ *and* GUILDENSTERN *enter from the stairway. They stand watching* HAMLET *like a pair of asylum attendants*)

HAMLET (*Puts his coat over the arm of the armchair; he sits and mutters*)   These tedious old fools.

POLONIUS (*Stops, overhearing* HAMLET'*s remark. Then, seeing* ROSENCRANTZ *and* GUILDENSTERN, *he says to them brusquely*) You go to seek the lord Hamlet? (*Crumples up the torn page, says hopelessly*) There he is!
(*He tosses the wad of paper away and exits by the ramp*)

GUILDENSTERN (*Bowing*)   My honoured lord.

ROSENCRANTZ (*Bowing*)   My most dear lord.

HAMLET (*Looks up from his book, puzzled for a moment; then, recognizing them, he tosses the book on the table and runs up on the platform between them, shaking their hands and greeting them cordially*)   My excellent good friends. How doest thou, Guildenstern? Ah, Rosencrantz! Good lads, how do ye both?

ROSENCRANTZ (*Forcing his mirth*)   As the indifferent children of the earth.

GUILDENSTERN (*Echoing his grinning manner*)　Happy in that we are not overhappy.
On Fortune's cap we are not the very button.

HAMLET　Nor the soles of her shoe?

ROSENCRANTZ　Neither, my lord.
(*The three cross down to the main stage*)

HAMLET　Then you live about her waist, or in the middle of her favours?

GUILDENSTERN　Faith, her privates we.

HAMLET　In the secret parts of Fortune. O most true, she is a strumpet! (ROSENCRANTZ *and* GUILDENSTERN *laugh a little too heartily.* HAMLET *looks at them sternly. There is an awkward pause*) What's the news?

ROSENCRANTZ　None, my lord, but that the world's grown honest.

HAMLET　Then is doomsday near! But your news is not true. (*He crosses to the armchair and sits;* GUILDENSTERN *crosses behind him and sits on the up left corner of the table;* ROSENCRANTZ *moves to the right of the armchair*) Let me question more in particular. What have you, my good friends, deserved at the hands of Fortune, that she sends* you *to prison hither?

GUILDENSTERN　(*Searching him out, thinking he is about to discover something*) PRISON, my lord?

HAMLET　Denmark's a prison.

ROSENCRANTZ　Then is the world one.

HAMLET　A goodly one, in which there are MANY confines, wards, and dungeons, Denmark being one of the worst.

ROSENCRANTZ　We think not so, my lord.
(GUILDENSTERN *steals a look at a few pages in* HAMLET'S *book*)

HAMLET Why then 'tis none to YOU. For there is nothing good or bad but thinking makes it so. (*He turns, sees* GUILDENSTERN *look at his book.* GUILDENSTERN *smiles and closes it*) To me it is a prison.

ROSENCRANTZ (*Trying another possible theory for* HAMLET's *behavior*) Why, then your AMBITION makes it one; 'tis too narrow for your mind.

HAMLET O God! I could be bounded in a nutshell, and count myself a king of INFINITE space, (*Dejectedly*) were it not that I have bad dreams.

GUILDENSTERN (*Pressing the point*) Which dreams, indeed, are AMBITION, for the very substance of the ambitious is merely the shadow of a dream.

HAMLET A dream itself is but a shadow.

ROSENCRANTZ Truly, and I hold AMBITION of so airy and light a quality that it is but a shadow's shadow.

HAMLET Then are our beggars bodies, and our monarchs and outstretched heroes the beggars' shadows. (*Stands*) Shall we to the court? For by my fay, I cannot reason.

GUILDENSTERN (*Crossing to* ROSENCRANTZ) We'll wait upon you.

HAMLET No such matter. I will not sort you with the rest of my servants; for to speak to you like an honest man, I am most dreadfully attended. (*He turns to go off right.* ROSENCRANTZ *and* GUILDENSTERN *hold a quick conference behind his back*) But—(*He turns back unexpectedly and catches them conferring*) in the beaten way of friendship, what make you at Elsinore?

ROSENCRANTZ To visit you, my lord, no OTHER occasion.

HAMLET Beggar that I am, I am even poor in thanks, but I thank you; and sure, dear friends, my thanks are too dear a

halfpenny. Were you not sent for? (*They look embarrassed*)
Is it your own inclining? Is it a free visitation? Come, deal
justly with me. Come, come—nay speak.

GUILDENSTERN (*Innocently*)　What should we say, my lord?

HAMLET　Why anything, but to the purpose. You WERE sent
for, and there is a kind of confession to your LOOKS, which
your modesties have not craft enough to colour. I KNOW the
good King and Queen have sent for you.

ROSENCRANTZ (*With an uneasy laugh*)　To what end, my lord?

HAMLET (*Comes to them appealingly*)　That you must teach
me. But let me conjure you, by the rights of our fellowship,
by the consonancy of our youth, by the obligation of our ever
preservèd love, and by what more dear a better proposer could
charge you withal, be even and direct with me, whether you
WERE sent for or no.
　　(*He crosses above the armchair to the table, leaving them
　　to confer*)

GUILDENSTERN (*Softly to* ROSENCRANTZ)　What say you? (RO-
SENCRANTZ *signals "no!"*)

HAMLET (*Overhearing this, he turns and says sharply*)　Nay
then, I have an eye of you! (*Slamming his fist on the table
with angry desperation*) If you LOVE me, hold not off!

GUILDENSTERN　My lord, (*Clears his throat*) we WERE sent for.

HAMLET (*Laughs, speaks gravely, somewhat reproachfully*)　I
will tell you why; (*They start to speak but he silences them*)
so shall my anticipation prevent your discovery, and your
secrecy to the King and Queen moult no feather. (*Searching
for words, he passes between them and comes around in front
of the armchair*)* I have of late—(*Adding facetiously*) but

---

* During the whole of this famous passage, Mr. Burton would often perform any one of several bizarre actions, the idea for which occurred to
him quite by accident during a matinée in the final week of the Boston
performances. On this occasion, Rosencrantz and Guildenstern had
moved so close to the armchair that Burton could not cross between it

wherefore I know not—lost all my mirth, forgone all custom of exercise, and indeed it goes so heavily with my disposition that this goodly frame, the earth, seems to me a sterile promontory. (*Throughout the speech he wavers between complete detachment and total involvement with what he is saying*) This most excellent canopy, the air, (*Pointing up*) look you, this brave o'erhanging firmament, this majestical roof fretted with golden fire, why it appears nothing to me but a foul and pestilent congregation of vapours. (*Holding a hand out to them*) What a piece of work is a man! How noble in reason, how infinite in faculties. In form and moving, how express and admirable. In action, how like an angel; in apprehension, how like a god! The beauty of the world, the paragon of animals. (*To himself*) And yet to me, (*sits*) what is this quintessence . . . of dust? Man delights not me. (ROSENCRANTZ *laughs.* HAMLET *continues angrily*) No, nor WOMAN neither—though by your smiling you seem to say so.

ROSENCRANTZ   My lord, there was no such stuff in my thoughts.

HAMLET   Why did you laugh then, when I said "man delights not me"?

ROSENCRANTZ   (*Quickly changing the subject*)   To think, my lord, if you delight not in man, what lenten entertainment the PLAYERS shall receive from you. We coted them on the way, and hither are they coming to offer you service.

HAMLET   (*Ironically*)   He that plays the KING shall be welcome. His majesty shall have tribute of me. (*Intensely interested*) What players are they?

ROSENCRANTZ   Even those you were wont to take such delight in, the tragedians of the city.

---

and them; so as a joke he climbed over the chair to get to his correct position. A few weeks later, after the New York opening, he repeated the climbing feat and added the action of bouncing up and down on the seat of the chair. By the final month of New York performances, Burton incorporated this as permanent business and would occasionally walk on the table as well during the last section of the speech—or then again he might not do any of the above movements.

HAMLET   How chances it they travel? Their residence, both in reputation and profit, was better both ways. Do they hold the same estimation they did when I was in the city? Are they so followed?

ROSENCRANTZ   No, indeed are they not.

HAMLET   It is not very strange, for my uncle is King of . . . (*Pretends he cannot remember, then snapping his fingers*) Denmark! And those that would make mows at him while my father lived, (*Scrutinizing the small portrait* ROSENCRANTZ *wears on his tie*) give twenty, forty, fifty, a hundred ducats apiece for his picture in little. 'Sblood! There is something in this more than natural, if philosophy could find it out.

> (A *happy little march played by a recorder and a drum is heard in the distance*)

GUILDENSTERN   There ARE the players!

HAMLET (*Jumping up*)   Gentlemen, you are welcome to Elsinore. Your hands! Come then, you're welcome. (*Confidentially*) But my uncle-father, and aunt-mother are deceived.

GUILDENSTERN (*Believing they are going to discover something at last*)   In what, my dear lord?

HAMLET (*Tricking them*)   I am but mad north-north-west; when the wind is southerly, I know a hawk from a handsaw.

POLONIUS (*Enters from the ramp—gleefully*)   Well be with you, gentlemen.

> (*The music stops*)

HAMLET   Hark you, Guildenstern, and you too, at each ear a hearer—(*Pointing at* POLONIUS) that great baby you see there is not yet out of his swaddling clouts.
> (*They laugh.* POLONIUS *goes out of the center doors for a brief moment*)

ROSENCRANTZ Happily he is the SECOND time come to them, for they say an old man is twice a child.

(POLONIUS *comes back reading a playbill*)

HAMLET I will prophesy he comes to tell me of the players; mark it. (*He slumps into the armchair and reclines casually with his legs over one of the arms*) You say right, sir, a Monday morning, 'twas so indeed.

POLONIUS (*Crosses to the platform, bustling with enthusiasm*) My lord, I have news to tell you!

HAMLET My lord, I have news to tell YOU. When Roscius was an actor in Rome—

POLONIUS The actors are come hither, my lord.

HAMLET (*Laughing at his ridiculous busy-ness*) Buzz, buzz!

POLONIUS (*Slightly affronted*) Upon mine honour.

HAMLET Then came actor on his ass—

POLONIUS (*Reading from the playbill as he comes down the side steps to stage center*) "The best actors in the world, either for tragedy, comedy, history, pastoral, pastoral-comical, historical-pastoral, tragical-historical, tragical-comical-historical-pastoral, scene indivisible, or poem unlimited." Seneca cannot be too heavy, nor Plautus too light; for the law of writ and the liberty, these are the only men.

HAMLET (*Rises, crosses center to him, and says intensely*) O Jeptha, judge of Israel, what a treasure hadst thou!

POLONIUS (*Suspiciously*) What treasure had he, my lord?

HAMLET (*Mysteriously*) Why
"One fair daughter, and no more,
The which he lovèd passing well."

(*He snatches the playbill from* POLONIUS, *crosses right, and gives it to* GUILDENSTERN, *who puts it on the table*)

POLONIUS (*Confidentially to* ROSENCRANTZ)   Still on my daughter.

HAMLET (*Overhearing him*)   Am I not in the right, Old Jeptha?

POLONIUS   If you call ME Jeptha, my lord, I have a daughter that I love "passing well."

HAMLET (*Perplexed*)   Nay, that follows not.

POLONIUS (*Still scenting the trail*)   What follows then, my lord.

HAMLET (*Baiting him*)   Why "As by lot, God wot," (*Music begins again*) and then you know, "It came to pass, as most like it was"—But look where my abridgement comes! (*Four* PLAYERS *enter, two of them carrying a trunk,** *one playing the recorder, the other playing a drum.* HAMLET *hurries up onto the platform to greet them*) You are welcome, masters, welcome all! (*The* PLAYERS *finish their music, set their instruments, coats, hats, and trunk down on the platform. They return* HAMLET'S *greeting;* HAMLET *shakes hands with each one*) I am glad to see thee well! Welcome, good friends! (*The four* PLAYERS *separate, making an aisle through which the* FIRST PLAYER *makes a grand solo entrance.* HAMLET, *on seeing him, claps an arm around him exuberantly*) Ahhh! My old friend! (*Seeing his beard*) Why, thy face is valanced since I saw thee last! Com'st thou to BEARD me in Denmark? (*To the boy-actress*) What, my young lady and mistress! By our lady, your "ladyship" is nearer to heaven than when I saw you last by the altitude of a chopine. Pray God your voice, like a piece of uncurrent gold, be not cracked within the ring! (*The* PLAYERS *laugh*) Masters, you are all welcome! (*Energetically, with excitement*) We'll e'en to it like French falconers, fly at anything we see. We'll have a speech straight. Come! Give us a taste of your quality. Come, a passionate speech!

---

* Two wooden chairs tied together were used as a rehearsal prop representing the trunk.

FIRST PLAYER (*Heartily*) What speech, my good lord?

HAMLET (*Takes off the* FIRST PLAYER's *scarf and puts it around his own neck*) I heard thee speak me a speech once, but it was never acted, or if it was, not above once, for the play I remember pleased not the million. (*Pointing at* POLONIUS, ROSENCRANTZ, *and* GUILDENSTERN) 'Twas caviar to the general. But it was, as I received it, an excellent play, well digested in the scenes, set down with as much modesty as cunning. One speech in it I chiefly loved. 'Twas Aeneas' tale to Dido! (*The* PLAYERS *nod. They all know it. One* PLAYER *rummages through the trunk quickly, finds the script, and hands it to the* FIRST PLAYER) And thereabout of it especially where he speaks of Priam's slaughter. If it live in your memory, begin as this line —(*Trying to remember*) Let me see, let me see—(*Quoting*) "The rugged Pyrrhus, like the Hyrcanian beast—" (*The* FIRST PLAYER, *who by this time has found the speech to which he is referring, shakes his head*) 'Tis not so. It begins with Pyrrhus—(*Continues quoting as he crosses down the side steps*) "The rugged Pyrrhus, he whose sable arms, Black as his purpose, doth the night resemble. With eyes like . . . (*For a moment he cannot remember the next word. Then, looking into* POLONIUS' *face, he recalls*) CARBUNCLES, the hellish Pyrrhus Old grandsire Priam seeks." So proceed you.
> (*He crosses to the armchair and sits.* ROSENCRANTZ *and* GUILDENSTERN *sit by the table*)

POLONIUS 'Fore God, my lord, well spoken, with good accent and good discretion.
> (*He sits on the stool down left. The* PLAYERS *sit around the sides of the platform*)

FIRST PLAYER (*Having glanced over the speech, he discards the script and takes the stage at the center of the platform; he*

venerably performs the speech in a grand style with classic
declamation and full broad gestures)
"Anon, he finds him
Striking too short at Greeks; his antic sword (*He snaps his*
fingers and instantly one of the PLAYERS *hands him a prop-*
sword from the trunk)
Rebellious to his arm, lies where it falls,
Repugnant to command. Unequal matched,
Pyrrhus at Priam drives, (*Brandishing the sword*) in rage
    strikes wide,
But with the whiff and wind of his fell sword,
The unnervèd father falls. (HAMLET *suddenly sits up and*
looks out front. The idea for playing The Murder of Gon-
zago *before* CLAUDIUS *occurs to him*) Then senseless Ilium,
Seeming to feel this blow, with flaming top
Stoops to his base, and with a hideous crash
Takes prisoner Pyrrhus' ear; for lo, his sword,
Which was declining on the milky head
Of reverend Priam, seemed in the air to stick.
So, as a painted tyrant Pyrrhus stood,
And like a neutral to his will and matter,
Did nothing. (*He comes partially down the side steps toward*
his audience)
But as we often see against some storm,
A silence in the heavens, the rack stand still,
The bold winds speechless, and the orb below
As hush as death, (*Rushing back bombastically*) anon the
    dreadful thunder
Doth rend the region! So after Pyrrhus' pause,
A rousèd VENGEANCE (*The word strikes* HAMLET) sets him
    new awork,
And never did the Cyclops' hammers fall
On Mars's armour forged for proof eterne
With less remorse than Pyrrhus' bleeding sword
Now falls on Priam
Out, out, thou strumpet, Fortune! A—"

POLONIUS (*Bored to death*)   This is too long!
(HAMLET *and the* PLAYERS *glare at him. He gets up and crosses center*)

HAMLET (*Crossing to the side steps*)   It shall to the barber's with your beard. (*To* FIRST PLAYER) Prithee, say on. He's for a jig. Or a tale of bawdry. Or he sleeps. Say on. (*Portentously*) Come to Hecuba.
(*He kneels on the side steps.* POLONIUS *sits in the armchair*)

FIRST PLAYER (*Hands the sword to one of the* PLAYERS. *He continues the speech for* HAMLET) "But who, O who had seen the mobled queen—"

HAMLET (*Puzzling over the meaning*)   "The mobled queen?"

POLONIUS (*Insisting peevishly*)   That's GOOD! "Mobled queen" is good.

(HAMLET *motions for the* FIRST PLAYER *to continue*)

FIRST PLAYER   "Run barefoot up and down, threatening the flames
With bisson rheum, a clout upon that head
Where late the diadem stood, and for a robe,
About her lank and all o'er-teemèd loins,
(*Seizing a coat from one of the* PLAYERS)
A blanket in the alarm of fear caught up—
Who this had seen, with tongue in venom steeped,
'Gainst Fortune's state would "TREASON" have pronounced.
But if the gods themselves did see her then,
When she saw Pyrrhus make malicious sport
In mincing with his sword her husband's limbs,
The instant burst of clamour that she made,
(*On the verge of tears*) Unless things mortal move them not at all
Would have made milch the burning eyes of heaven,

(*Broken*) And passion in the gods."
(*He muffles his face in the coat and falls to the platform*)

POLONIUS (*Revulsed*)   Look whether he has not turned his colour, and has tears in his eyes. Prithee, no more.

HAMLET (*Helping* FIRST PLAYER *up, he says gently and appreciatively*)   'Tis well. I'll have thee speak out the rest of this soon. (*To* POLONIUS) Good my lord, will you see the players well bestowed? Do you hear? Let them be well used, for they are the abstract and brief chronicles of the time. After your death you were better have a bad epitaph than their ill report while you live.

POLONIUS (*Crossing to the side steps, he says disdainfully*)   My lord, I will use them according to their desert.

HAMLET   God's bodykins, man, much better. Use every man after his desert (*Pointing at* ROSENCRANTZ *and* GUILDENSTERN) and who should 'scape whipping? Use them after your own honour and dignity—the less they deserve, the more merit is in your bounty. (*He places* POLONIUS' *hand in the* FIRST PLAYERS' *hand*) Take them in.

POLONIUS (*Starts off right for the side platform*)   Come . . . (*Adds saccharinely for* HAMLET's *benefit*) SIRS!

HAMLET (*Impatiently*)   Follow him, friends, We'll hear a play tomorrow. (PLAYERS *react excitedly, pick up their paraphernalia, and follow* POLONIUS *off from the side platform, right.* HAMLET *catches the* FIRST PLAYER *by the arm as he is about to leave, takes him to the left of the platform, and says to him softly and intensely*) Dost thou hear me, old friend, can you play *The Murder of Gonzago?*

FIRST PLAYER   Aye, my lord.

HAMLET (*Nervously, eagerly*)   We'll have it tomorrow night. You could, for a need, study a speech of some dozen or sixteen lines which I would set down and insert in't, could you not?

FIRST PLAYER   Aye, my lord.

HAMLET   Very well. (*Pointing after* POLONIUS) Follow that lord
—(*Putting the scarf back around his neck, he adds kindly*)
And look you, mock him not. (FIRST PLAYER *bows and exits*)
       (HAMLET *crosses down to* ROSENCRANTZ *and* GUILDEN-
       STERN, *stage right*)
My good friends, I'll leave you till night. You are welcome
to Elsinore.

ROSENCRANTZ (*Trying to talk to him*)   Good my lord—

HAMLET (*Vituperously*)   Aye, so God . . . be . . . with . . .
you. (ROSENCRANTZ *and* GUILDENSTERN *hurry off up right.*
HAMLET *crosses center stage, then says with great relief*) Now
I am alone. (*The following soliloquy pours out with passion-
ate excoriation*)
O what a rogue and peasant slave am I!
(*Pointing at the platform*) Is it not monstrous that this
    player here,
But in a fiction, in a dream of passion,
Could force his soul so to his own conceit,
That from her working all his visage wanned.
Tears in his eyes, distraction in his aspect,
A broken voice, and his whole function suiting
With forms to his conceit—and all for nothing.
For (*Pronouncing each syllable with disgust*) Hec . . . u
    . . . ba!
What's Hecuba to him, or he to Hecuba,
That he should weep for her? What would he do
Had he the motive and the cue for passion
That I have? He would drown the stage with tears
And cleave the general ear with horrid speech,
Make mad the guilty and appal the free,
Confound the ignorant, and amaze indeed
The very faculties of eyes and ears. Yet I,
A dull and muddy-mettled rascal, peak
Like John-a-dreams, unpregnant of my cause,

And can say . . . nothing. No, not for a KING!
Upon whose property and most dear life
A damned defeat was made. Am I a coward?
(*Looking from side to side*) Who calls me villiain, breaks my
   pate across,
Plucks off my beard and blows it in my face,
Tweaks me by the nose, gives me the lie i' the throat
As deep to the lungs—(*Whirls completely around*) Who
   does me this, HA?
(*Tearfully*) Swounds, I should take it, for it cannot be
But I am pigeon-livered, and lack gall
To make oppression bitter,
(*Crossing onto the side steps*) or ere this
I should ha' fatted all the region kites (*Pointing at the arm-
chair*)
With this slave's offal. (*Each of the following words builds
with tremendous intensity of emotion*) Bloody, bawdy, villain!
Remorseless, treacherous, lecherous, kindless villain!
(*A long, loud, descending glissando*) Aaaaaaaaaaaaahhhhhh
(*Tearfully, almost inaudibly*) vengeance. (*Having raised his
arm to strike, he looks up at his hand, laughs, and drops it in
desperation*)
Why, what an ass am I!
(*Crossing center stage*) This is most brave,
That I, the son of a dear father murdered,
Prompted to my revenge by heaven and hell,
(*With acerbity*) Must, like a whore, unpack my heart with
   words
And fall a-cursing like a very drab,
A scullion!
Fie upon't! Foh! (*His mind racing*) About, my brain. (*Cross-
ing down on the apron*) I have heard
That GUILTY creatures sitting at a play
Have by the very cunning of the scene
Been struck so to the soul, that presently
They have proclaimed their malefactions.
For murder, though it have no tongue, will speak

With most miraculous organ. I'll have these players
Play something like the murder of my father
Before mine uncle. I'll observe his looks.
I'll tent him to the quick. If he but BLENCH,
I know my course. The spirit that I have seen
May be the devil, and the devil hath power
To assume a pleasing shape; yea, and perhaps
Out of my weakness and my melancholy,
As he is very potent with such spirits,
Abuses me to damn me. (*Goes to the armchair for his coat.
He stops and sees* CLAUDIUS *off, up right. He picks up the coat
quickly and bounds onto the platform*) I'll have grounds
More relative than this. (*Pointing toward* CLAUDIUS, *he gives
a cunning little laugh and then whispers with fiendish de-
light*) The play's the thing
Wherein I'll catch the conscience of the King.
        (*He runs off by the ramp*)

SCENE 7

CLAUDIUS *enters up right, followed by* GERTRUDE, ROSENCRANTZ,
and GUILDENSTERN. CLAUDIUS *crosses the stage, goes up the side
steps to the platform.* GERTRUDE *follows him and stands on the
side steps.* ROSENCRANTZ *and* GUILDENSTERN *wait center stage.*

CLAUDIUS (*Looks off the ramp after* HAMLET, *puzzled. Turns
    back and asks* ROSENCRANTZ *and* GUILDENSTERN)
    And can you by no drift of circumstance
    Get from him why he puts on this confusion,
    Grating so harshly all his days of quiet
    With turbulent and dangerous lunacy?

ROSENCRANTZ   He does confess he feels himself distracted,
    But from what cause he will by no means speak.

GUILDENSTERN   Nor do we find him forward to be sounded,
But with a crafty madness keeps aloof,
When we would bring him on to some confession
Of his true state.

GERTRUDE   Did he receive you well?
(CLAUDIUS *puts his hands on her shoulders and caresses her*)

ROSENCRANTZ   Most like a gentleman.

GUILDENSTERN   But with much FORCING of his disposition.

ROSENCRANTZ   Niggard of question, but of our demands
Most free in his reply.

GERTRUDE   Did you assay him
To any pastime?

   (POLONIUS *enters down left carrying a small white prayer book.* OPHELIA *follows him on. He bows to* CLAUDIUS *and* GERTRUDE, *then shows* OPHELIA *where to stand at left of the front steps*)

ROSENCRANTZ   Madam, it so fell out that certain PLAYERS
We o'er-raught on the way. Of these we told him,
And there did seem in him a kind of joy
To hear of it. (CLAUDIUS *comes down center on the platform, takes* OPHELIA'*s hand. She curtsies to him*) They are about
   the court,
And, as I think, they have already order
This night to play before him.

POLONIUS (*Crossing to center stage*)   'Tis most true,
And he beseeched ME to entreat your Majesties
To hear and see the matter.

CLAUDIUS (*Enthusiastically*)   With all my heart. (*Crossing back to* GERTRUDE) And it doth much content me
To hear him so inclined.

Good gentlemen, give him a further edge,
And drive his purpose on to these delights.

ROSENCRANTZ   We shall, my lord.

(ROSENCRANTZ *and* GUILDENSTERN *bow and exit down right*)

CLAUDIUS (*Lovingly*)   Sweet Gertrude, leave us too,
For we have closely sent for Hamlet hither,
That we, as 'twere by accident, may here
Affront Ophelia. (POLONIUS *joins him on the platform*)
Her father and myself, lawful espials,
Will so bestow ourselves, that seeing, unseen,
We may of their encounter frankly judge,
And gather by him, as he is behaved,
If't be the affliction of his love or no
That thus he suffers for.

GERTRUDE (*Graciously*)   I shall obey you. (*She crosses down left on the platform;* OPHELIA *comes up on the platform to her and takes her hand*)
And for your part, Ophelia, I do wish
That your good beauties be the happy cause
Of Hamlet's wildness; so shall I hope your virtues
Will bring him to his wonted way again,
To both your honours.

OPHELIA (*Kneeling to her*)   Madam, I wish it may.
(GERTRUDE *exits by the stairway*)

POLONIUS (*Directing the scene, he points to the side platform*)
Ophelia, walk you here. (*To* CLAUDIUS) Gracious, so please you,
We will bestow ourselves. (*Hands her the prayer book*) Read on this book,
That show of such an exercise may colour
Your loneliness. (*Sotto voce*)
I hear him coming, let's withdraw, my lord.

(POLONIUS and CLAUDIUS go down the steps behind the platform and conceal themselves behind the clothing rack. OPHELIA sees HAMLET coming up the ramp. She has a moment of indecision, then hurries off the side platform, left)

HAMLET (Enters from the ramp, comes to down left corner of platform; he speaks quickly, quietly, musing to himself throughout the soliloquy)
To be, or not to be; that is the question.
Whether 'tis nobler in the mind to suffer
The slings and arrows of outrageous fortune,
Or to take arms against a sea of troubles,
And by opposing, end them. To die, to sleep—
Nor more; and by a sleep to say we end
The heart-ache, and the thousand natural shocks
That flesh is heir to; 'tis a consummation
Devoutly to be wished; to die, to sleep.
(Troubled) To sleep? Perchance to dream. Aye, there's the rub;
For in that sleep of death, what dreams may come
When we have shuffled off this mortal coil,
Must give us pause. (Crossing down front steps) There's the respect
That makes calamity of so long life.
For who would bear the whips and scorns of time,
The oppressor's wrong, the proud man's contumely,
The pangs of disprized love, the law's delay,
The insolence of office, and the spurns
That patient merit of the unworthy takes, (Sits on the stool)
When he himself might his quietus make
With a bare bodkin? Who would fardels bear,
To grunt and sweat under a weary life,
But that the dread of something after death,
The undiscovered country, from whose bourn
No traveller returns, puzzles the will,
And makes us rather bear those ills we have,

Than fly to others that we know not of.
Thus conscience does make cowards of us all,
And thus the native hue of resolution
Is sicklied o'er with the pale cast of thought,
And enterprises of great pitch and moment
With this regard their currents turn awry,
> (OPHELIA *enters up right, crosses below the table to center stage*)

And lose the name of action. (*Seeing her*) Soft you now,
The fair Ophelia. (*Rises, crosses to her, says weightedly*)
  Nymph, in thy orisons
Be all my sins remembered.
> (*He kisses her softly on the cheek*)

OPHELIA (*Caressing his cheek with her hand*) Good my lord, *Hamlet.*
How does your honour for this many a day?

HAMLET (*Pained*) I humbly thank you, well, well, well.

> (*She takes her hand away and looks toward the clothing rack. He senses something is wrong*)

OPHELIA (*Holding out a locket*) My lord, I have remembrances of yours
That I have longèd long to re-deliver.
I pray you now receive them.

HAMLET (*With a little laugh*) No, not I. (*Shrugs*)
I never gave you aught. *Hamlet*

OPHELIA My honoured lord, you know right well you DID;
And with them words of so sweet breath composed
As made the things more rich. (HAMLET *laughs again; she continues, injured*) Their perfume lost,
Take these again, for to the noble mind
Rich gifts wax poor when givers prove unkind.
There, my lord.
> (*She places the locket in his hand and turns away to hide her tears. Just at that moment, unknown to her, a slight movement of the clothing rack catches* HAMLET's *eye*)

HAMLET (*Crosses a few steps upstage, looks behind the rack, and then says softly to himself*) Ah haa! (*He crosses to the armchair, sits, plays with the locket, and then says casually*) Are you honest?

OPHELIA (*Turning back to him, bewildered*) My lord?

HAMLET Are you fair?

OPHELIA What means your lordship?

HAMLET (*Softly*) That if you BE honest and fair, your honesty should admit no discourse to your BEAUTY.

OPHELIA Could beauty, my lord, have better commerce than with honesty?

HAMLET (*Beginning to anger*) Aye, truly, for the power of beauty will sooner transform honesty from what it is to a BAWD, than the force of honesty can translate beauty into his likeness. This was sometime a paradox, but now the time gives it proof. (*He throws the locket on the table*) I did love you once.
  (*He rises and crosses a few steps center*)

OPHELIA (*Shaken*) Indeed, my lord, you made me believe so.

HAMLET (*Turns to her angrily*) You should NOT have believed me. For virtue cannot so inoculate our old stock, but we shall relish of it. I loved you not!

OPHELIA (*Lowers her eyes, turns away, walks despairingly down right, and says softly*) I was the more deceived.

HAMLET (*Glances at the clothing rack, turns back, and says to her quietly and with genuine concern*) Get thee to a nunnery. Why wouldst thou be a breeder of sinners? I am myself indifferent honest, but yet I could accuse me of such things, (*Grief-stricken*) it were better my mother had not borne me. (*He braces himself on the back of the armchair, overcome with misery*) I am very proud, revengeful, ambitious, with more offences at my beck than I have thoughts to put them in, imagination to give them shape, or time to act them in. (*She crosses behind the table to the armchair to comfort him*) What should such fellows as I do crawling between earth and heaven? (*He crosses to the side steps*) We are arrant knaves all, believe none of us. Go thy ways to a nunnery. (*She comes to him again; he turns on her forcefully, clenches her wrist, and says to her slowly and deliberately, giving her the most terrible test*) Where's your father?

OPHELIA (*Avoiding his stare, she speaks with great difficulty*) At home, my lord.

HAMLET (*Releases his grasp as if to say "That's done it." He starts to leave without saying anything, then turns back and says quickly*) Let the doors be shut upon him, that he may play the fool no where but in his own house. Farewell.

(*He starts up the side steps*)

OPHELIA (*Going back to the table, crossing herself*) O help him, you sweet heavens.

HAMLET (*Hearing her, he comes back, and lashes out at her*) If thou dost marry, I'll give thee this plague for thy dowry— be thou as chaste as ice, as pure as snow, thou shalt not escape calumny. Get thee to a nunnery! Go, farewell! (*Crosses to the platform, turns back, and adds vindictively*) Or if thou will needs marry, marry a fool, for wise men know well enough what monsters you make of them. To a nunnery, go, and quickly too. Farewell.

OPHELIA (*Rushing desperately up the steps to him*) Heavenly powers, restore him!

HAMLET (*Raging, he seizes her forearm and forces her down the steps*) I have heard of your paintings too, well enough. God hath given you one face (*Waving his hand in her face*) and you MAKE yourselves another. (*Dragging her around in a circle*) You jig, you amble, and you lisp, you nickname God's creatures, and make your (*With a sweeping gesture he*

indicates her body) WANTONNESS your ignorance. Go to!
(*Throws her down roughly on the steps*) I'll no more on't!
(*Shouting*) IT HATH MADE ME MAD! (*He darts up the
steps and crouches down to her*) I say we will have no more
marriages! Those that are married already, (*Looking at the
clothing rack*) all but ONE, shall live. (*Stands*) The rest
shall keep as they are. (*Woefully*) To a nunnery—go!
(*About to burst into tears, he dashes off the ramp, left*)

OPHELIA (*Pulling herself up on the steps*)　　O what a noble mind
is here o'erthrown!
The courtier's, soldier's, scholar's, eye, tongue, sword,
The expectancy and rose of the fair state,
The glass of fashion, and the mould of form,
The observed of all observers, quite, quite down.
(*She crosses in front of the table, sadly picks up her locket,
and says despondently*) And I, of ladies most deject and
wretched,
That sucked the honey of his music vows,
(*Leaning on the table*)
Now see that noble and most sovereign reason,
Like sweet bells jangled, out of tune and harsh;
That unmatched form and feature of blown youth
Blasted with ecstasy. (*Crosses to the stool, right of the table*)
O woe is me
To have seen what I have seen, (*Sits*) see what I see.

(CLAUDIUS *comes out from behind the right end of the
rack, goes up on the platform, and looks down the ramp
after* HAMLET. POLONIUS *comes around the left end and
goes across the side stage to center stage, shaking his
head in bewilderment. He looks briefly at* OPHELIA *and
then turns to* CLAUDIUS)

CLAUDIUS (*Agitated, in turmoil, says with a sneer*)
Love? His affections do not THAT way tend!
Nor what he spake, though it lacked form a little,
Was not like madness. There's something in his soul

O'er which his melancholy sits on brood, (POLONIUS *glances*
at OPHELIA)
And I do doubt the hatch and the disclose
Will be some danger; (*Crosses to the front steps and says*
with resolve) which for to prevent,
I have in quick determination
Thus set it down—he shall with speed to England—
    (OPHELIA *looks up with alarm. He adds as an after-*
    thought)
For the demand of our neglected tribute.
Haply the seas, and countries different
With variable objects, shall expel
This something-settled matter in his heart,
Whereon his brains still beating puts him thus
From fashion of himself. What think you on't?

POLONIUS (*Nodding*)   It shall do well. But yet do I believe
The origin and commencement of his grief
Sprung from neglected love. (*Looks over to* OPHELIA, *crosses*
to her, and says in a child-comforting tone) How now,
Ophelia,
You need not tell us what Lord Hamlet said;
We heard it all. (*Gives her a kiss on the forehead; she recoils*
in horror and rushes off up right, sobbing. POLONIUS *looks*
after her amazed, then turns back to CLAUDIUS *and says with*
considerable concern) My lord, do as you please,
(*Crossing center stage*) But if you hold it fit, after the play
Let his queen mother all alone entreat him
To show his grief; let her be round with him,
And I'll be placed, so please you, in the ear
Of all their conference. If she find him not,
To England send him, or confine him where
Your wisdom best shall think.

CLAUDIUS   It shall be so. (*He turns and starts off, then turns*
back and adds in a somber tone)
Madness in great ones must not unwatched go.

(He leaves quickly up the stairway. POLONIUS *watches him go up a few steps and then turns back, giving a worried look after* OPHELIA *as the curtain falls)*

INTERMISSION

(fifteen minutes)

ACT TWO

SCENE 8

The curtain goes up to reveal the following changes in set properties: the table has been removed; the armchair and straight-backed chair have been placed on the platform at the top of the side steps, facing the main stage, the armchair in the downstage position; there is a small wooden bench at the center of the side platform; a twofold piece of scenery representing a castle has been placed stage right, parallel to the side and rear walls of the set, a stool is set in front of the castle flat; four candle footlamps have been placed in a row along the front of this impromptu stage.

At the rise of the curtain, the five PLAYERS *are busy making preparations for* The Murder of Gonzago. PLAYER-MUSICIAN *is setting two chairs on the side stage, on which two court ladies will sit during the play.* PLAYER-LUCIANUS *is sitting on the stool in front of the flat helping the* PLAYER-QUEEN *into his costume.* PLAYER-PROLOGUE *is sitting on the front steps;* FIRST PLAYER-KING *is leaning against the back of the armchair, both studying their scripts.*

HAMLET (*Enters from the ramp. He speaks anxiously, nervously; the* PLAYERS *all stop what they are doing and listen*) Speak the speech, I pray you, as I pronounced it to you, trippingly on the tongue; but if you mouth it, as many of your players do, I had as lief the town crier spoke my lines. (*Sits in the armchair;* PLAYERS *sit on the platform and steps*) Nor do not saw the air too much with your hand thus, but use all gently; for in the very torrent, tempest, and, as I may say, whirlwind

of your passion, you must acquire and beget a temperance
that may give it smoothness. O, it offends me to the soul to
hear a robustious periwig-pated fellow tear a passion to tatters,
to very rags, to split the ears of the groundlings, who for the
most part are capable of nothing but inexplicable dumb
shows and noise. I would have such a fellow whipped for
o'erdoing Termagant; it out-Herod's Herod! Pray you, avoid
it. (*He comes forward and sits among them at the top of the
front steps*)

FIRST PLAYER (*Good-naturedly*)   I warrant your honour.

HAMLET   Be not too tame neither, but let your own discretion
be your tutor. Suit the action to the word, the word to the
action—with this special observance, that you o'erstep not
the modesty of nature. For anything so overdone is from the
purpose of playing, whose end, both at the first and now,
was and is, to hold, as 'twere, the mirror up to nature; to show
virtue her own feature, scorn her own image, and the very
age and body of the time his form and pressure. (*He becomes involved with the advice, for a moment putting aside
the urgency of the occasion*) Now this overdone, or come
tardy off, though it make the unskillful laugh, cannot but
make the judicious grieve; the censure of the which ONE
must in your allowance o'erweigh a whole theatre of others.
O there be players that I have seen play, and heard others
praise, and that highly—not to speak it profanely—that
having neither the accent of Christians, not the gait of Christian, pagan, NOR man, (PLAYERS *laugh*) have so strutted and
bellowed, that I have thought some of nature's journeymen
had made men, and not made them well, they imitated
humanity so abominably.

FIRST PLAYER   I hope we have reformed that indifferently with
us, sir.

HAMLET   O reform it altogether! (*To* PLAYER-LUCIANUS) And
let those that play your clowns speak no more than is set

down for them; for there be of them that will themselves
laugh, to set on some quantity of barren spectators to laugh
too, (PLAYERS *laugh*. HAMLET *adds by way of caution*) though
in the meantime some necessary question of the PLAY be
then to be considered. That's villainous, and shows a most
pitiful ambition in the fool that uses it. (*He turns, sees* POLO-
NIUS *coming up the ramp, followed by* ROSENCRANTZ, GUIL-
DENSTERN, *and* HORATIO. *He rises, says to the* PLAYERS *urgently*) Go! Make you ready! (PLAYERS *start to cross off right;
to* POLONIUS) How now, my lord, will the King hear this piece
of work?
　　(PLAYERS *stop to hear the answer*)

POLONIUS　And the Queen too, and that presently. (PLAYERS
react excitedly and exit up right)

HAMLET　Bid the players make haste.
　　(POLONIUS *follows them off, up right*)

GUILDENSTERN　(*Still trying to corner him*)　My lord—

HAMLET　Will you two help to hasten them?

GUILDENSTERN　We will, my lord.
　　(*He and* ROSENCRANTZ *exit up right*)

HAMLET　(*Watches them go; then he turns back and expresses
great relief at seeing* HORATIO)　What, ho, Horatio.
　　(*He motions him forward to the front steps*)

HORATIO　Here, sweet lord, at your service.

HAMLET　(*Sits on the stool;* HORATIO *sits on the front steps be-
side him*)
Horatio, thou art e'en as just a man
As e'er my conversation coped withal.

HORATIO　(*Protesting*)　O, my dear lord.

HAMLET　Nay, Do not think I flatter. (*With a sad smile*)
For what advancement may I hope from thee

That no revénue hast but thy good spirits
To feed and clothe thee? Why should the poor be flattered?
Dost thou hear—
Since my dear soul was mistress of her choice,
And could of men distinguish, her election
Hath sealed thee for herself. For thou hast been
As one, in suffering all, that suffers nothing;
A man that Fortune's buffets and regards
Hast ta'en with equal thanks. And blessed are those
Whose blood and judgment are so well comingled
That they are not a pipe for Fortune's finger
To sound what stop she please. Give me that man
That is not passion's slave, (*With deep feeling*) and I will
　　wear him
In my heart's core, aye, in my heart of heart,
As I do thee. (*Laughter of the Courtiers is heard off left.*
HAMLET *and* HORATIO *rise; he speaks more urgently*) Some-
　　thing too much of this.
There is a play tonight before the King.
One scene of it comes near the circumstance
Which I have told thee of my father's death.
I prithee, when thou seest that act afoot,
Even with the very comment of thy soul
Observe my uncle. If his occulted guilt
Do not itself unkennel in one speech, (POLONIUS *enters up*
right, followed by ROSENCRANTZ *and* GUILDENSTERN; *for a mo-*
ment the old man conceals himself behind the castle flat,
trying to overhear what HAMLET *is saying*)
It is a damnèd ghost that we have seen,
And my imaginations are as foul
As Vulcan's stithy. (POLONIUS, ROSENCRANTZ, *and* GUILDEN-
STERN *come out from behind the flat.* HAMLET, *seeing them,*
takes HORATIO *down left on the side stage*) Give him HEED-
　　FUL note,
For I mine eyes will rivet to his face,
And after we will both our judgments join
In censure of his seeming.

HORATIO Well, my lord,
  If he steal aught the whilst this play is playing,
  And 'scape detecting, I will pay the theft.

> (*Courtiers' voices are heard off left*)

HAMLET They are coming to the play. I must be idle.
Get you a place.

> (HORATIO *crosses up left on the main stage;* POLONIUS,
> ROSENCRANTZ *and* GUILDENSTERN *cross up on to the plat-
> form.* CLAUDIUS *enters from the stairway with* GERTRUDE.
> *He carries a wine goblet from which he drinks frequently
> during the scene. They are followed by* OPHELIA, *who car-
> ries a fan, seven Courtiers, two ladies and three attend-
> ants, two carrying candelabra, and one carrying a wine
> pitcher. The assembly group themselves about the plat-
> form and engage in conversation*)

CLAUDIUS (*Gaily*) How fares our cousin Hamlet?

HAMLET Excellent i' faith, of the chameleon's dish; I eat the
air, promise-crammed. You cannot feed capons so.

CLAUDIUS (*Baffled, but unconcerned, laughs with the Courtiers*)
I have nothing with this answer, Hamlet. These words are
not mine. (*He stands behind the armchair, next to* GERTRUDE,
and drinks)

HAMLET No. Nor mine now. (*To* POLONIUS) My lord, you
played once in the university, you say.

POLONIUS (*Coming forward to the front steps*) That did I,
my lord, and was accounted a good actor.

HAMLET (*He moves down left*) What did you enact?

POLONIUS I did enact Julius Caesar. I was killed i' the Capitol.
Brutus killed me.

HAMLET It was a brute part of him to kill so capital a calf
there. (POLONIUS *leads* OPHELIA *down the front steps to a*

*stool down left, then crosses back to the front steps. The
Courtiers continue talking among themselves*) Be the players
ready?

ROSENCRANTZ (*Crossing up to the knuckle of the two platforms*)
Aye, my lord. They stay upon your patience.
    (*He motions off right, signaling the* PLAYERS *to speed
things up.* OPHELIA *sits on the stool*)

GERTRUDE   Come hither, my dear Hamlet, sit by me.

HAMLET   No, good mother. (*Seeing* OPHELIA) Here's metal
more attactive.

POLONIUS (*Crossing up to* CLAUDIUS, *says to him confidentially*)
O ho! Do you mark that?

HAMLET (*Crossing to* OPHELIA)   Lady, shall I lie in your lap?
    (*He sits behind her on the corner of the platform*)

OPHELIA (*Looks away from him, terribly embarrassed; she fans
herself nervously*)   No, my lord.

HAMLET   I mean my HEAD upon your lap.
    (CLAUDIUS *begins fondling* GERTRUDE)

OPHELIA   Aye, my lord.

HAMLET   Do you think I meant COUNT-ry matters?

OPHELIA   I think nothing, my lord.

HAMLET   That's a fair thought to lie between maid's legs.

OPHELIA   What is, my lord?
    (POLONIUS *comes forward to the front steps, listening in
on the conversation*)

HAMLET (*Rises and moves right of her*)   Nothing.

OPHELIA (*Trying to cheer him*)   You are merry, my lord.

HAMLET   Who, I?
    (GERTRUDE *begins laughing boisterously as* CLAUDIUS *whis-*

pers in her ear; her laughter is echoed by the chatter of the Courtiers)

OPHELIA   Aye, my lord.

HAMLET   O God! Your only jig-maker. What should a man do but be merry, (*Loudly, for all to hear*) FOR LOOK YOU HOW CHEERFULLY MY MOTHER LOOKS! (*There is a sudden shocked silence*) and my father DIED within these two hours.

OPHELIA   Nay, 'tis twice two months, my lord.

HAMLET   (*Crossing to the front steps*)   So long? Nay, then let the devil wear black, for I'll have a suit of sables. O heavens, die two months ago, and not forgotten yet? Then there's hope a great man's memory may outlive his life half a year! But by'r Lady, he must build churches then!

(*Music, "Fata La Parte,"* * *begins. PLAYER-MUSICIAN enters from the side platform playing a recorder, accompanied on a tabour by COURTIER-HARZ. The two musicians sit on the bench. The two court ladies sit in the straight-backed chairs on the side stage; HORATIO sits on the edge of the side platform, left, where he can watch CLAUDIUS. GERTRUDE sits in the straight-backed chair. PLAYER-PRO-LOGUE enters with a piece of scenery painted to look like a tree, which he places in front of the castle flat. The dumb show begins. The PLAYER-KING enters with the PLAYER-QUEEN. She curtsies to him and sits on the stool in front of the tree. PLAYER-KING kneels beside her, pantomimes offering his heart to her, which she takes and places next to her own heart. PLAYER-KING puts his wrist to his brow as if to faint. PLAYER-QUEEN expresses alarm and gives him her hand, which he kisses. They both rise and exit arm in arm behind the flat. PLAYER-LUCIANUS comes out from behind the flat, triumphantly*

---

* This and the piece indicated on page 247 are sixteenth-century villancicos by Spanish composer Juan del Encina. They were both taken from Columbia record album ML 5875, "Sweet Pipes," recorded by Bernard Krainis and the Krainis Consort.

*holds up a small golden vial, and then exits behind the
flat.* CLAUDIUS, *meanwhile, has not been paying much
attention to the play. He has remained standing, so-
cializing with the Courtiers, who regard the play as
quaint and amusing.* HAMLET *crosses up on the platform,
takes* CLAUDIUS' *goblet away from him, and points at the
play, forcing him to watch.* PLAYER-QUEEN *returns, sweeping on in horror. She kneels by the stool and indicates
bemoaning with her hand to her brow.* PLAYER-LUCIANUS
*enters and offers her his heart. She refuses. He panto-
mimes offering her jewels. She accepts them and gives
him her hand. They bow to the court and exit as the
music ends. All of the above action happens rapidly, in
time to the spritely music, taking a total of forty-five
seconds. It is performed with broad, stylized gestures
similar to Chinese theatre movements. At the end of the
dumb show,* HAMLET *and* HORATIO *exchange looks; there
was no sign of guilt from* CLAUDIUS)

OPHELIA (*Puzzled*)　　What means this, my lord?
(CLAUDIUS *sits in the armchair*)

HAMLET (*Standing next to* CLAUDIUS)　　Marry, this is miching
mallecho; it means mischief.

OPHELIA　　Belike this show imports the argument of the PLAY.

(PLAYER-PROLOGUE *comes in front of the castle flat wearing a tragedy mask*)

HAMLET　　We shall know by this fellow. The players cannot
keep counsel—(*Returning the goblet to* CLAUDIUS *with a
smile*) they'll tell ALL.

OPHELIA　　Will he tell us what this show meant?

HAMLET (*Crossing down the side steps to her*)　　Aye, or any
show that you will show him. Be not you ASHAMED to SHOW,
he'll not SHAME to SHOW you what it means.
(*A court lady laughs lewdly*)

OPHELIA (*With injured dignity*) You are naught, you are naught. I'll mark the play.

(*Music, "Triste Espana," begins.* COURTIER-HARZ *plays the lute,* PLAYER-MUSICIAN, *the recorder*)

PLAYER-PROLOGUE For us and for our tragedy,
Here stooping to your clemency,
We beg your hearing patiently.
(*He exits behind the flat*)

HAMLET (*To* OPHELIA) Is this a prologue, or the posy of a ring?

OPHELIA 'Tis brief, my lord.

HAMLET (*Bitterly*) As woman's love!
(*He crosses upstage and sits next to* HORATIO *on the side platform*)

PLAYER-KING (*Enters with* PLAYER-QUEEN *and stands upstage of her in front of the flat*)
Full thirty times hath Phoebus' cart gone round
Neptune's salt wash, and Tellus' orbèd ground,
And thirty dozen moons with borrowed sheen
About the world have times twelve thirties been,
(*Both place their hands on their hearts*) Since love our hearts,
(*Both hold up wedding rings*) and Hymen did our hands,
Unite commutual in most sacred bands.

(*They promenade in a half circle and reverse their positions*)

PLAYER-QUEEN (*Falsetto*) So many journeys may the sun and moon
Make us again count o'er ere love be done.
(PLAYER-KING *falters and sits weakly on a stool*)
But woe is me, you are so sick of late, (*Kneels behind him*)
So far from cheer and from your former state,
That I distrust you. Yet though I distrust,
Discomfort you, my lord, it nothing must.

Where love is great, the littlest doubts are fear;
Where little fears grow great, great love grows there.

PLAYER-KING   Faith, I must leave thee love, and shortly too,
(PLAYER-QUEEN *despairs*)
My operant powers their functions leave to do,
And thou shalt live in this fair world behind,
   (CLAUDIUS *sits forward and begins to watch intently*)
Honoured, beloved, and haply one as kind
For husband shalt thou—

PLAYER-QUEEN (*Rises*)   O confound the rest,
Such love must needs be treason in my breast.
   (HAMLET *notices* CLAUDIUS' *concentration. He nudges*
   HORATIO; *both stand—*HAMLET *down on the main stage,*
   HORATIO *up on the platform*)
In second husband let me be accursed;
None wed the second but who killed the first.

HAMLET (*Crosses up to the front steps, stands behind* GERTRUDE,
and says to her slyly, with a laugh)   That's wormwood . . .
wormwood.
   (*He signals the* PLAYERS *to continue and keeps his stare
   fixed on* CLAUDIUS)

PLAYER-QUEEN   The instances that second marriage move
Are base respects of thrift, but none of love.
A second time I kill my husband dead,
When second husband kisses me in bed.

   (GERTRUDE *looks to* HAMLET *as if this is in the worst
   possible taste*)

PLAYER-KING   I do believe you think what now you speak,
But what we do determine, oft we break.
Purpose is but the slave to memory,
Of violent birth, but poor validity.
   (POLONIUS, *noticing* CLAUDIUS' *discomfort, brings him a
   pitcher of wine and is about to pour a goblet full when*
   HAMLET *stops him*)

What to ourselves in passion we propose,
The passion ending, doth the purpose lose.
(HAMLET *takes* CLAUDIUS' *goblet from him and hands it
to a Courtier*)
Our wills and fates do so contrary run,
That our devices still are overthrown;
Our thoughts are ours, their ends none of our own.
So think thou wilt no second husband wed,
But die thy thoughts when thy first lord is dead.
(*The music stops*)

·PLAYER-QUEEN (*Kneeling*) Nor earth to me give food, nor
heaven light,
Sport and repose lock from me day and night,
To desperation turn my trust and hope,
And anchor's cheer in prison be my scope;
Both here and hence pursue me lasting (*The voice almost
cracks*) strife,
If once a widow, ever I be wife!

HAMLET (*Tossing it off lightly, to* GERTRUDE) If she should
break it now.

(CLAUDIUS *rises, crosses back to* POLONIUS, *and confers
with him*)

PLAYER-KING 'Tis deeply sworn. (*Stands and gives his hand to*
PLAYER-QUEEN) Sweet, leave me here awhile;
My spirits grow dull, and fain I would beguile
The tedious day with SLEEP.
(*The music continues*)

PLAYER-QUEEN SLEEP rock thy brain,
And never come mischance between us twain.
(*He exits behind the flat. Throughout the next lines the*
PLAYER-KING *goes through an elaborate pantomime of pre-
paring to sleep; he lays down and rests his head on his
hands on the stool*)

HAMLET Madam, how like you this play?

GERTRUDE The lady doth PROTEST too much, methinks.

HAMLET O, but she'll keep her word.

CLAUDIUS (*Sternly*) Have you heard the argument? Is there no offence in't?

HAMLET (*Lightly*) No, no. They do but jest. Poison, in jest. No offence in the world.

CLAUDIUS (*Regaining his control, he crosses back to the arm-chair and sits*) What do you call the play?

HAMLET The Mouse-trap. Marry, how? Trapically! (*The Courtiers laugh; POLONIUS shushes them*) This play is the image of a murder done in Vienna. Gonzago is the duke's name, his wife Baptista; You shall see anon; 'tis a knavish piece of work, but what of that? Your Majesty, and we that have FREE SOULS, it touches US not. (*Pushing GUILDENSTERN's face away*) Let the galled jade wince, OUR withers are unwrung. (PLAYER-LUCIANUS *enters, circles the sleeping* PLAYER-KING, *summoning the evil spirits*) This is one Lucianus, nephew to the King.

OPHELIA You are as good as a chorus, my lord.

HAMLET (*Coming forward to the side steps, he snatches her fan away from her*) I could interpret between you and your love, if I could see the puppets dallying.

OPHELIA (*Tortured*) You are keen, my lord, you are keen.

HAMLET It would cost YOU a groaning to take off my edge. (*Sits on the side steps directly beneath* CLAUDIUS) Begin, murderer! Pox! Leave thy damnable faces and begin. Come, the croaking raven doth bellow for revenge.

PLAYER-LUCIANUS (*Hovering over the* PLAYER-KING, *he hisses his incantation*)
Thoughts black, hands apt, drugs fit, and time agreeing;
Confederate season, else no creature seeing;
    (*He pulls a vial from his cloak and holds it up*)

Thou mixture rank, of midnight weeds collected,
With Hecate's ban thrice blasted, thrice infected,
Thy natural magic and dire property,
On wholesome life usurp immediately.

> (*He pours the vial contents into the* PLAYER-KING'S *ear.* CLAUDIUS *clenches his chair and bites his lip. The* PLAYER-KING *rises with violent spasms.* CLAUDIUS *shudders.* PLAYER-KING *falls to the floor*)

HAMLET (*Rolls over on to his haunches in front of* CLAUDIUS. *He begins speaking softly, lightly, offhandedly, then builds in intensity, volume, and speed, advancing toward* CLAUDIUS *and putting the pressure on him*) He poisons him in the garden for his estate. (CLAUDIUS *gasps*) His name's Gonzago. (HAMLET *stands*) The story is extant, and written in very choice Italian. (*Meanwhile the* PLAYER-QUEEN *has returned to the scene; she reacts in horror on seeing the* PLAYER-KING *but soon embraces* PLAYER-LUCIANUS. HAMLET *points at the* PLAYERS *with the fan, marking the action*) You shall see anon . . . how the murderer . . . gets the love . . . of Gonzago's . . . (*He turns on* CLAUDIUS, *pointing the fan at him*) WIFE!

> (CLAUDIUS *lurches forward at him furiously*)

OPHELIA (*Hysterically*) The King rises!

HAMLET (*Shrieking in* CLAUDIUS' *face*) What, frighted with false fire?

GERTRUDE How fares my lord?

POLONIUS Give o'er the play!

CLAUDIUS (*Feverishly, through clenched teeth*) Give me some light. (*Shouts*) AWAY!

> (*There is pandemonium.* CLAUDIUS *flees up the stairway. Ladies scream. Attendants race about in confusion, remove the side-stage chairs and a candelabra. The* PLAYERS *grab up their lanterns, bench, and tree and rush off with them, leaving the castle-flat folded up in its place. Cries*

of "Lights, lights," "Look to the King," etc., are heard
as the entire court exits, all but HAMLET *and* HORATIO)

HAMLET (*Roaring with laughter through the turmoil*)
Why let the stricken deer go weep,
The hart ungalled play,
For some must watch while some must sleep,
Thus runs the world away. (*The shouts fade offstage.* HAMLET
speaks excitedly) O good Horatio, I'll take the ghost's word
for a thousand pound! Didst perceive?

HORATIO Very well, my lord.

HAMLET Upon the talk of the poisoning?

HORATIO I did very well note him.
    (ROSENCRANTZ *and* GUILDENSTERN *re-enter from the stair-*
    way; they approach HAMLET *cautiously*)

HAMLET (*Laughing demonically*) Ha haa! Come, some music!
Come, the recorders.
    (HORATIO *dashes off for them up right*)
For if the King like not the comedy,
Why then, belike—he likes it not, perdy.

    (*Sits in the armchair and bounces up and down*)
Come, some music!

GUILDENSTERN (*Coming down on the platform behind* HAMLET)
Good my lord, vouchsafe me a word with you.

HAMLET (*With a grand gesture*) Sir, a whole history!

GUILDENSTERN The King, sir—

HAMLET (*Turning on him*) Aye sir, what of HIM?

GUILDENSTERN Is in his retirement marvellous distempered.

HAMLET With drink, sir?

GUILDENSTERN No, my lord, rather with choler.

HAMLET (*Rises and crosses down on the main stage*) Your wisdom should show itself more richer to signify this to the doctor; for, for me to put him to his purgation would perhaps plunge him into far MORE choler.

GUILDENSTERN (*Following after him*) Good my lord, put your discourse into some frame, and start not so wildly from my affair.

HAMLET I am tame, sir, pronounce.

GUILDENSTERN (*Entreating*) The Queen, your mother, in most great affliction of spirit hath sent me to you.

HAMLET (*Laughs*) You are welcome.

GUILDENSTERN Nay, good my lord, this courtesy is not of the right breed. If it shall please you to make me a wholesome answer, I will do your mother's commandment; if not, your pardon and my return shall be the end of my business.

HAMLET Sir, I cannot.

GUILDENSTERN What, my lord?

HAMLET (*Crosses around him and begins backing him up, right*) Make you a wholesome answer. My wit's diseased. But sir, such answer as I can make, you shall command, or rather, as you say, my mother. Therefore no more, but to the matter. My mother, you say—

ROSENCRANTZ (*Crossing down onto the main stage, he says impatiently*) Then thus she says! Your behaviour hath struck her into amazement and admiration.

HAMLET (*Sarcastically*) O wonderful son that can so astonish a mother! But is there no sequel at the heels of this mother's admiration? Impart.

ROSENCRANTZ She desires to speak with you in her closet ere you go to bed.

HAMLET We shall obey, were she ten times our mother. Have you any further "trade" with us?

ROSENCRANTZ (*Playing for sympathy*) My lord, you once did love me.

HAMLET (*Crosses up on the platform*) And do still, (*Wiggling his fingers*) by these pickers and stealers.

ROSENCRANTZ (*Angrily, following him to the steps*) Good my lord, what is your cause of distemper? You do surely bar the door upon your own liberty if you deny your griefs to your friend.

HAMLET Sir, (*Points at the armchair and says facetiously*) I lack advancement.

ROSENCRANTZ How can that be, when you have the voice of the King himself for your succession in Denmark?

HAMLET Aye sir, but "While the grass grows—" the proverb is something musty. (*The* PLAYER-MUSICIAN *enters up right, comes center stage with two recorders**) O the recorders! (*Meeting him center*) Let me see one. (*He takes the smaller of the two. The* PLAYER-MUSICIAN *exits.* HAMLET *crosses right and speaks to* GUILDENSTERN, *forcing him down on the stool*) To withdraw with you—Why do you go about to recover the wind of me, as if you would drive me into a toil?

GUILDENSTERN O my lord, if my duty be too bold, my love is too unmannerly.
        (*He starts to get up*)

HAMLET (*Pushing him down again*) I do not well understand that. (*Kneels left of him, says beguilingly*) Will you play upon this pipe?

GUILDENSTERN My lord, I cannot.

HAMLET I pray you.

---

* Two sticks of dowel painted brown and tapered at one end represented the recorders.

GUILDENSTERN   Believe me, I cannot.

HAMLET   I beseech you.

GUILDENSTERN   (*Insisting*)   I know no touch of it, my lord.

HAMLET   (*Pleasantly*)   It is as easy as lying. (*Demonstrating how to hold the instrument*) Govern these ventages with your fingers and thumb, give it (*Trilling the R*) brrrreath with your mouth, and it will discourse most eloquent music. Look you, these are the stops.

GUILDENSTERN   But these cannot I command to any utterance of harmony! I have not the SKILL!

HAMLET   (*Rises angrily*)   Why look you now how unworthy a thing you would make of ME! (GUILDENSTERN *stands*) You would play upon me, you would seem to know MY stops, you would pluck out the heart of my mystery, you would sound me from my lowest note to the top of my compass—and there is much music, excellent voice (*Indicates his head by rotating the recorder about it*) in this little organ. Yet cannot you make it speak? Sblood! Do you think I am easier to be played on than a PIPE? Call me what instrument you will, though you can fret me, yet you cannot play upon me. (POLONIUS *enters from the stairway.* HAMLET *meets him at the platform, says to him contemptuously*) God bless you, sir!

POLONIUS   My lord, the Queen would speak with you, and presently.
    (*He starts to go*)

HAMLET   (*Grabs him by the coattail, pulls him down to the front steps and points up in the air with the recorder*)   Do you see yonder cloud that's almost in shape of a camel?

POLONIUS   (*Looks up, then looks sternly at* HAMLET)   By the mass, and 'tis like a camel indeed.

HAMLET   (*Still looking up*)   Methinks it is like a weasel.

POLONIUS   (*Still looking at* HAMLET)   'Tis backed like a weasel!

HAMLET   Or like a whale?

POLONIUS (*Playing along disgruntedly*)   VERY like a whale.

HAMLET   Then I will come to my mother by and by. (*Pointing at* ROSENCRANTZ *and* GUILDENSTERN) They fool me to the top of my bent. I will come by and by.

POLONIUS   I will say so. (*Starts up the stairway*)

HAMLET (*Crossing center*)   "By and by" is easily said. (POLONIUS *stops, looks back at him, shakes his head in disgust, and exits*) Leave me, (*He tosses the recorder to* GUILDENSTERN, *adds scornfully*) FRIENDS!
> (GUILDENSTERN *catches the recorder and exits hastily with* ROSENCRANTZ, *down right. The lights begin to fade.* HAMLET *crosses down center, says to himself softly with intense excitement*)

'Tis now the very witching time of night,
When churchyards yawn, and hell itself breathes out
Contagion to this world. Now could I drink HOT BLOOD,
And do such bitter business as the day
Would quake to look on. Soft! (*He crosses to the platform, picks up the one remaining candelabrum, and says sadly*)
   Now to my mother.
O heart, lose not thy nature. Let not ever
The soul of Nero enter this firm bosom.
Let me be cruel, not unnatural,
I will SPEAK daggers to her, but USE none;
> (*Looks up to the stairway*)

My tongue and soul in this be hypocrites;
How in my words soever she be shent,
To give them seals, never my soul consent.
> (*He exits up the stairway*)

SCENE 9

A dim light remains on the main-stage area. During the first part of the scene the furniture on the platform is shifted into place for the closet scene.

ROSENCRANTZ *hurries on from the right entrance, crossing to the side platform; his sword is drawn and he carries a lantern. He is followed by* GUILDENSTERN, *who carries a heavy sword in a scabbard. The two cronies cross to the stairway, watching* HAMLET *go up them. They then cross to the right of the main stage.* ROSENCRANTZ *places the lantern on the stool, right.*

CLAUDIUS (*Follows them on, looks after* HAMLET, *crosses to the side steps; he says agitatedly*)
I like him not! Nor stands it safe with us
To let his madness range; therefore prepare you;
(*Crossing right*) I your commission will forthwith dispatch,
And he to England shall along with you. (*Takes the sword from* GUILDENSTERN)
The terms of our estate may not endure
Hazard so near us as doth hourly grow
Out of his lunacies.

GUILDENSTERN   We will ourselves provide.
Most holy and religious fear it is
To keep those many many bodies safe
That live and feed upon your majesty.

ROSENCRANTZ   The cease of majesty
Dies not alone; but like a gulf doth draw
What's near it with it. 'Tis a massy wheel
Fixed on the summit of the highest mount,
To whose huge spokes ten thousand lesser things
Are mortised and adjoined. Never ALONE
Did the king sigh, but with a GENERAL groan.

CLAUDIUS   Arm you, I pray you, to this speedy voyage,
For we will fetters put about this fear
Which now goes too free-footed.

ROSENCRANTZ   We will haste us.
(*He exits right with* GUILDENSTERN, *carrying a lantern*)

POLONIUS   (*Enters from the ramp and comes onto the main
stage;* CLAUDIUS *starts on seeing him*)
My lord, he's going to his mother's closet.
Behind the arras I'll convey myself
To hear the process. I'll warrant she'll tax him home.
And as you said, and wisely was it said,
'Tis meet that some more audience than a mother,
Since nature makes them partial, should o'erhear
The speech, of vantage.
(*With grave concern*) Fare you well, my liege.
(*He starts off left, then turns back and adds, sotto voce*)
I'll call upon you ere you go to bed,
And tell you what I know.

CLAUDIUS   Thanks, dear my lord. (POLONIUS *exits from the
ramp.* CLAUDIUS *unsheathes the sword part way, then closes
it forcefully and throws it down on the stage. He then crosses
to the side steps and kneels on the bottom step. He folds his
hands, says painfully*)
O my offence is rank. It smells to heaven;
It hath the primal eldest curse upon't—
A brother's murder. (*Unfolds his hands and sits on the steps*)
Pray can I not!
Though inclination be as sharp as will
My stronger guilt defeats my strong intent,
And like a man to double business bound,
I stand in pause where I shall first begin,
And both neglect.
(*Staring at his palm*) What if this cursèd hand
Were thicker than itself with brother's blood?

Is there not rain enough in the sweet heavens
To wash it white as snow? Whereto serves mercy
But to confront the visage of offence?
And what's in prayer but this twofold force,
To be forestallèd ere we come to fall,
(*Hopefully*) Or pardoned, being down. Then I'll look up!
My fault is past . . . (*Gets up, says despondently, pacing
down left*) But O, what form of prayer
Can serve my turn? Forgive me my foul murder?
That cannot be, since I am still possessed
Of these effects for which I did the murder—
My crown, mine own ambition, and . . .
(*With affection*) my Queen.
May one be pardoned and retain the offence?
In the corrupted currents of THIS world,
Offence's gilded hand MAY shove by justice,
And oft 'tis seen the wicked prize itself
Buys out the law.
(*Looks up, hopelessly*) But 'tis not so above;
THERE is no shuffling, there the action lies
In his true nature, and we ourselves compelled
Even to the teeth and forehead of our faults
To give in evidence. (*Pacing slowly down center*) What
    then? What rests?
Try what repentance can—what can it not? (*Pacing down
right in agony*)
Yet what can it, when one cannot repent?
        (*Presses his clasped hands to his forehead, weeping*)
O wretchèd state. O bosom black as death.
O limèd soul, that struggling to be free
Art MORE engaged. (*His arms entreating the heavens*) Help,
    angels; make assay. (*Fall resignedly to his knees*)
Bow, stubborn knees, and heart with strings of steel,
Be soft as sinews of the new-born babe.
All MAY be well.
        (*He lowers his brow to his clasped hands, attempting to
        pray; the light on him dims slightly*)

HAMLET (*Enters from the side platform right, hurrying past. He stops, seeing* CLAUDIUS *and the sword behind him, and whispers*)
Now might I do it . . . pat! (*He climbs down over the edge of the platform cautiously and comes forward*) Now he is praying; (*Carefully, silently, he picks up the sword, removes it from the scabbard, and sets the scabbard down. He comes up quickly behind* CLAUDIUS)
And now I'll do it! (*He swings the sword in an arc behind his head and is about to slash it down when* CLAUDIUS, *still in prayer, moves slightly, causing* HAMLET *to hesitate*) And so he goes to heaven?
And so am I revenged? That would be scanned.
A villain kills my father, and for that,
I, his sole son, do this same villain send
To heaven. (*Moves right of him, says preposterously*)
Why, this is hire and salary, not revenge!
He took my father grossly, full of bread,
With all his crimes broad blown, as flush as May;
(*Sadly*) And how his audit stands who knows save heaven—
But in our circumstance and course of thought,
'Tis heavy with him. And am I then revenged
To take him in the purging of his soul,
When he is fit and seasoned for his passage?
No. (*He looks at the sword and places it over his arm*)
Up, sword, and know thou a more horrid hent,
When he is drunk, asleep, or in his rage,
Or in the incestuous pleasure of his bed,
At game, a-swearing, or about some act
That has no relish of salvation in't—
Then TRIP him that his heels may KICK at heaven,
And that his soul may be as damned and black
As hell, whereto it goes. (*Looks off right anxiously*) My mother stays. (*Looking at* CLAUDIUS)
This physic but prolongs thy sickly days.

    (*He tiptoes out down right*)

CLAUDIUS (*Rising dejectedly*)   My words fly up, my thoughts
remain below.
   (*He picks up the empty scabbard mechanically*)
Words without thoughts never to heaven go.

   (*He feels the top of his empty scabbard and looks at it,
   gasping in horror; he backs off quickly, down right, petri-
   fied*)

SCENE 10

The lights reveal the clothesrack placed up center on the platform. The armchair has been placed on the down left corner of
the platform, with the straight-back chair in front of it, center.
   GERTRUDE *enters hurriedly up the ramp, followed by* POLO-
NIUS. *She sits in the armchair and begins arranging her hair.*

POLONIUS (*Urgently*)   He will come straight.
   (*Admonishingly*) Look you lay home to him,
Tell him his pranks have been too broad to bear with,
And that your Grace hath screened and stood between
Much heat and him. I'll sconce me even here. (*He climbs
through the capes hanging on the clothing rack, then peeks
through them and adds*)
Pray you, be round with him!

GERTRUDE (*Nervously*)   I'll warrant you, fear me not.

HAMLET (*Calling from off left*)   Mother, mother, mother!

GERTRUDE (*Stands*)   Withdraw, I hear him coming. (POLONIUS
ducks his head in)

HAMLET (*Runs up the ramp, his sword over his right arm; he
crosses the platform right and asks resignedly*)
Now, mother, what's the matter?

GERTRUDE   Hamlet, thou hast thy father much offended.

HAMLET   Mother, YOU have my father "much offended."

GERTRUDE   (*Severely*)   Come, come, you answer with an idle tongue.

HAMLET   (*Bitterly*)   Go, go, you question with a WICKED tongue.

GERTRUDE   Why, how now, Hamlet!

HAMLET   What's the matter NOW?

GERTRUDE   Have you forgot me?

HAMLET   No, by the rood, not so.
You are the QUEEN. Your husband's . . . brother's . . . wife.
(*Sadly*) And would it were not so, you are my mother.

GERTRUDE   (*Starting off left*)   Nay then, I'll set those to you that CAN speak.

HAMLET   (*Grasping her firmly by the arm, he forces her into the chair, center*)
Come, come, and sit you down. You shall not budge.
You go not till I set you up a glass
Where you may see the inmost part of you.

GERTRUDE   (*Seeing the sword, frightened*)
What wilt thou do? Thou wilt not murder me?
(*Cries out*) Help, help! Ho!

POLONIUS   (*Shouting from behind the rack*)   What ho? Help, help, help!

what sound?

HAMLET   (*Turns upstage*)   How now? A RAT? (*Rushes to the rack*) DEAD, for a ducat, (*Plunges the sword in between the capes*) DEAD!

> (GERTRUDE *screams;* POLONIUS *cries out in agony; his hand is seen to clench the top bar of the rack, but it soon releases its grasp and drops out of sight*)

GERTRUDE   O me, what hast thou done?

HAMLET (*Shouting triumphantly*)   Nay, I know not! Is it the KING?

GERTRUDE   O what a rash and bloody deed is this!

HAMLET (*Trying to wrench the sword free from the rack, he says accusingly*)
A bloody deed—almost as bad, good mother,
As kill a King, and marry with his brother.

GERTRUDE (*Slowly, with great astonishment*)   As KILL a King?

HAMLET   Aye, lady, it was my word (*With extreme effort he pulls the sword out with* POLONIUS *impaled on it.* POLONIUS *makes a helpless, entreating gesture to* HAMLET. HAMLET *pulls the sword out of him and drops it in revulsion as* POLONIUS *topples forward and rolls over on his back, dead.* HAMLET *speaks woefully*)
Thou wretched, rash, intruding fool, farewell.
I took thee for thy better. Take thy fortune;
Thou find'st to be too busy is some danger. (GERTRUDE *sobs, supporting herself on the back of the armchair.* HAMLET *speaks firmly*) Leave wringing of your hands.
(*Forcing her to sit in the chair*) Peace, sit you down,
And let me wring your heart, for so I shall,
If it be made of penetrable stuff;
If damnèd custom have not brassed it so,
That it be proof and bulwark against sense.

GERTRUDE (*Hysterically*)   What have I DONE, that thou dar'st wag thy tongue
In noise so rude against me?

HAMLET (*Turbulently*)   Such an act
That blurs the grace and blush of modesty,
Calls virtue hypocrite, takes off the rose
From the fair forehead of an innocent love,
And sets a blister there, makes marriage vows
As false as dicers' oaths; O such a deed

As from the body of contraction plucks
The very soul, and sweet religion makes
A rhapsody of words. (*She turns away; he forces her to look
at him*)   Heaven's face doth glow
And this solidity and compound mass
With tristful visage, as against the doom,
Is thought-sick at the ACT.

GERTRUDE   Aye me, what ACT
That roars so loud and thunders in the index?

HAMLET (*Kneeling left of her, he holds up a portrait miniature*
of his father, which hangs around his neck, and says tenderly,
patiently*)
Look here upon this picture, (*Holding up the portrait minia-
ture of* CLAUDIUS *that she wears*) and on THIS.
The counterfeit presentment of two brothers.
(*Showing her his*) See what a grace was seated on this brow;
Hyperion's curls, the front of Jove himself,
An eye like Mars, to threaten and command;
A station like the herald Mercury,
New-lighted on a heaven-kissing hill;
A combination and a form indeed
Where every god did seem to set his seal
To give the world assurance . . . of a MAN!
This WAS your husband. (*Bitterly*) Look you now what fol-
lows. (*Holding up her portrait of* CLAUDIUS)
Here IS your husband (*Mocking*) like a mildewed ear,
Blasting his wholesome brother. Have you eyes?
Could you on this fair mountain leave to feed
And batten on this MOOR? Ha, have you EYES?
You cannot call it love, for at your age
The heyday in the blood is tame, it's humble,
And waits upon the judgment. And what judgment
Would step from (*Pointing to his portrait*) THIS, to (*Point-
ing to hers*) THIS.

---

* This business was pantomimed.

(*She turns away tormented. He stands, says uncomprehendingly*)
O shame, where is thy blush? Rebellious hell,
If thou canst mutine in a matron's bones,
To flaming youth let virtue be as wax
And melt in her own fire. Proclaim no shame
When the compulsive ardour gives the charge,
Since frost itself as actively doth burn,
And reason panders will.

GERTRUDE (*Flabbergasted, she speaks with self-reproach*)
O Hamlet, speak no more.
Thou turn'st mine eyes into my very soul,
And there I see such black and grainèd spots
As will not leave their tinct.

HAMLET (*Continuing his tirade*)   Nay, but to live
In the rank sweat of an enseamèd bed,
(*She takes him by the arm*)
Stewed in corruption, honeying and making love
Over the nasty sty—

GERTRUDE (*Holding his arm and kneeling in front of him*)
O speak to me no more!
These words like daggers enter in mine ears;
No more, sweet Hamlet.

HAMLET (*With mounting fury*)   A murderer and a villain,
A slave that is not twentieth part the tithe
Of your precedent lord; a vice of kings,
A cutpurse of the empire and the rule,
That from a shelf the precious diadem stole
And put it in his pocket.

GERTRUDE   No more! (*The lights dim and the shadow of the*
GHOST *fills the rear wall*)

HAMLET   A King of shreds and patches—(*Wrenching himself
free from her grasp, he looks up and sees the* GHOST *out front.*

She falls to the floor; he gasps and crosses himself, is awe-struck)
Save me and hover o'er me with your wings,
You heavenly guards. What would your gracious figure?

GERTRUDE (*Aghast*)　Alas, he's mad.

HAMLET (*With his eyes fixed straight ahead*)
Do you not come your tardy son to chide,
That, lapsed in time and passion, lets go by
The important acting of your dread command?
O say!

GHOST (*Urgingly*)　Do not forget. (HAMLET *cringes*) This visitation
Is but to whet thy almost blunted purpose. (GERTRUDE *rises to her knees and looks into* HAMLET's *face*)
But look! Amazement on thy mother sits;
(*Sympathetically*) O step between her and her fighting soul—
Conceit in weakest bodies strongest works—
Speak to her, Hamlet.

HAMLET (*With a dead voice, his eyes frozen on the* GHOST)
How is it with you, lady?

GERTRUDE (*Rises*)　Alas, how is't with you,
That you do bend your eye on vacancy, (*Looking out, she sees nothing*)
And with the incorporal air do hold discourse?
Forth at your eyes your spirits wildly peep.
(*Smoothing his hair*) O gentle son,
Upon the heat and flame of thy distemper
Sprinkle cool patience. (*She looks out again*) Whereon do you look?

HAMLET (*Watching the* GHOST, *transfixed*)　On him, on him!
Look you how pale he glares.
His form and cause conjoined, preaching to stones
Would make them capable. (*Fearfully*) Do not look upon me,

Lest with this piteous action you convert
My stern effects; then what I have to do
Will want true colour; tears, perchance, for blood.

GERTRUDE   To whom do you speak this?

HAMLET   Do you see nothing there?

GERTRUDE   (*Looking around*)   Nothing at all, yet all that is I
see.

HAMLET   Nor did you nothing hear?

GERTRUDE   No, nothing but ourselves.
         (*The shadow enlarges until it fills the wall and vanishes*)

HAMLET   (*Pointing ahead*)   Why look you there! Look how it
steals away—
MY FATHER (GERTRUDE *cries*) in his habit as he lived—
Look where he goes, even now, out at the portal!

GERTRUDE   This is the very coinage of your brain;
This bodiless creation ecstasy
Is very cunning in.

HAMLET   Ecstacy? (*Fearful for a moment that she may be
right, he feels his pulse, convincing himself of his own sanity*)
My pulse as yours doth temperately keep time,
And makes as healthful music. It is not madness
That I have uttered. Bring me to the test,
And I the matter will re-word, which madness
Would gambol from. (*Takes her in his arms and says softly,
pleading*) Mother, for love of grace,
Lay not that flattering unction to your soul,
That not your trespass but my madness speaks.
It will but skin and film the ulcerous place,
Whilst rank corruption, mining all within,
Infects unseen. (*Helping her to the chair, center, he seats her,
stands left of her*) Confess yourself to heaven,
Repent what's past, avoid what is to come,

And do not spread the compost on the weeds
To make them ranker.

GERTRUDE (*Weeping softly*)   O Hamlet, thou has cleft my
heart in twain.

HAMLET (*Gloriously*)   O throw away the worser part of it,
And live the purer with the other half.
Good night; (*Pleading*) but go not to my uncle's bed.
ASSUME a virtue, if you have it not.
Refrain tonight,
And that shall lend a kind of EASINESS
To the next abstinence, the next more easy;
(*Sadly*) Once more good night, (*Kneels next to her*)
And when you are desirous to be blessed (*His voice breaks*)
I'll blessing beg of you. (*He weeps, she takes his head to her
bosom, comforting him. Pointing back to* POLONIUS, *he says
through his tears*) For this same lord,
I do repent; but heaven hath pleased it so
To punish me with this, and this with me,
That I must be their scourge and minister.
I will bestow him, and will answer well
The death I gave him. So again, good night. (*Rises*)
(*With difficulty*) I must be cruel only to be kind. (*He crosses
up left*) Thus bad begins, (*He starts to go; then, as he looks
off to the ramp, he is reminded of his purpose*) and worse re-
mains behind.
  (*Returns to her, down right platform, and says sharply*)
One word more, good lady.

GERTRUDE (*Dazed*)   What shall I do?

HAMLET (*Another invective*)   Not this, by no means, that I
bid you do:
Let the bloat King tempt you again to bed,
Pinch wanton on your cheek, call you his mouse,
And let him for a pair of reechy kisses,
Or paddling in your neck with his DAMNED fingers,

Make you to ravel all this matter out
That I essentially am not in madness,
But mad in CRAFT. 'Twere good you let him know.

GERTRUDE (*Immobile*)   Be thou assured, if words be made of
  breath
And breath of life, I have no life to breathe
What thou hast said to me.

HAMLET (*Flatly, with a touch of irony*)   I must to England—
  you know that?

GERTRUDE (*Rises and hugs him*)   Alack,
  I had forgot 'tis so concluded on.

HAMLET   There's letters sealed, and my two schoolfellows,
  Whom I will trust as I will adders fanged,
  They bear the mandate; they must sweep my way,
  And marshal me to knavery. (*Lightheartedly*) Let it work,
  For 'tis sport to have the enginer
  Hoist with his own petar; and it shall go hard
  But I will delve one yard below their mines,
  And blow them at the moon. (*Laughs*) O 'tis most sweet
  When in one line two crafts directly meet. (*He kisses her
  lightly, then crosses up left and points at* POLONIUS)
  This "MAN" shall set me packing.
  I'll lug the guts into the neighbor room.
  Mother, good night. (*Laughs*) Indeed, this counsellor
  Is now most still, most secret, and most grave,
  Who was in life a foolish, prating . . . (*Sorrowfully*) knave.
  Come, sir! (*Lifts* POLONIUS' *shoulders*) to draw toward an end
  with you.
      (*He touches* POLONIUS' *face softly; then, grabbing him by
      the wrists and dragging him off down the ramp, he calls
      back*)
  Good night, mother!
      (GERTRUDE *weeps softly. The lights slowly begin to cross
      fade to the main stage*)

CLAUDIUS (*Enters up right, crosses up the side steps onto the platform. Seeing the sword, he picks it up and asks sharply*) Where is your son?

GERTRUDE (*Rises, crosses dazedly down the side steps to the main stage*) Ah, mine own lord, what have I seen tonight.

CLAUDIUS (*Alarmed*)　What, Gertrude? How does Hamlet?

GERTRUDE　Mad as the sea and wind when both contend
Which is the mightier. In his lawless fit,
Behind the arras hearing something stir
Whips out his rapier, cries, "A rat, a rat!"
And in this brainish apprehension kills
The unseen good old man.

CLAUDIUS　O heavy deed!
It had been so with US had we been there. (*Crossing down to her*) His liberty is full of threats to ALL;
To you yourself, to us, to every one.
Alas, how shall this bloody deed be answered?
(*A scheme occurs to him*) Where is he gone?

GERTRUDE　To draw apart the body he hath killed,
O'er whom his very madness, like some ore
Among a mineral of metals base,
Shows itself pure. He weeps for what is done.

CLAUDIUS　O Gertrude, come away. (*Leading her to a stool, down right*)
The sun no sooner shall the mountains touch,
But we will ship him hence. (*Seats her*) And this vile deed
We must with all our majesty and skill
Both countenance and excuse. (*Calling off, up right*) Ho
Guildenstern!
(ROSENCRANTZ *and* GUILDENSTERN *enter up right*)
Friends both, go join you with some further aid.
Hamlet in madness hath POLONIUS slain,

And from his mother's closet hath he dragged him.
Go seek him out, speak fair, and bring the body
Into the chapel. I pray you, haste in this.
    (GUILDENSTERN *exits up right,* ROSENCRANTZ *exits from*
    the left ramp)
Come, Gertrude, we'll call up our wisest friends
And let them know both what we mean to do
And what's untimely done.
    (*Somewhat irritated by her apathy*) O come away!
    (*She rises; he ushers her off down right*)
My soul is full of discord (*She exits. He looks back toward*
the platform and adds sinisterly) and dismay!
    (*He exits down right*)

SCENE 11

The lights fade to a blackout. The chairs and clothing rack
are quickly removed from the platform. A dim light comes up on
the main stage.

HAMLET (*Enters from the ramp, runs onto the main stage, stops*
    to catch his breath, claps his hands together, and rubs them)
    Safely stowed!

ROSENCRANTZ (*Calling from off left*)   Hamlet!

GUILDENSTERN (*Calling from off right*)   Lord Hamlet!

HAMLET (*Jocularly*)   But soft, what noise? Who calls on Ham-
    let? (*Laughs ironically*) O! Here they come.

        (ROSENCRANTZ *enters down left,* GUILDENSTERN *up right,*
        both with drawn swords. They converge on HAMLET *and*
        circle him at sword point)

ROSENCRANTZ   What have you done, my lord, with the dead
    body?

HAMLET (*Saucily*) Compounded it with dust, whereto 'tis kin. (*He moves to go*)

ROSENCRANTZ (*Threatening with his sword*) Tell us where 'tis, that we may take it thence and bear it to the chapel.

HAMLET Do not believe it.

ROSENCRANTZ Believe what?

HAMLET (*Jesting*) That I can keep your counsel, and not mine own. Besides, to be demanded of a SPONGE, what replication should be made by the son of a king?

ROSENCRANTZ Take you ME for a SPONGE, my lord?

HAMLET (*Flippantly*) Aye, sir, that soaks up the King's countenance, his rewards, his authorities. But such officers do the King best service in the end; He keeps them like an apple in the corner of his jaw, first mouthed, to be last . . . (*Gulps*) swallowed. When he needs what you have gleaned, it is but squeezing you, and, (*Inflecting the word up and down*) SPONNNGE, you shall be dry again.

ROSENCRANTZ I understand you not, my lord.

HAMLET I am glad of it. A knavish speech sleeps in a foolish ear.

ROSENCRANTZ (*Furiously*) My lord, you must tell us where the body is, and go with us to the King.

HAMLET (*Whimsically*) The body is with the King, but the King is not with the body. The King, is a thing—

GUILDENSTERN A thing, my lord?

HAMLET Of no . . . thing. (*Laughs*) Bring me to him.
(*He starts off up right; they follow him a few steps; then he suddenly doubles back and makes a dash for the stairway. They chase him up the stairway, shouting "Hamlet!" and "Lord Hamlet!" after him*)

SCENE 12

The lights come up slightly on the main stage and the plat-form as CLAUDIUS *enters up right with* CORNELIUS. *They are flanked by four Courtiers, two armed with swords, two carrying lanterns.*

CLAUDIUS (*Crossing center, says to* CORNELIUS)
　How dangerous is it that this man goes loose;
　Yet must not we put the strong law on him.
　He's loved of the distracted multitude,
　Who like not in their judgment, but their eyes.
　To bear all smooth and even,
　This sudden sending him away must seem
　Deliberate pause. Diseases desperate grown
　By desperate appliance are relieved,
　Or not at all. (ROSENCRANTZ *enters from the stairway*) How
　now, what hath befallen?

ROSENCRANTZ　Where the dead body is bestowed, my lord,
　We cannot get from him.

CLAUDIUS　But where is HE?

ROSENCRANTZ　Without, my lord, guarded, to know your
　pleasure.

CLAUDIUS　Bring him before us.

ROSENCRANTZ (*Calling*) Ho Guildenstern, bring in my lord!
　(GUILDENSTERN *brings* HAMLET *down the stairway at
　sword point; the Courtiers draw their swords and step
　forward to protect* CLAUDIUS)

CLAUDIUS　Now, Hamlet, where's Polonius? ⟩ *Poo-lone-e-us*

HAMLET (*Quips*) At supper.

CLAUDIUS (*Angrily*) At supper? Where?

HAMLET Not where he eats, but where he is eaten. A certain convocation of politic WORMS are e'en (*Savagely*) AT HIM. (*Quizzically*) Your worm is your only emperor for diet. We fat all creatures else to fat us, and we fat ourselves for maggots. Your (*Pointing at* CLAUDIUS) FAT King, and your (*Pointing at* GUILDENSTERN) LEAN BEGGAR is but variable service; two dishes, but to one table—that's the end.

CLAUDIUS (*Hopelessly, to* CORNELIUS) Alas, alas!

HAMLET A man may fish with the worm that hath eat of a king, and eat of the fish that hath fed of that worm.

CLAUDIUS (*Pushing the Courtiers' swords aside, he crosses up to* HAMLET *on the platform and asks sternly*) What dost thou mean by this?

HAMLET Nothing! . . . But to show you how a King MAY go a progress through the guts of a beggar.

CLAUDIUS (*Fighting back his anger*) Where is Polonius?

HAMLET In heaven. Send thither to see. If your messenger find him not there, seek him (*Points down*) in the other place yourself. (*Crossing down the steps to the main stage*) But, indeed, if you find him not within this month, you shall (*sniffs*) NOSE him, as you go up the stairs into the lobby.

CLAUDIUS (*To a Courtier*) Go seek him there.
    (*Courtier with a lantern exits up the stairway*)

HAMLET (*Calling after him*) He will stay till you come.

CLAUDIUS Hamlet, this deed, for thine especial safety—
    Which we do tender, as we dearly grieve
    For that which thou hast done—must send thee hence
    With fiery quickness. Therefore prepare thyself.
    The bark is ready, and the wind at help;
    The associates tend, and everything is bent
    For England.

HAMLET (*Bluntly*)   England.

CLAUDIUS   Aye, Hamlet.

HAMLET   Good!

CLAUDIUS   So is it, if thou knew'st our purposes.

HAMLET (*Laughs, says slyly*)   I see a cherub that sees them. But come, for England. (*He starts to go off up right, but then turns and makes a sudden dash for the platform and kisses* CLAUDIUS *on the cheek*) Farewell, dear MOTHER.
　　(*He turns and starts down the steps*)

CLAUDIUS   Thy loving FATHER, Hamlet.

HAMLET   My MOTHER! (*Vehemently*) Father and mother is man and wife, man and wife is one . . . FLESH; and so— (*Blows him a kiss*) my MOTHER. Come, for England.
　　(*He exits up right, closely guarded by the Courtiers*)

CLAUDIUS (*Angrily to* ROSENCRANTZ, GUILDENSTERN, *and* CORNELIUS)
Follow him at foot, tempt him with speed aboard,
Delay it not; I'll have him hence tonight.
Away! For everything is sealed and done
That else leans on the affair. Pray you, make haste. (*They exit up right. He comes forward, says sinisterly*)
And England, if my love thou hold'st at aught—
As my great power thereof may give thee sense,
Thou mayst not coldly set
Our sovereign process, which imports at full,
By letters conguring to that effect,
The present DEATH OF HAMLET!
(*Feverishly*) Do it, England!
For like the hectic in my blood he rages,
And thou must cure me. Till I know 'tis done,
Howe'er my haps, my joys were ne'er begun.

　　(*He exits left. There is a blackout*)

SCENE 13

The castle flat and stool are removed, right. The center doors are open. An intense white light comes up full on the side and main platforms. In the distance is heard the sound of men marching and whistling a jaunty tune.* A Standard Bearer enters up right with a banner and stands at attention right of center stage. FORTINBRAS *and his* CAPTAIN *enter from the side platform, right. The two cross to the center of the main platform and watch the passing army, offstage, down right.*

FORTINBRAS Go, Captain. *(Points at the center doors)* From
   me greet the Danish King.
   Tell him that by his license, Fortinbras
   Craves the conveyance of a promised march
   Over his kingdom. *(Handing him a document)* You know
   the rendezvous. *(*CAPTAIN *nods)*
   If that his Majesty would aught with us,
   We shall express our duty in his eye,
   And let him know so.

CAPTAIN *(Saluting him)* I will do't, my lord.

FORTINBRAS *(Crossing right, he points offstage with his sword
   and commands the Standard Bearer)*
   Go softly on!
      (They exit right. The CAPTAIN *turns to go, then sees* HAM-
      LET, ROSENCRANTZ, *and* GUILDENSTERN *entering from the
      centers doors)*

HAMLET *(Crossing to the* CAPTAIN*)* Good sir, whose powers are
   these?

---

* The tune whistled was a version of "Sweete Kate" composed by Robert
Jones in 1609 for his *Fourth Booke of Ayres.* The score can be found in
An Elizabethan Song Book by Auden, Kallman, and Greenberg (Double-
day-Anchor book #A56).

CAPTAIN   They are of Norway, sir.
(*The marching and whistling fade down*)

HAMLET   How purposed, sir, I pray you?

CAPTAIN   Against some part of Poland.

HAMLET   Who commands them, sir?

CAPTAIN   (*Still watching the army*)   The nephew to old Norway, Fortinbras.

HAMLET   Goes it against the MAIN of Poland, sir,
Or for some FRONTIER?

(*The marching and whistling fade up as if another troop were passing*)

CAPTAIN   Truly to speak, and with no addition,
We go to gain a little patch of ground
That hath in it no profit but the name.
To pay five ducats, five, I would not FARM it.

HAMLET   Why, then the Polack never will defend it.

CAPTAIN   Yes, it is already garrisoned.

(*The marching and whistling fade down*)

HAMLET   (*To himself*)   Two thousand souls, and twenty thousand ducats
Will not debate the question of this straw.
This is the imposthume of much wealth and peace,
That inward breaks, and shows no cause without
Why the man dies. (*To* CAPTAIN) I humbly thank you, sir.

CAPTAIN   God be wi' you, sir.
(*Salutes him and exits through the center doors*)

ROSENCRANTZ   Will it please you go, my lord?
(*The marching fades up, whistling ends*)

HAMLET (*Nods*) I'll be with you straight. (*Imploringly*) Go
a little before.
> (ROSENCRANTZ *and* GUILDENSTERN *exit through the center
> doors*)

How all occasions do inform against me,
And spur my dull revenge! What is a man,
If his chief good and market of his time
(*Marching fades down*)
Be but to sleep and feed? A beast, no more.
(*Marching fades out*)
Sure he that made us with such large discourse,
Looking before and after, gave us not
That capability and godlike reason
To fust in us unused. Now whether it be
Bestial oblivion, or some craven scruple
Of thinking too precisely on the event—
A thought which quartered hath but one part wisdom,
And ever three parts (*The word repulses him*) COWARD—I
do not know
Why yet I live to say this thing's to do,
Since I have cause, and will, and strength, and means
To do't. (*Marching fades in*) Examples gross as earth exhort
me.
Witness this army of such mass and charge,
Led by a delicate and tender Prince,
Whose spirit with divine ambition puffed
Makes mouths at the invisible event,
Exposing what is mortal and unsure (*Marching fades down*)
To all that fortune, death, and danger dare,
Even for an eggshell. (*Marching fades out;* HAMLET *speaks
heroically*) Rightly to be great
Is not to stir without great argument,
But greatly to find quarrel in a straw
When honour's at the stake. How stand I then?
That have a father killed, a mother stained,
Excitements of my reason and my blood,

And let all sleep (*Marching and whistling fade up*) while to
   my shame I see
The imminent death of twenty thousand men,
That for a fantasy and trick of fame
Go to their graves like beds; fight for a plot
Whereon the numbers cannot try the cause,
Which is not tomb enough and continent
To hide the slain. (*Firmly resolved*) O from this time forth,
My thoughts be bloody, or be nothing worth!

   (*The marching and whistling reach a crescendo, the
   whistlers dividing their tune into a canonic "echo" effect
   as* HAMLET *turns on his heel and exits center with great
   determination*)

ACT THREE

SCENE 14

Four Courtiers quickly reset the table, armchair, and stool right of the main stage, as in the first act, only with the narrow end of the table facing the audience. The lights go up on the entire stage.

GERTRUDE *enters from the stairway pursued by* HORATIO, *who is trying to speak with her. The* GENTLEMAN *enters from the center doors, confronts* GERTRUDE *on the platform, and says something urgent to her softly.*

GERTRUDE (*Crossing right on the platform and shaking her head*)   I will not speak with her.

GENTLEMAN (*Following her, persisting*)   She is importunate, indeed DISTRACT.
Her mood will needs be pitied.

GERTRUDE   What would she have?

GENTLEMAN (*Cautiously*)   She speaks much of her father, says she hears
There's TRICKS i' the world; and hems, and beats her heart,
Spurns enviously at straws, speaks things in doubt
That carry but half sense.

HORATIO (*Urging gently*)   'Twere good she were spoken with, for she may strew
Dangerous conjectures in ill-breeding minds.

GERTRUDE Let her come in. (GENTLEMAN *bows to her, looks questioningly to* HORATIO, *who gives him a nod, then exits through the center doors.* GERTRUDE *crosses slowly right to the armchair, says dejectedly to herself*)
To my sick soul, as sin's true nature is,
Each toy seems prologue to some great amiss. (*Sits*)
So full of artless jealousy is guilt,
It spills itself, in fearing to be spilt.

OPHELIA (*Enters from the center doors, disheveled; she goes to* HORATIO, *looks at him strangely, then demands*)
Where is the beauteous majesty of Denmark?

GERTRUDE How now, Ophelia?

OPHELIA (*Turns and looks blankly at her, then, distracted, walks slowly down the side steps; she sings*)
How should I your true-love know
From another one?
By his cockle hat and staff,
And his sandal shoon.*
     (*She sits on the side steps*)

GERTRUDE Alas, sweet lady, what imports this song?

OPHELIA (*Childishly*) Say you? Nay, pray you, mark.
     (*Sings*)
He is dead and gone, lady,
He is dead and gone,
     (*Laughs*)
At his head a grass-green turf,
At his heels a stone.

GERTRUDE Nay, but Ophelia—
     (CLAUDIUS *enters up right and crosses to the armchair*)

---

* The traditional melodies were used for Ophelia's songs, the scores of which are quoted in the H. H. Furness Variorum edition of the play, published by J. P. Lippincott in 1877, reprinted by Dover Paperbacks in 1963. This song is found on p. 330.

OPHELIA (*Crossly*)   Pray you, mark!
(*Sings*) White his shroud as the mountain snow—

GERTRUDE   Alas, look here, my lord.

OPHELIA (*Sings*)   Larded—(*She breaks off, seeing* CLAUDIUS, *then continues*) with sweet flowers, (*She gets up, frightened and shivering, crosses to down right corner of the platform, and sits*)
Which bewept to the grave did go
With true-love showers.

CLAUDIUS (*Crossing center*)   How do you, pretty lady?

OPHELIA   Well, God 'ild you. (HORATIO *crosses down front steps and tries to comfort her*) They say the owl was a baker's daughter. (*Ominously*) Lord, we know what we are. But we know not what we . . . MAY be. (*Naïvely*) God be at your table.

CLAUDIUS (*To* GERTRUDE)   Conceit upon your father.

OPHELIA (*Overhearing* CLAUDIUS, *she says violently*)   Pray you, let's have no words of this! But when they ask you what it means, say you this—
    (*Sings lightly*)
Tomorrow is Saint Valentine's Day,
All in the morning betime, (*Stroking her hair*)
And I a maid at your window,
To be your Valentine.*
    (*Gets up and crosses up side steps; she speaks nervously*)
Then up he rose, and donned his clothes,
And dupped the chamber door,
Let in the maid, that out a maid,
Never departed more.

CLAUDIUS   Pretty Ophelia.

* See Furness Variorum, p. 333.

OPHELIA (*Walking precariously along the right edge of the platform*) Indeed, la, without an oath, I'll make an end on't. (*She falls off the front edge of the platform.* HORATIO *catches her.* GERTRUDE *rises and crosses down to her, attempting to hold her.* OPHELIA *sings violently*)

By Gis and by Saint Charity,
Alack, and fie for shame,
Young men will do't if they come to't,
    (*Beating on* HORATIO's *chest*)
By cock they are to blame!
Quoth she, before you tumbled me,
    (HORATIO *sets her on the stool*)
You promised me to wed.
    (*Speaks fearfully*)
He answers:
So would I ha' done by yonder sun,
And thou hadst not come to my bed.

    (*She runs up onto the platform.* GERTRUDE *crosses down left to the stool*)

CLAUDIUS How long hath she been thus?

OPHELIA (*To* CLAUDIUS, *frightened*) I hope all will be well. We must be patient, (*Tearfully*) but I cannot choose but weep to think they should lay him in the cold ground. (*Angrily*) My brother shall know of it. (*Cordially*) And so I thank you for your good counsel. (*With fashionable dignity*) Come, my coach. (*Curtsying to many imaginary ladies*) Good night, ladies, good night, sweet ladies, good night, good night.
    (*She runs out center*)

CLAUDIUS Follow her close; give her good watch, I pray you.
    (HORATIO *exits center*)
O this is the poison of deep grief. It springs
All from her father's death. (*Crossing down left*) O Gertrude, Gertrude—

When sorrows come, they come not single spies,
But in battalions. First, her father slain,
Next, your son gone, and he most violent author
Of his own just remove; the people muddied,
Thick and unwholesome in their thoughts and whispers,
For good Polonius' death. And we have done but greenly
In hugger-mugger to inter him. Poor Ophelia
Divided from herself and her fair judgment;
Last, and as much containing as all these,
Her brother is in secret come from France,
And wants not buzzers to infect his ear
With pestilent speeches of his father's death.

(*Noise of an angry crowd is heard in the distance*)

GERTRUDE (*Crossing up side steps*)　Alack, what noise is this?

CLAUDIUS (*Crossing up onto the platform*)　Where are my
　　Switzers? Let THEM guard the door!

GENTLEMAN (*Rushing in through the center doors*)　My lord,
　　my lord!

CLAUDIUS　What is the matter?

GENTLEMAN　Save yourself, my lord!
　　The ocean, overpeering of his list,
　　Eats not the flats with more impetuous haste
　　Than young LAERTES in a riotous head
　　O'erbears your officers. The rabble call him lord,
　　They cry, "Choose we Laertes shall be king!"
　　Caps, hands, and tongues applaud it to the clouds,
　　"Laertes shall be king! Laertes king!"

GERTRUDE　How cheerfully on the false trail they cry!
　　O this is counter, you false Danish dogs.

(*A great yell goes up from the offstage crowd*)

CLAUDIUS　The doors are broke!

LAERTES (*appears with a sword in the center doorway, followed by the head members of the crowd, some carrying pikes. The* GENTLEMAN *rushes to the door, attempting to block their entrance.* LAERTES *seizes him, throws him down on the platform, and, holding the sword at his throat, demands*) Where is this King? (*To the crowd*) Sirs, stand you all without.

CROWD (*Cries*) "No, let us in," "We will come in!" etc.

LAERTES I pray you give me leave. (*Crowd noises fade off-stage*)

CROWD (*Cries*) "We will," "Give Laertes leave," etc.

LAERTES I thank you. Keep the door. (*The* GENTLEMAN *gets up and stands in the doorway with the crowd;* LAERTES *sees* CLAUDIUS) O thou vile King, Give me my father!

GERTRUDE (*Restraining him*) Calmly, good Laertes.

LAERTES That drop of blood that's calm proclaims me bastard,
Cries cuckold to my father, brands the harlot
Even here between the chaste unsmirchèd brows
Of my true mother.

CLAUDIUS (*Crossing center stage calmly*)
What is the cause, Laertes,
That thy rebellion looks so giant-like?
(LAERTES *raises his sword;* GERTRUDE *holds his arm.* CLAUDIUS *speaks firmly*) Let him go, Gertrude, do not fear our person.
There's such divinity doth hedge a king,
That treason can but PEEP to what it would,
Acts little of his will. Tell me, Laertes,
Why thou art thus incensed—let him go, Gertrude. (*She does*) Speak, man.

LAERTES (*Crossing onto the side steps*) Where is my father?

CLAUDIUS (*Looks first to* GERTRUDE, *then says sharply*) Dead!

GERTRUDE (*Protecting*)   But not by him!

CLAUDIUS   Let him demand his fill. (*Sits in the armchair*)

LAERTES (*Crossing above the table to right*)
How came he dead? I'll not be juggled with.
To hell, allegiance; vows to the blackest devil,
Conscience and grace to the profoundest pit!
(*Threatening him across the table with his sword*)
I dare damnation! To this point I stand,
That both the worlds I give to negligence,
Let come what comes, only I'll be revenged
Most thoroughly for my father.

CLAUDIUS   Who shall stay you?

LAERTES   My will, not all the world.
And for my means, I'll husband them so well,
They shall go far with little.

CLAUDIUS   Good Laertes,
If you desire to know the certainty
Of your dear father's death, is't writ in your revenge,
That swoopstake you will draw both friend and foe,
Winner and loser?

LAERTES   None but his enemies.

CLAUDIUS   Will you KNOW them then?

LAERTES (*Putting his sword on the table, he spreads his arms*)
To his good friends thus wide I'll ope my arms,
And like the kind life-rendering pelican,
Repast them with my blood.

CLAUDIUS   Why, now you speak
Like a good child, and a true gentleman.
That I am guiltless of your father's death, (GERTRUDE *makes
a move toward him; he turns, gives her a stern look, then
continues*)
And am most sensibly in grief for it,

It shall as level to you judgment pierce
As day does to your eye.
        (OPHELIA *sings offstage*)

CROWD   Let her come in!

LAERTES   How now, what noise is that?
        (OPHELIA *re-enters, having heard the commotion. She is
        carrying a bunch of weeds* and is covered with water
        and muck.* LAERTES *runs to greet her, stops, side steps,
        horrified*)
O heat, dry up my brains! Tears seven times salt,
Burn out the sense and virtue of mine eye.
By heaven, thy madness shall be paid with weight,
Till our scale turn the beam. O rose of May,
Dear maid, kind sister, sweet Ophelia. (*She looks at him
blankly and turns away*)
O heavens, is't possible a young maid's wits
Should be as mortal as an old man's life?

OPHELIA   (*Crossing down the front steps, she sings woefully*)
        They bore him barefaced on the bier;
        Hey non-nonny, nonny, hey nonny,
        And in his grave rained many a tear—
        (*She breaks off from her song; then, watching an imaginary
        bird take flight, she says*) Fare you well, my dove.

LAERTES   Hadst thou thy wits, and didst persuade revenge,
It could not move thus.

OPHELIA   (*Watching the bird up in the air, she crosses center*)
You must sing down, a-down and you call him a-down-a.
(*Watching the bird soar*) O how the wheel becomes it!
(CLAUDIUS *crosses to her; she bumps into him, then gives a
terrified cry and runs to* LAERTES) It is the false steward that
stole his master's daughter!

LAERTES   (*Trying to comfort her*)   This nothing's more than
matter.

* Twine was substituted as the rehearsal prop.

OPHELIA (*Giving a weed to* LAERTES) There's rosemary. That's for remembrance. Pray you, love, remember. And pansies, that for thoughts.

LAERTES A document in madness, thoughts and remembrance fitted.

OPHELIA (*Crosses to* CLAUDIUS) There's fennel for you, and columbines. (*Crossing down right to* GERTRUDE) There's rue for you—and here's some for me; we may call it herb-of-grace a-Sundays—O you must wear your rue with a difference. There's a daisy. I would give you some violets, (*Sadly*) but they withered all when my father died. They say he made a good end.
　　(*Sings prettily*)
　For bonny sweet Robin is all my joy.

LAERTES Thought and affliction, passion, hell itself,
She turns to favour and to prettiness.

OPHELIA (*Sings* the following song heavily, frequently losing the tune and speaking the lines, searching for their meaning*)
　And will 'a not come again?
　And will 'a not come again?
　　(*Crossing up onto the platform, she kneels and strokes the ground*)
　No, no, he is dead,
　Go to thy death-bed
　He never will come again.
　His beard was as white as snow,
　All flaxen was his poll. (*Tormented*)
　He is gone, he is gone,
　And we cast away moan,
　God 'a mercy on his soul.
And of all Christian souls, I pray God. (LAERTES *goes to her and kneels beside her. She looks blankly at him, then slaps his face harshly; she gets up*) God be with you!

* See Furness Variorum, p. 350.

*(She walks slowly to the door, looks slyly at the men
standing there, and then suddenly breaks through them,
as they try to catch her.* GERTRUDE *hurries out after her.
The crowd disperses)*

LAERTES *(Burning through his tears)* Do you SEE this, O God?

CLAUDIUS *(Taking him to the armchair)*
Laertes, I must commune with your grief
Or you deny me right.
     (He seats him)

LAERTES Let this be so.
His means of death, his obscure funeral
No trophy, sword, nor hatchment o'er his bones,
No noble rite, nor formal ostentation,
Cry to be heard, as 'twere from heaven to earth,
That I MUST call't in question.

CLAUDIUS So you shall;
And where the offence is, let the great axe fall.
Now must your conscience my acquittance seal,
And you must put me in your heart for friend,
Since you shall know that HAMLET *(LAERTES stands, CLAUDIUS
braces him)*
Who hath your noble father slain,
Pursued MY life.

LAERTES *(Crossing down center)*
And so have I a noble father lost,
A sister driven into desperate terms,
Whose worth, if praises may go back again,
Stood challenger on mount of all the age
For her perfections. *(With determined anger)* But my re-
     venge will come.

CLAUDIUS *(Crossing to his right)*
Break not your sleeps for that. You must not think
That we are made of stuff so flat and dull,
That we can let our beard be shook with danger

And think it pastime. (MESSENGER *enters down right and kneels*) You shortly shall hear more.
(*Crossing right to* MESSENGER)
How now, what news?

MESSENGER (*Handing him two letters*)
Letters, my lord, from Hamlet (CLAUDIUS *starts*)
This to your Majesty, this to the Queen.

CLAUDIUS (*Astonished*)   From Hamlet? Who brought them?

MESSENGER   Sailors, my lord, they say; I saw them not.

CLAUDIUS   Laertes, you shall hear them.
Leave us! (MESSENGER *bows and exits down right.* CLAUDIUS *reads*) "High and mighty, you shall know I am set naked on your kingdom. Tomorrow shall I beg leave to see your kingly eyes, when I shall, first asking your pardon thereunto, recount the occasion of my sudden and more strange return. Hamlet."
What should this mean?
(*Furiously*) Are all the rest come back?
Or is it some abuse and no such thing?

LAERTES (*Looking over* CLAUDIUS' *shoulder*)   Know you the hand?

CLAUDIUS   'Tis Hamlet's character. "Naked"?
And in a postscript here he says "alone."
Can you advise me?

LAERTES   I am lost in it, my lord. But let him come!
(*Vengefully*) It warms the very sickness in my heart
That I shall live and tell him to his teeth,
"THUS didest thou."

CLAUDIUS   If it be so, Laertes—
Will you be ruled by me?

LAERTES   Aye, my lord,
So you will not O'ERrule me to a peace.

CLAUDIUS (*Leading him to the table, he sits in the armchair*)
To thine OWN peace. If he be now returned, (LAERTES *sits
in the stool*)
As checking at his voyage, and that he means
No more to undertake it, I will work him
To an exploit, now ripe in my device,
Under the which he shall not choose but fall;
And for his death no wind of blame shall breathe,
But even his mother shall uncharge the practice,
And call it accident.

LAERTES My lord, I will be ruled:
The rather if you could devise it so
That I might be the organ.

CLAUDIUS (*Stands and looks around to check that no one is lis-
tening*) It falls right.
You have been talked of since your travel much,
And that in Hamlet's hearing, for a quality
Wherein they say you shine.

LAERTES What part is that, my lord?

CLAUDIUS A very riband in the cap of youth.
Two months since,
Here was a gentleman of Normandy.
He made confession of you,
And gave you such a masterly report
For art and exercise in your defence,
And for your rapier most especial,
That he cried out "It would be a sight indeed
If one could match you." Sir, this report of his
Did Hamlet so envenom with his envy,
That he could nothing do but wish and beg
Your sudden coming o'er to play with him
Now out of this—

LAERTES (*Stands and asks reluctantly*)
What out of this, my lord?

CLAUDIUS (*Enkindling him*)
Laertes, was your father dear to you?
Or are you like the painting of a sorrow,
A face without a heart?

LAERTES (*Angered*)   Why ask you this?

CLAUDIUS   Hamlet comes back, what would you undertake
To show yourself your father's son in deed
More than in words?

LAERTES (*Hotly*)   To cut his throat i' the church!

CLAUDIUS (*Showing a sinister smile, he crosses to the side stage.*
LAERTES follows)
No place, indeed, should murder sanctuarize.
Revenge should have no bounds. But good Laertes,
Will you do this? Keep close within your chamber;
Hamlet returned shall know YOU are come home (*Sits on*
the edge of the platform)
We'll put on those shall praise your excellence,
And set a double varnish on the fame
The Frenchman gave you, bring you in fine together,
And wager on your heads. He, being remiss,
Most generous, and free from all contriving,
Will not peruse the foils, so that with ease,
Or with a little shuffling, you may choose
A sword unbated, and in a pass of practice (*Thrusting his*
arm forward)
Requite him for your father.

LAERTES (*Sits on the stool, down right*)   I will do't.
And for that purpose I'll anoint MY sword.
(*Menacingly*) I bought an unction of a mountebank,
So mortal that, but dip a knife in it,
Where it draws blood no cataplasm so rare,
Collected from all simples that have virtue
Under the moon, can save the thing from death
That is but SCRATCHED withal. I'll touch my point

With this contagion, that if I gall him SLIGHTLY,
It may be death.

CLAUDIUS (*Pleased*)   Let's further think of this.
If this should fail? Soft, let me see. . . . I ha't!
When in your motion you are hot and dry,
As make your bouts more violent to that end,
And that he calls for drink, I'll have prepared him
A chalice for the nonce, whereon but sipping,
If he by chance escape your venomed stuck,
Our purpose may hold there.

GERTRUDE (*Calling from offstage*)   My lord, my lord!

(CLAUDIUS *and* LAERTES *stand;* CLAUDIUS *puts his fingers
to his lips indicating secrecy, then crosses to the table.*
GERTRUDE *enters from the center doors*)

CLAUDIUS   How now, sweet Queen?

GERTRUDE (*Leaning against the wall, overcome*)
One woe doth tread upon another's heel,
So fast they follow! Your sister's drowned, Laertes.

LAERTES (*Crossing to the side steps*)   Drowned! Wh-where?

GERTRUDE (*Crossing to the center of the platform*)
There is a willow grows aslant a brook,
That shows his hoar leaves in the glassy stream;
There with fantastic garlands did she come,
Of crowflowers, nettles, daisies, and long purples
That liberal shepherds give a grosser name,
But our cold maids do dead men's fingers call them.
There on the pendant boughs, her coronet weeds
Clambering to hang, an envious sliver broke,
When down her weedy trophies and herself
Fell in the weeping brook. Her clothes spread wide,
And mermaid-like awhile they bore her up,
Which time she chanted snatches of old tunes,
As one incapable of her own distress,

Or like a creature native and indued
Unto that element; but long it could not be
Till that her garments, heavy with their drink,
Pulled the poor wretch from her melodious lay
To muddy death.

LAERTES (*Collapsing on the steps*)   Alas, then she is drowned.

GERTRUDE (*Crossing to him*)   Drowned, drowned.

LAERTES (*Fighting back his tears*)
Too much of water hast thou, poor Ophelia,
And therefore I forbid my tears. (*His voice breaks*) But yet
It is our trick; nature her custom holds,
Let shame say what it will.
(*Weeping*) When these are gone,
The woman will be out. (*Rises angrily*) Adieu, my lord.
I have a speech of fire that fain would blaze,
But that this folly doubts it.
        (*He exits up right*)

CLAUDIUS (*Excitedly*)   How much I had to do to calm his rage!
Now fear I this will give it start again.
Therefore let's follow, Gertrude.
        (*They exit up right*)

SCENE 15

A *distant bell tolls. Four Courtiers enter from the right and carry the table to stage center; they turn the table on its side, with the top facing the audience, to represent a barricade in front of a grave. The stool is placed at the right end of the table, the armchair is removed. Courtiers exit.*

The FIRST GRAVEDIGGER *enters through the center doors carrying a lantern. He is followed by the* SECOND GRAVEDIGGER, *who carries a spade and a pick and whistles, ironically, "Tomorrow is Saint Valentine's Day."*

FIRST GRAVEDIGGER (*Sets his lantern down on the stool above the side steps, crosses to the grave, looks into it, turns, and speaks with a Warwickshire Midlands dialect*)   Is she to be buried in Christian burial, that willfully seeks her own salvation?

SECOND GRAVEDIGGER   I tell thee she is, and therefore make her grave, straight; The crowner hath sat on her, and finds it Christian burial.

FIRST GRAVEDIGGER   How can that be? Unless she drowned herself in her own defence.

SECOND GRAVEDIGGER   Why, 'tis found so.
    (*The sound of the bell fades out*)

FIRST GRAVEDIGGER   It must be "se offendendo," it cannot be else. For here lies the point: If I drown myself wittingly, it argues an act, and an act hath three branches; it is to act, to do, to perform; argal, she drowned herself wittingly.

SECOND GRAVEDIGGER   Nay, but hear you, goodman delver—

FIRST GRAVEDIGGER   Give me leave! (SECOND GRAVEDIGGER *sits on the side steps*) (*Pointing down into the grave*) Here lies the water—good? (*Pointing to the table ledge*) Here stands the man—good! (*Illustrating each point literally with his hands*) If the man go to this water and drown himself, it is willy-nilly he goes, mark you that! But, (*Pointing first to the grave, then to the ledge*) if the water come to HIM and drown him, he drowns not himself; (*Greatly pleased with his own logic*) Argal, he that is not guilty of his own death shortens not his own life!
    (*He goes behind the barricade down into the grave* and prepares to dig*)

---

* The actor created the illusion of descending a few feet by gradually lowering himself to his knees.

SECOND GRAVEDIGGER (*Trying to disprove him*) But is this LAW?

FIRST GRAVEDIGGER Aye, marry is't. Crowner's Quest law.

SECOND GRAVEDIGGER Will you ha' the truth on't? If this had not been a gentlewoman, she should have been buried OUT o' Christian burial.

FIRST GRAVEDIGGER (*Leaning over the barricade*) Why, there thou sayst! And the more pity that great folk should have countenance in this world to drown or hang themselves, more than their even-Christian. Come, my spade. (SECOND GRAVEDIGGER *rises, hands him the spade*) There is no ancient gentlemen but gardeners, ditchers, and grave-makers—they hold up ADAM's profession.
(*He starts digging*)

SECOND GRAVEDIGGER Was he a gentleman?

FIRST GRAVEDIGGER 'A was the first that ever bore arms.

SECOND GRAVEDIGGER (*Preposterously*) Why, he had none.

FIRST GRAVEDIGGER (*Angrily*) What, art a heathen? How dost thou understand the Scripture? The Scripture says Adam digged. (*Pointing to his arm*) Could he dig without arms? I'll put another question to thee; if thou answerest me not to the purpose, confess thyself—

SECOND GRAVEDIGGER Go to.

FIRST GRAVEDIGGER (*With a merry twinkle*) What is he that builds stronger than either the mason, the shipwright, or the carpenter?

SECOND GRAVEDIGGER (*Racks his brain, then comes up with an idea*) The gallows-maker! For that frame outlives a thousand tenants.
(*Both laugh*)

FIRST GRAVEDIGGER   I like thy wit well, i' good faith! The gallows does well! But (*Catching him pawkily*) HOW does it well? It does well to those that do ILL. Now THOU dost ill to say the gallows is built stronger than the church; argal, the gallows may do well to THEE. (*Laughs*) To't again, come.
(*He digs*)

SECOND GRAVEDIGGER   (*Picking up the lantern, he crosses to the right of the grave*)   Who builds stronger than a mason, a shipwright, or a carpenter?

FIRST GRAVEDIGGER   Aye, tell me that and unyoke.

SECOND GRAVEDIGGER   (*An idea strikes him*)   Marry, now I can tell!

FIRST GRAVEDIGGER   To't!

SECOND GRAVEDIGGER   (*Sits on the stool, dejectedly*)   Mass, I cannot tell.

FIRST GRAVEDIGGER   Cudgel thy brains no more about it, for your dull ass will not mend his pace wi' beating; and when you are asked this question next, say "a GRAVE-MAKER." (*With a macabre delight*) The houses HE makes last till DOOMSDAY. (*Giving him a coin from his pocket*) Go, get thee to Yaughan, fetch me a stoup of liquor. (SECOND GRAVE-DIGGER *exits up right with his pick and lantern.* FIRST GRAVE-DIGGER *digs and sings**)
In youth when I did love, did love,
Methought it was very sweet,
   (HAMLET *and* HORATIO *enter center, cross to the side steps, and watch him, amused*)
To contract, oh the time for-a my behove,
O me thought there-a was nothing a-meet.

HAMLET   (*Quizzically*)   Has this fellow no feeling of his business, that he sings at grave-making?
   (FIRST GRAVEDIGGER *looks up at them*)

* The actor improvised his own melody.

HORATIO   Custom hath made it in him a property of easiness.

HAMLET (*Laughs*) 'Tis e'en so. The hand of little employment hath the daintier sense.

FIRST GRAVEDIGGER (*Laughs, sings broadly, with great embellishment, to* HAMLET)
 But age with his stealing steps
 Hath clawed me in his clutch,
 And hath shippèd me intil the land,
 As if I had never been such.

 (*Picks up a skull and shows it to* HAMLET)

HAMLET (*Laughing with* HORATIO) That skull had a tongue in it, and could sing once. (FIRST GRAVEDIGGER *throws the skull back down in the grave*) How the knave jowls it to the ground, as if it were Cain's jawbone that did the first murder. This might be the pate of a politician, which this ass now o'er-reaches; one that would circumvent God, might it not?

HORATIO   It might, my lord.
 (FIRST GRAVEDIGGER *resumes his digging*)

HAMLET   Or of a courtier, which could say, (*Assuming an affected manner, similar to the one we will see in* OSRIC) "Good morrow, sweet lord, how dost thou, good lord?" This might be my lord such-a-one, that praised my lord such-a-one's horse, when he meant to beg it, might it not?

HORATIO (*Laughing*) Aye, my lord.

HAMLET   Why e'en so! And now my Lady Worm's—chopless, and knocked about the mazzard with a sexton's spade. Here's fine revolution, and we had the trick to see it. (*To* FIRST GRAVEDIGGER) Did these bones cost no more the breeding, but to play at loggats with 'em? (FIRST GRAVEDIGGER *laughs and nods*) Mine ache to think on't!

FIRST GRAVEDIGGER (*Sings to* HAMLET)
 A pickaxe and a spade, a spade,

For and a shrouding sheet,
O a pit of clay for to be made
For such a guest is meet.

HAMLET (*Sits on the steps;* HORATIO *stands beside him*)   Whose grave's this, sirrah?

FIRST GRAVEDIGGER (*Rouguishly*)   Mine, sir! (*Laughs uproariously, sings outrageously*)
O a pit of clay for to be made
  (*Gleefully picks up another skull*)
For such a guest is meet.

  (*He sets the skull on the ledge of the table*)

HAMLET   I think it be thine, indeed, for thou LIEST in it.

FIRST GRAVEDIGGER (*Bantering*)   You lie out on't, sir, and therefore 'tis not yours. For my part, I do not lie in't, yet it is mine.

HAMLET   Thou dost lie in't to be in't and say it is thine. 'Tis for the dead, not for the quick—therefore thou liest.

FIRST GRAVEDIGGER   'Tis a quick lie sir, 'twill away again from me to you.
  (*He guffaws*)

HAMLET   What man dost thou dig it for?

FIRST GRAVEDIGGER   For no MAN, sir.

HAMLET   What woman then?

FIRST GRAVEDIGGER   For none neither.

HAMLET   Who is to be buried in it?

FIRST GRAVEDIGGER   One that WAS a woman sir, but, rest her soul, she's dead.

  (*He turns his back and continues digging*)

HAMLET (*To* HORATIO)   How absolute the knave is! We must speak by the card, or equivocation will undo us. (FIRST GRAVEDIGGER *smiles*) How long hast thou been a grave-maker?

FIRST GRAVEDIGGER (*Scratches himself, leans over the barricade, and speaks as a guide to a tourist*) Of all the days i' the year, I came to it that day that our last King Hamlet o'ercame Fortinbras.

HAMLET (*Reflectively*) How long is that since?

FIRST GRAVEDIGGER Why cannot you tell that? Every fool can tell that. It was that very day that YOUNG Hamlet was born —he that is mad and sent into England.

HAMLET Aye, marry, why was he sent into England?

FIRST GRAVEDIGGER Why, because he was mad. He shall recover his wits there, or if he do not, 'tis no great matter there. (*He turns and digs*)

HAMLET Why?

FIRST GRAVEDIGGER (*Stops digging*) 'Twill not be seen in him there. There the men are as mad as he.

HAMLET How came he mad?

FIRST GRAVEDIGGER (*Digging*) Very STRANGELY, they say.

HAMLET How strangely?

FIRST GRAVEDIGGER (*As if the answer were obvious*) Faith, e'en with losing his wits.

HAMLET Upon what ground?

FIRST GRAVEDIGGER (*As if speaking to a dullard*) Why, here in Denmark! (HAMLET *covers his face in amused exasperation;* FIRST GRAVEDIGGER *speaks to* HORATIO) I have been sexton here, man and boy, thirty years. (*Pause; he digs*)

HAMLET (*Pensively*) How long will a man lie in the earth ere he rot?

FIRST GRAVEDIGGER Faith, if he be not rotten afore he die, (*Scratching his behind*) as we have many POCKY corses nowadays that will scarce hold the laying in, he will last you some eight year, or nine year. A tanner will last you nine year.

HAMLET   Why he more than another?

FIRST GRAVEDIGGER   Why, sir, his hide is so tanned with his trade that he will keep out water a great while. And your water is a sore decayer of your whoreson dead body. (*Picking up a skull from the ledge*) Here's a skull now! This skull hath lain you in the earth three and twenty years.

HAMLET   Whose was it?

FIRST GRAVEDIGGER   (*Recollecting fondly*)   A whoreson mad fellow's it was! Whose do you think it was?

HAMLET   (*Amused*)   Nay, I know not.

FIRST GRAVEDIGGER   (*Smacking the skull*)   A pestilence on him for a mad rogue! (*Laughing, he holds his hand over his head as if pouring a bottle of wine on it*) He poured a flagon of Rhenish on my head once! (*Affectionately*) This same skull, sir, was Yorick's skull, the King's jester.

HAMLET   (*Amazed*)   This?

FIRST GRAVEDIGGER   E'en that.

HAMLET   Let me see. (FIRST GRAVEDIGGER *hands him the skull; he gives a little laugh, recalling fondly*) Alas, poor Yorick!— I knew him, Horatio. A fellow of infinite jest, of most excellent fancy. (FIRST GRAVEDIGGER *smiles and nods;* HAMLET *reminisces with a boyish quality*) He hath borne me on his back a thousand times, and now how abhorred in my imagination it is—my gorge rises at it. Here hung those lips that I have kissed I know not how oft. Where be your gibes now? Your gambols, your songs, your flashes of merriment, that were wont to set the table on a roar? Not one now to mock your own grinning? Quite chop-fallen. (*Sharper, some of his former bitterness recalled*) Now get you to my lady's chamber, and tell her, let her paint an inch thick, to this favour she must come. Make her laugh at that. Prithee, Horatio, tell me one thing.

HORATIO   What's that, my lord?

HAMLET   Dost thou think Alexander looked o' this fashion in the earth?

HORATIO   E'en so.

HAMLET (*Sniffing*)   And smelt so? Pah!
    (*He tosses the skull back to the* FIRST GRAVEDIGGER)

HORATIO   E'en so, my lord.

HAMLET (*Laughs*)   To what base uses we may return, Horatio! Why may not imagination trace the noble dust of Alexander till he find it stopping a bung-hole?

HORATIO   'Twere to consider too curiously to consider so.

HAMLET   No, faith, not a jot—as thus—Alexander died, Alexander was buried, Alexander returneth to dust. The dust is earth, of earth we make loam, and why of that loam whereto he was converted might they not stop a beer barrel? (FIRST GRAVEDIGGER *laughs;* HAMLET *chants*)
    Imperious Caesar, dead and turned to clay,
    Might stop a hole to keep the wind . . . (*Speaks*) away.
    O that that earth which kept the world in awe
    Should patch a wall to expell the winter's flaw! (*Bell tolls;*
FIRST GRAVEDIGGER *quickly gives a few last-minute smoothings to the grave, crosses up right, and stands over his spade;* HAMLET *looks off center*)
But soft, but soft awhile. Here comes the King,
The Queen, the courtiers. Who is this they follow?
And with such maimèd rights? This doth betoken
The corse they follow did with desperate hand
Fordo its own life. 'Twas of some estate.
Couch we awhile and mark.

(HAMLET *and* HORATIO *cross down right. Six Courtiers
enter from the center doors carrying a coffin;* they are
followed by* LAERTES, *a* PRIEST, CLAUDIUS *and* GERTRUDE
*and the two court ladies. Courtiers cross down the side
steps and wait center stage*)

LAERTES (*Standing on the side steps, asks* PRIEST *solemnly*)
What ceremony else?

HAMLET (*Aside to* HORATIO)   That is Laertes,
A very noble youth. Mark.
(*The sound of the bell fades out*)

LAERTES (*Repeating more emphatically*)   What ceremony else?

PRIEST (*Gravely*)   Her obsequies have been as far enlarged
As we have warranty. Her death was doubtful,
And but that great command o'ersways the order,
She should in ground unsanctified have lodged
Till the last trumpet. For charitable prayers,
Shards, flints, and pebbles should be thrown on her;
Yet here she is allowed her virgin crants,
Her maiden strewments, and the bringing home
Of bell and burial.

LAERTES   Must there no more be done?

PRIEST   No more be done?
We should profane the service of the dead
To sing a requiem and such rest to her
As to peace-parted souls.

LAERTES   Lay her in the earth. (*Courtiers place the coffin in
the grave, then retire up left and right*)
And from her fair and unpolluted flesh
May violets spring. I tell thee, churlish priest,
A ministering angel shall my sister be
When thou liest howling!

* A black cloth, held taut, was used to represent the coffin.

HAMLET (*Anguished*)   What, the fair Ophelia!
(*He and* HORATIO *withdraw, down right*)

GERTRUDE (*Laying a bunch of flowers on the grave*)
Sweets to the sweet, farewell.
I hoped thou shouldst have been my Hamlet's wife.
I thought thy bride-bed to have decked, sweet maid,
And not have strewed thy grave.

LAERTES (*Kneeling in front of the grave, he wails vindictively*)
O treble woe
Fall ten times treble on that cursèd head
Whose wicked deed thy most ingenious sense
Deprived thee of. (FIRST GRAVEDIGGER *comes forward to the
grave with his spade*) Hold off the earth awhile!
Till I have caught her once more in my arms. (*Vaults over
the barricade into the grave*)
Now pile your dust upon the quick and dead,
Till of this flat a mountain you have made
To o'ertop old Pelion or the skyish head
Of blue Olympus!

HAMLET (*Appears right on the side platform and cries out, in-
censed*) What is he whose grief
Bears such an emphasis, whose phrase of sorrow
Conjures the wandering stars, and makes them stand
Like wonder-wounded hearers? This is I,
Hamlet, the Dane!
(*He leaps in the grave*)

LAERTES (*Wrestling with him*)   The devil take thy soul!

(*Courtiers rush to the grave and try to part them*)

HAMLET (*Struggling*)   Thou pray'st not well.
I prithee, take thy fingers from my throat,
For though I am not splenitive and rash,
Yet have I in me something dangerous
Which let thy wisdom fear. Hold off thy hand!

CLAUDIUS   Pluck them asunder!

GERTRUDE   Hamlet, Hamlet!

HORATIO   (*Helping to part them*)   Good, my lord, be quiet.

> (*Courtiers haul them out of the grave; two men take* HAMLET *down right and three drag* LAERTES *left to the side stage*)

HAMLET   (*Struggling to free himself from the Courtiers*)
Why, I will fight with him upon this theme
Until my eyelids will no longer wag!

GERTRUDE   O my son, what theme?

HAMLET   I loved Ophelia! Forty thousand brothers
Could not with all their quantity of love
Make up my sum. What wilt thou do for her?

CLAUDIUS   O he is mad, Laertes.

GERTRUDE   For love of God, forbear him.

HAMLET   (*Enraged, he breaks free from the Courtiers and crosses center*)
SWOUNDS, show me what thou'lt do!
Would weep? Would fight? Would fast? Would tear thyself?
Would drink up eisell, eat a crocodile?
I'll do it! (*Advancing toward* LAERTES *down left*) Dost come here to whine,
To outface ME with leaping in her grave?
(*Pushes Courtiers away from* LAERTES)
Be buried quick with her, and so will I,
And if thou prate of mountains, let them throw
Millions of acres on us, (*With mounting fury*) till our ground,
Singeing his pate against the burning zone,
Make OSSA LIKE A WART! (*Pause; he waits for* LAERTES'
reply, but LAERTES *is speechless*) Nay, and thou'lt mouth,
I'll rant as well as thou.

GERTRUDE　This is mere madness,
And thus awhile the fit will work on him.
Anon, as patient as the female dove
When that her golden couplets are disclosed,
His silence will sit drooping.

HAMLET (*Sadly*)　Hear you, sir,
What is the reason that you use me thus?
I loved you ever. But it is no matter.
(*Crossing up front steps*)
Let Hercules himself do what he may,
The cat will mew, and (*He says the word in* CLAUDIUS' *face*)
　DOG will have his day.
　　　(*He exits through the center doors*)

CLAUDIUS　I pray thee, good Horatio, wait upon him. (HORATIO
exits center; Courtiers and FIRST GRAVEDIGGER *exit down right
and left.* CLAUDIUS *comes forward on the platform, says softly
to* LAERTES)
Strengthen your patience in our last night's speech
We'll put the matter to the present push. (*Looking back, he
sees* GERTRUDE *standing by the center doors; he says impa-
tiently*)
Good Gertrude, set some watch over your son. (*She exits
center with her ladies.* CLAUDIUS *speaks to* LAERTES)
This grave shall have a LIVING monument.
　　　(*Taking him across the platform to the center doors*)
An hour of quiet shortly shall we see,
Till then in patience our proceeding be.
　　　(*They exit. The doors close*)

SCENE 16

---

*The Courtiers reset the table, armchair, and stool, similar to
their positions in the first act, only further upstage right and*

at a raked angle, thus opening more space center stage. HAMLET
and HORATIO *enter from the ramp, conversing as they cross
down the front steps to the side stage.*

HAMLET   Sir, in my heart there was a kind of fighting
  That would not let me sleep; Rashly—
  And praised be rashness for it, let us know
  Our indiscretion sometimes serves us well
  When our deep plots do pall, and that should learn us
  There's a divinity that shapes our ends,
  Rough-hew them how we will.

HORATIO   That is most certain.
  So Guildenstern and Rosencrantz go to it?

HAMLET   (*Unconcerned*)   Why, man, they did make love to
    this employment.
  They are not near my conscience.
  'Tis dangerous when the baser nature comes
  Between the pass and fell-incensèd points
  Of mighty opposites.

HORATIO   (*Incredulously*)   Why, what a King is this!

HAMLET   Does it not, think thee, stand me now upon—
  He that hath killed my King, and whored my mother,
  Popped in between the election and my hopes,
  Thrown out his angle for my proper life,
  And with such cozenage—is't not perfect conscience
  To quit him with his arm? And is't not to be damned
  To let this canker of our nature come
  In further evil?

HORATIO   It must be shortly known to him from England
  What is the issue of the business there.

HAMLET   It will be short. The interim is mine,
  And a man's life no more than to say,
  (*Snaps his fingers*) "one."
  But I am very sorry, good Horatio,
  That to Laertes I forgot myself;

For by the image of MY cause, I see
The portraiture of his. (OSRIC *enters from the stairway, carrying a plumed hat; he tries to overhear their conversation*)
　　I'll court his favours.
But sure the bravery of his grief did put me
Into a towering passion.

HORATIO (*Crossing right of* HAMLET, *he sees* OSRIC)
Peace, who comes here?

OSRIC (*Crossing down left on the platform; he speaks with over-articulate diction*) Your lordship is right welcome back to Denmark.
　　(*He bows, flourishing his hat*)

HAMLET (*Stands*) I humbly thank you, sir. (*Turns to* HORATIO) Dost know this water-fly?

HORATIO No, my lord.
　　(OSRIC *momentarily drops his affected façade and casts a sinister stare at* HAMLET)

HAMLET Thy state is the more gracious, for 'tis a vice to know him.

OSRIC (*Crossing down the front steps to the side stage, left of* HAMLET) Sweet lord, if your lordship were at leisure, I should impart a thing to you from his Majesty.

HAMLET I will receive it, sir, with all diligence of spirit. (OSRIC *bows and flourishes his hat*) Put your bonnet to his right use —'tis for the head.

OSRIC (*Unwinding the scarf about his neck*) I thank your lordship, it is very hot.

HAMLET No, believe me, 'tis very cold. The wind is northerly.

OSRIC (*Fawning to him, he rewinds the scarf about his neck*) It is INDIFFERENT cold, my lord, indeed.

HAMLET (*Badgering him*) But yet methinks it is very sultry and hot for my complexion.

OSRIC   Exceedingly, my lord. It is very sultry, as 'twere, I cannot
tell how. But, my lord, his Majesty bade me signify to you
that he has laid a great wager on your head. Sir, here is the
matter—
(*Another flourish*)

HAMLET   (*Pointing to* OSRIC's *head*)   I beseech you, remember—

OSRIC   (*Protesting, he almost lets his anger show*)   Nay, good
my lord, for mine ease, (*With a covering laugh*) in good
faith. Sir, here is newly come to court Laertes; believe me,
an absolute gentleman, full of most excellent differences, of
very soft society, and great showing.

HAMLET   (*Crossing right to the main stage*)   What imports the
nomination of this gentleman?

OSRIC   Of Laertes?

HAMLET   Of HIM, sir.

OSRIC   You are not ignorant of what excellence Laertes is? I
mean, sir, for his weapon.

HAMLET   What's his weapon?

OSRIC   Rapier and dagger.

HAMLET   That's two of his weapons. (OSRIC *forces a laugh*)
But, well?

OSRIC   (*Crossing to him*)   The King, sir, hath laid, sir, that in
a dozen passes between yourself and him, he shall not exceed
you three hits. He hath laid on twelve for nine, and it would
come to immediate trial, if your lordship would vouchsafe
the answer.

HAMLET   (*Suddenly apprehensive; he paces a bit and then asks*)
How if I answer no?

OSRIC   (*With a menacing undertone*)   I mean, my lord, the
opposition of your person in trial.

HAMLET (*Resolved, he crosses back to the side stage and sits on a corner of the platform*)　Sir, I will walk here in the hall. If it pleases his Majesty, it is the breathing time of day with me; let the foils be brought, the gentleman willing, and the King hold his purpose, I will win for him if I can. If not, I will gain nothing but my shame and the odd hits.

OSRIC　Shall I re-deliver you e'en so?
　　　(*He starts to bow*)

HAMLET (*Beating* OSRIC *to it, he makes an elaborate flourish with his hand*)　To this effect, sir, after what flourish your nature will.

OSRIC (*Crossing up the side steps to the platform*)　I commend my duty to your lordship.
　　　(*He bows*)

HAMLET (*Mocking him*)　Yours, yours. (OSRIC *exits by the stairway*) He does well to commend it himself, there are no tongues else for his turn.

HORATIO (*Worried*)　You will lose this wager, my lord.

HAMLET　I do not think so. Since he went into France, I have been in continual practice. I shall win at the odds. But . . . (*Forebodingly*) thou wouldst not think how ill all's here about my heart—(HORATIO *starts fearfully; attempting to allay* HORATIO's *fears,* HAMLET *says reassuringly*) but it is no matter.

HORATIO　Nay, good my lord—

HAMLET　It is but foolery. But it is such a kind of gaingiving as would perhaps trouble a woman.

HORATIO　If your mind dislike anything, obey it. I will forestall their repair hither and say you are not fit.

HAMLET　Not a whit! We defy augury. There is special providence in the fall of a sparrow. (*Openly*) If it be now, (*Rises*) 'tis not to come; (*Introspectively*) if it be not to come, it will be now; (*Warmly to* HORATIO) if it be not now, yet it will

come—the readiness is all. Since no man hath aught of what
he leaves, what is't to leave betimes? (*Putting a hand on*
HORATIO's *shoulder*) Let be.

> (*Offstage voices are heard. Courtiers enter; two carry the
> armchair up the side steps, placing it center of the plat-
> form facing the main stage; another enters with a small
> table and places it on the down left corner of platform;
> one brings on rapier and fencing-foils, another the dag-
> gers; a third enters with two wine cups and stands left on
> the platform.* CLAUDIUS *enters from the stairway with*
> LAERTES, *followed by* OSRIC. GERTRUDE *enters from the
> side platform, crosses to the armchair, and sits*)

CLAUDIUS (*Crossing to the side steps with* LAERTES)
Come, Hamlet, come and take this hand from me.

HAMLET (*Crossing center*)   Give me your pardon, sir. I have
    done you wrong;
But pardon it as you are a gentleman.
This presence knows,
And you must needs have learned, how I am punished
With a sore distraction. Sir, in this audience,
Let my disclaiming from a purposed evil
Free me so far in your most generous thoughts,
That I have shot my arrow o'er the house
And hurt my brother.

LAERTES   I am satisfied in nature,
    Whose motives, in this case, should stir me most
    To my revenge; but in my terms of honour
    I stand aloof, and will no reconcilement
    Till by some (*Pointing at the foils*) elder masters of known
        honour
    I have a voice and precedent of peace,
    To keep my name ungored. (*Crosses center to* HAMLET) But
        till that time
    I do receive your offered love like love,
    And will not wrong it.

HAMLET (*Taking* LAERTES' *hand*)   I embrace it freely,
And will this brother's wager frankly play.
Give us the foils. Come on.

> (HORATIO *crosses down right, moving the stool from right of the table to the down right corner of the stage*)

LAERTES   Come, one for me.

> (OSRIC *crosses up center and takes the foils from a Courtier*)

HAMLET   I'll be your foil, Laertes; in mine ignorance
Your skill shall like a star in the darkest nights
Stick fiery off indeed.

LAERTES   You mock me, sir?

HAMLET   No, by this hand.

CLAUDIUS   Give them the foils, young Osric. (OSRIC *crosses to* HAMLET *and forces a regular foil on him*) Cousin Hamlet,
You know the wager?

HAMLET (*Flexing his foil*)   Very well, my lord. (*Takes a dagger from a Courtier*)
Your Grace has laid the odds o' the weaker side.

CLAUDIUS   I do not fear it. I have seen you both.
But since he is bettered, we have therefore odds.

> (OSRIC *crosses left to* LAERTES; *they exchange looks;* LAERTES *purposely takes the wrong foil*)

LAERTES (*Whipping the foil*)   This is too heavy. Let me see another.

> (*Returning the first foil to* OSRIC, *he takes the poisoned one*)

HAMLET   This likes me well. These foils have all a length?

OSRIC   Aye, my good lord. (LAERTES *chooses his dagger*)

CLAUDIUS Set me the stoops of wine upon that table.
If Hamlet give the first or second hit,
Or quit in answer of the third exchange,
The King shall drink to Hamlet's better breath,
And in the cup an union shall he throw
Richer than that which four successive Kings
In Denmark's crown have worn. Come, begin—
And you the judges bear a wary eye.
> (OSRIC *stands up center, prepared to judge.* HORATIO *acts as* HAMLET's *judge*)

HAMLET Come on, sir.

LAERTES Come, my lord.
> (*They play.* HAMLET *makes two or three thrusts which* LAERTES *parries. Suddenly, catching* LAERTES' *dagger guard open,* HAMLET *touches him on the left side*)

HAMLET One!

LAERTES No!

HAMLET Judgment?

OSRIC A hit! A very palpable hit.

LAERTES Well-again.
> (*They assume the on-guard position for the next bout*)

CLAUDIUS Stay! Give me a drink. (HAMLET *crosses down right;* LAERTES *crosses left to the side stage.* CLAUDIUS *takes the poisoned cup from the table and says, holding up a pearl*) Hamlet, this pearl is thine. (*Drops it in the cup and hands the cup to a Courtier; he picks up the other cup and offers a toast*) Give him the cup. Here's to thy health.

> (*All eyes watch as the Courtier carries the cup across the full width of the stage and kneels before* HAMLET, *offering it to him*)

HAMLET (*Taps the cup with his foil*)
I'll play this bout first;
Set it by awhile. (*Courtier places the cup on the table, right*)
Come! (*They play again. This time* LAERTES *initiates the attacks,* HAMLET *remaining defensive. After a few exchanges* HAMLET *sees his opening and thrusts cleanly, touching* LAERTES *in the center of the chest*)
Another hit! What say you?

LAERTES   A touch, a touch, I do confess it. (*Courtiers applaud.* HAMLET *crosses down right and sits on the stool;* HORATIO *relieves him of his foils.* LAERTES *crosses left to the side stage*)

CLAUDIUS (*Smiles to* GERTRUDE)   Our son shall win.

GERTRUDE (*Rising*)   He's faint and scant of breath. (*Goes down the side steps and crosses down right to* HAMLET, *giving him her handkerchief*) Here, Hamlet, take my napkin, rub thy brows. (*She takes the poisoned cup from the table*) The Queen carouses to thy fortune, Hamlet.

HAMLET   Good madam.

CLAUDIUS (*Cries out in alarm*)   GERTRUDE! (*Realizing that all are watching him, he says with a low steady tone*) Do not drink.

GERTRUDE   I will, my lord, I pray you, pardon me. (*She drinks part of the contents and hands the cup to* HORATIO, *who places it on the table*) Come, let me wipe thy face.

LAERTES (*Standing on the front steps, says secretly to* CLAUDIUS)
My lord, I'll hit him now.

CLAUDIUS (*Defeatedly*)   I do not think't.
    (*He crosses to the armchair and sits*)

LAERTES (*Turns; coming down the steps, he says to himself*)
And yet it is almost against my conscience.

HAMLET (*Crossing center with his weapons, says jokingly*)
Come for the third, Laertes, you do but dally.

I pray you, pass with your best violence;
I am afeard you make a wanton of me.

LAERTES (*Crossing center*) Say you so? Come on.

(*They begin the third bout,* LAERTES *fencing with all
his skill and energy,* HAMLET *parrying and reposting with
equal technique and spirit. In the course of their maneuvers they half-circle the stage so that* LAERTES *comes
stage right and* HAMLET *stage left.* OSRIC *and* HORATIO
also circle, staying behind their respective contestants.
LAERTES *makes a sudden lunge at* HAMLET *with both his
weapons, but* HAMLET *thwarts him with a double engage
so that the two remain locked center stage, rapiers to
daggers*)

OSRIC Nothing, neither way.

(*They part.* HAMLET *crosses down left to* HORATIO *and
hands him his foil and dagger*)

LAERTES (*Coming up behind* HAMLET) Have at you now!

(*He deliberately sticks his unbated foil into* HAMLET's
arm. HAMLET *clasps his arm in pain.* CLAUDIUS *rises.
Courtiers freeze.* LAERTES *backs off down center. Bewildered,* HAMLET *crosses to* LAERTES *and, lifting the blade
of his foil, he examines the tip. He looks questioningly
to* LAERTES, *who avoids his eyes. With* LAERTES *offering
no resistance,* HAMLET *takes the fatal weapon from him
and crosses back to* HORATIO, *left. He then takes his first
foil from* HORATIO *and tosses it to* LAERTES; *then, advancing on* LAERTES, *he begins attacking furiously**)

CLAUDIUS Part them, they are incensed!

HAMLET Nay, come again.

(*Circling* LAERTES, *he forces him back against the side
steps; beating his foil savagely, he disarms and stabs him*)

---

* Mr. Burton was so energetic in his fencing that he broke four foils in the
course of the run.

OSRIC (*Seeing* GERTRUDE *sway*)　Look to the Queen there, ho!

HORATIO (*Crossing center to* HAMLET)
They bleed on both sides. How is it, my lord?

OSRIC (*Helping* LAERTES *across the platform to the front steps*)
How is't, Laertes?

LAERTES　Why, as a woodcock to mine own springe, Osric.
I am justly killed with mine own treachery.

HAMLET (*Crossing to* GERTRUDE)　How does the Queen?

CLAUDIUS (*Coming forward to the side steps*)　She swoons to
see them bleed.

GERTRUDE　No, no, the drink—O, my dear Hamlet—(*He helps
her to the stool*)
The drink, the drink! I am poisoned.

HAMLET　O villainy! Ho, let the door be locked.
　　　(HORATIO *leaps to the center doors to guard them*)
Treachery! Seek it out.

LAERTES　It is HERE, Hamlet! Hamlet, thou art slain. (GERTRUDE
wails)
No medicine in the world can do thee good.
　　　(*Summoning all his strength, he crosses down center*)
In thee there is not half an hour of life.
The treacherous instrument is in thy hand,
Unbated and envenomed. The foul practice
Hath turned itself on me. (*Falls to the floor*) Lo, here I lie,
Never to rise again. Thy mother's poisoned—(*Gasping*)
I can no more—the King . . . the King's to blame.

HAMLET (*Picks up the poisoned cup from the table*)
The point envenomed too!
Then, venom, to thy work!
　　　(*Stalking him with the foil in one hand and the cup in
　　　the other, he pursues him up on the platform, around the*

armchair to down center of the platform, then slashes the rapier across his chest)

CLAUDIUS   O yet defend me, friends, I am but hurt!

HAMLET (*Throwing down the rapier, he seizes* CLAUDIUS *by the neck, forces him over the arm of the chair, and pours the poison down his throat*)
Here, thou incestuous, murderous, damnèd Dane,
Drink off this potion. Is thy union here?
Follow my mother!

(CLAUDIUS *writhes in agony, hanging over the arm of the chair.* HAMLET *gives the cup to* HORATIO)

LAERTES   He is justly served;
It is a poison tempered by himself.
Exchange forgiveness with me, noble Hamlet.
Mine and my father's death come not upon thee,
Nor thine on me.

HAMLET (*Crosses down the steps to him and takes his hand*)
Heaven make thee free of it. (LAERTES *falls dead*) I follow
    thee.
I am dead, Horatio. (GERTRUDE *falls from her stool, also dead*) Wretchèd Queen, adieu. (*Crossing to the side steps, weakly*)
You that look pale, and tremble at this chance,
That are but mutes or audience to this act,
Had I but time, as this fell sergeant Death
Is strict in his arrest, O, I could tell you—
But let it be. Horatio, I am dead.
Thou livest. Report me and my cause aright
To the unsatisfied.

HORATIO (*Holding the cup, crosses to the side steps*)   Never
    believe it!
I am more an antique Roman than a Dane.
Here's yet some liquor left! (*Starts to drink*)

HAMLET (*In a last surge of energy*)　As thou art a man,
　Give me the cup—let go, by heaven, I'll ha't!
　　　(*He wrests the cup from him and dashes it to the floor.
　　　Crossing up on the platform, he pushes* CLAUDIUS *off the
　　　arm of the chair to the floor, then falls into the chair,
　　　breathing heavily*)
　O good Horatio, what a wounded name,
　Things standing thus unknown, shall live behind me.
　If thou didst ever hold me in thy heart,
　Absent thee from felicity awhile,
　And in this harsh world draw thy breath in pain,
　To tell my story. (*Two distant cannon shots are heard*)
　What warlike noise is this?

OSRIC (*Dropping his affectations*)
　Young Fortinbras, with conquest come from Poland,
　To the ambassadors of England gives
　This warlike volley.

HAMLET (*Gets up and comes forward to* HORATIO)
　O, I die, Horatio.
　The potent poison quite o'er-crows my spirit.
　I cannot live to hear the news from England,
　But I do prophesy the election lights
　On Fortinbras. He has my dying voice;
　So tell him, with the occurrents more and less
　Which have solicited—(*He breaks off; a sudden death-like
　hush falls over the entire theatre;** HAMLET *looks down, sees*
　CLAUDIUS *dead at his feet, and gives a sad little laugh*) The rest
　. . . is silence.

　　　(*He falls forward into* HORATIO's *arms*)

---

* The means of achieving this striking effect came about accidentally during the first few weeks of performances. One night a house electrician,
eager to finish his duties, turned off the theatre air-conditioner in the
middle of Hamlet's death speech. The effect was so striking that Mr.
Burton incorporated it into the show permanently. Every night, on the
above line, the stage manager gave the cue over the backstage intercom to
"kill the air-conditioner."

HORATIO (*Easing him back into the armchair*)
  Now cracks a noble heart. Good night, sweet prince,
  And flights of angels sing thee to thy rest.
  (*Drum cadence is heard offstage*)
  Why does the drum come hither?

          (*The center doors open*)

FORTINBRAS (*Entering center, followed by Ambassadors*)
  Where is this sight?

HORATIO   What is it you would see? (*The drum stops*)
  If aught of woe or wonder, cease your search.

FORTINBRAS (*Seeing the bodies*)
  This quarry cries on havoc. O proud Death,
  What feast is toward in thine eternal cell,
  That thou so many princes at a shot
  So bloodily hast struck?

HORATIO   Give order that these bodies
  High on a stage be placèd to the view;
  And let me speak to the yet UNKNOWING world
  How these things came about.

FORTINBRAS   Let us haste to hear it,
  And call the noblest to the audience.
  For me, with sorrow I embrace my fortune.
  I have some rights of memory in this kingdom,
  Which now to claim my vantage doth invite me.
  Let four captains
  Bear Hamlet like a soldier to the stage,
  For he was likely, had he been put on,
  To have proved most royally. And for his passage,
  The soldiers' music and the rites of war
  Speak loudly for him.
  Take up the bodies. (*Six Courtiers cross to* HAMLET) Such
    a sight as this
  Becomes the field, but here shows much amiss.
  Go, bid the soldiers shoot.

(Funeral drums play. A distant cannon fires three shots. Courtiers lift HAMLET *high above their heads and march slowly out the center doors)*

CURTAIN

PART THREE

Interviews

---

‡   ‡   ‡

An Interview with
Richard Burton on Hamlet

THIS INTERVIEW *was tape-recorded on August 3, 1964, on Monday of the closing week of* Hamlet. *It began at seven* P.M. *in Richard Burton's hotel suite on the twentieth floor of the Regency Hotel in New York.*

Q: What was your first association with the play?
A: First time I saw it was in 1944 at Oxford when I was a student at the University. First time I read it was when I was about eleven or twelve years old. First time I learned it was when I was thirteen years old. So I've known the play fairly intimately for over twenty years.
Q: Who was the first Hamlet you ever saw?
A: John Gielgud. It's the best Hamlet I've ever seen. Very different, of course, from mine. His was emblematic of the Renaissance scholar and poet, unable to make up his mind; certainly not bloody, certainly not vengeful in my sense of the word, or in our production's sense of the word. But quite the best I've ever seen.
Q: How many times have you been in *Hamlet?*
A: This is my third. I played it once in a semiprofessional

production mixed up with the RAF and Oxford—that was about 1945—and then I did it at the Old Vic in 1953, and this one. So this is the third. I haven't played anything except Hamlet in it, so I've never been in the play in any other capacity. I've seen about twenty Hamlets: I saw Redgrave, Gielgud, Scofield twice, Robert Helpmann twice, Alan Bidel, John Neville, Griffith; I saw Olivier's film . . . there must be more, but I've forgotten them. I saw Maurice Evans play it, too.

Q: How is your third Hamlet different from the other two?

A: Well, I think it changes all the time, as you know. I'm not likely to sit back on one set performance. Even in this production I must have changed it vastly during the course of the playing. I think probably the first one was just sheer animal exuberance at the enjoyment of playing such a marvelous part. The second one was much more tearful and, I think, was a sort of unconscious imitation of John Gielgud. This one is, I think, for better or worse, uniquely my own. I think that I've matured as an actor sufficiently to rely absolutely on myself and not become derivative. But how they would differ specifically I don't know. It would take a large volume to write of the differences.

Q: What are your favorite scenes in the play?

A: I don't know . . . they vary from night to night. Some nights I like the Ghost thing—seeing the Ghost for the first time. I like the kind of wildness of it. On nights when I'm not as energetic as usual I prefer the more sedentary scenes, like the scene with Polonius and the book. And some nights I like doing "To be or not to be" more than I like doing "O, what a rogue and peasant slave." But it depends on whether I feel in good fettle or not. You can sort of sit back on "To be or not to be," and you can't on "O, what a rogue." Sometimes I like the play-within-the-play scene— some nights it bores me. I *never* like "How all occasions do inform against me," and I never like particularly—I have once or twice, I think—the advice to the players, largely because I don't agree with the advice. But I'm talking rela-

tively, you know. The whole thing is a magnificent joy to
play—but it does have its ups and downs.

Q: Some nights you play your opening court scene sadly and
and other nights intensely angered. What determines how
you play it?

A: That I don't know. And that I've never been able to know
about my acting on the stage. I never preplan any variation
on anything I do—it just occurs. And afterwards I sometimes try to analyze why I did such-and-such a thing in
such-and-such a way—and there's no reason I can give it.
Sometimes I think it's something that might have happened
during the day, or perhaps a cough in the wrong place in
the audience. But it's not sufficient reason, really, because
some nights the cough in the audience or the something that
happened that day has no effect on what you do that night
and sometimes it does. Having set the pattern for the performance I don't become a creature of circumstance—I
become very wayward. I let the mood take me—which I'm
sure is not strictly super-professional. But with a part like
Hamlet or a part like Lear, or a part like Macbeth, I think
you can do such things. You couldn't possibly do it with
Romeo because it's not large enough in scope. I think you
can do it with Hamlet. I've never played Romeo—never
want to.

Q: In the second platform scene with Horatio and Marcellus,
after the Ghost has vanished, you now contrive to deceive
them—obviously tricking them on "There's ne'er a villain
dwelling in all Denmark, but he's an arrant knave." You
used to play it as if you had suddenly caught yourself about
to spill the beans.

A: Yes. That came about, I think, largely because I received
a letter from my old professor at Oxford who said that it
had been discovered from an old diary that the words "old
Mole" in Elizabethan days meant a jocular reference to the
devil—Old Nick, you know, as we would say now. He therefore suggested in his letter that since this was a joking refer-
erence to the devil, the whole scene might be a deliberate

pulling of the wool over Horatio's and Marcellus' eyes—and so I do sometimes play it like that and sometimes I go back to the old version, depending again on how I feel.

Q: What amuses Hamlet so about hearing the Ghost under the stage? How can it be so humorous to him as you play it?

A: Well, because already his schizophrenia, I suppose, has taken place: that is, half of him wants to believe that the Ghost is right and half of him can't accept it. If he absolutely believed that the Ghost was right, he would immediately go off and kill the King in any normal play. But if there's a half of him that doubts it, if his self-mockery is so great, and his self-distrust is great enough, then one half of him would be humorously inclined to believe that this Ghost is a devil and is making fun of him, and the other half will say, "No, it is true." The self-mockery that is there exists right throughout *Hamlet*.

Any other major tragic figure has no sense of humor; certainly Macbeth, for example, has no humor about himself, neither does Lear, really; certainly not Othello; perhaps Mark Antony does in *Antony and Cleopatra*, a little. But Hamlet is continually making fun of himself at the moment of high pity and terror and great passion. For instance, in the middle of "O, what a rogue and peasant slave," at the height of his agony when he says, "O, vengeance," then he says, "Why, what an ass am I," quite clearly making fun of himself. This is very rare in a tragic protagonist.

Q: You deliberately play for a laugh, then, on "Why, what an ass am I"?

A: Sometimes I do, sometimes I don't. When I first tried to get it, it didn't work. And then I discovered that I was raising the wrong arm on "O, vengeance." I was using the upstage arm, but it seemed the audience couldn't see my face when I looked up at the hand on "What an ass am I." So I changed to the downstage arm and it worked. Purely a technical thing. It seems that unless they can see your face when you make fun of yourself they don't get the joke.

Sometimes it doesn't work, even with the downstage arm —mostly it does.

Q: Your celebrated reading of "O, vengeance"—the long sustained descending glissando on the "O," followed by an almost inaudible and tearful "vengeance"—you did first on opening night in New York. Did it come to you then, or had you thought about it before?

A: No. I think Hume Cronyn said when he played Hamlet, when he said the word "vengeance" he found it very difficult to sustain because it's such a closed vowel sound, whereas "O" is endless; like any vowel at the end of an Italian aria, it's almost inevitably an open vowel so that they can sustain it. And so I thought that might be interesting. I don't know when he told me that. I think he told me in Toronto. And if you say I did it on opening night, that's when I did it, because I don't remember when I first did it. But it's certainly a much more practical way of doing it.

Q: How do you justify Hamlet's drawing a sword on Horatio in the second platform scene on "I say, away"?

A: Well, frankly, I don't agree with that bit—that's a bit of direction of John's. But I think "I say, away" is to the Ghost. I don't think it is to Horatio. But John was absolutely adamant that it was to Horatio and I thought it works equally well either way, so I do it to Horatio. But I think that at this point, Hamlet has said "By heaven, I'll make a ghost of him that lets me," which is sufficient of a threat to keep Horatio away; and then "I say, away, go on; I'll follow thee" is all one line. But since he's already threatened Horatio with violence—he says "I will kill you if you don't let me go"—the addition of "I say, away" is no more antagonistic than the other. In fact, it's less.

Q: What was Hamlet's former relationship with Rosencrantz and Guildenstern?

A: Well, I don't know. It's very difficult. I think if they were good friends, he was certainly easily deceived. And Hamlet doesn't seem to be easily deceived by anybody else. So I can only think they were very nodding acquaintances, with Rosencrantz and Guildenstern doing most of the nodding. I don't think he can have been all that close to them, because he immediately perceives their purpose. And it doesn't take more than three or four minutes of dialogue for him to see that there is something very odd about these two men.

Q: You used to have a piece of business where you would catch Rosencrantz and Guildenstern talking to each other behind your back. It was on the line "But in the beaten way of friendship." Now you have eliminated it. Why?

A: I think Redfield and Fowler and I discussed it and we decided that since it was perfectly clear that Hamlet knew what they were up to anyway, that it was an extraneous piece of business—it was unnecessary action with the words. I think we sometimes still half do it, but I think it's more or less cut out for good now.

Q: Can you tell me what brought about the business of climbing up on the chair during the "I have of late" speech?

A: Yes. That's a speech that's so mellifluous and so beautiful —actually my favorite speech in the play—that I tend to go off somewhat too lyrically in it. And I know that when I do, or really when any actor does, the audience are generally lulled into a sort of sleep. They're not listening, really, to what you're saying. So I thought I must unpoeticize it. This I didn't plan, I may say. But I knew that there was something that I had to do to change it—to make them listen actually to what I was saying. And the one way to find out was if they laughed. You can't be sure if they *are* listening unless there's a physical reaction from the audience. So one night I went up on the chair. Then that became rather celebrated, that piece, so I thought I'd go one step further and get up on the table too. And it's quite clear that they do listen now, whereas I wasn't sure whether they were listening before. It's really sort of practical.

Q: Why is it that you *don't* do it some nights?

A: I feel as if the audience is totally gripped and I don't need
to do it.

Q: You mentioned that you think the meaning of the "To be
or not to be" soliloquy is that Hamlet is contemplating
suicide.

A: Yes.

Q: Is it in any way related to the action of the play?

A: No. Well, I suppose it's *possible* to relate it. I've read critics
who say he's not saying "Shall I kill myself or not?" He's
rather saying "Shall I be King or not?", or "Shall I kill the
King or not?" In other words, "to be" the boss, "or not to
be" the boss. But that, it seems to me, is a bit far fetched,
because everything else applies to death and heaven and
hell, and so on. An actor friend of mine has always wanted
to cut "To be or not to be" as being a hold-up of the play.
But it would be like—let me think—like cutting your knee
off and still walking. It wouldn't be very pleasant. No, I
rather like "To be or not to be."

Q: I think the scene you change the most from night to night
is the nunnery scene.

A: Yes, I do change that considerably. Again, I think the audience more or less tells me how to do that. I try not to
impose myself on the audience, and I let them tell me what
they want. And sometimes, too, if Ophelia's in a certain
mood, she's sometimes tangible with other actors. Then I
play to her mood rather than to the audience or myself. But
also it's a scene of infinite variety. There are infinite ways of
playing it. In fact, the nunnery scene is almost one long
soliloquy, you know. If you count how many words Ophelia
says and how many Hamlet says—until she says, "Oh, what
a noble mind is here o'erthrown"—it's all Hamlet. She's
hardly allowed to get a word out before he's at her. So really
it's again another thing like doing the soliloquies. One can
change it enormously, because one's alone.

Q: In all your experimentations, have you found one way to
be the key to the scene?

A: Well, I think the playing of it that works best is one great, sustained, passionate cry—from the moment he discovers somebody's behind the arras and that she's deceived him. From then on it's just a rolling kind of huge cataract of words—almost incoherent. And, indeed, I've noticed that if I do it that way, as I sometimes do—as just a tremendous outburst of passion and sustain it for the three of four minutes that it's necessary, I get an enormous round at the end. Whereas if I do it in a subtler way, with more self-contained agony, then I might get a round, or might not, but it's dubious. Again, rounds are indicative of what the audience is feeling. I think rounds actually are bad things, and that the bigger the round, probably the less well you've done that particular scene. Because if you really have done a perfect piece of acting, the audience is too overwhelmed to react with applause. That's a debatable subject. I may be wrong, but I've always felt that.

Q: Is Hamlet's reason for breaking with Ophelia in this scene because she has deceived him? Or is it because he must carry out his vengeance alone?

A: Well, I think it could be either of them, depending on how one felt that night. Some nights it can be the fact that she's deceived him—that she actually knows that her father and the King are hiding behind the wall; and other nights he's predetermined before he sees her to cut her off and continue on his own.

Q: Was Hamlet in love with Ophelia?

A: I'm not sure that even *he* knew. I think that probably he was very attracted to her and liked her very much and found her sweet and intelligent. Perhaps the streak of moodiness in her, which quite clearly exists, also appealed to the waywardness of his nature. It's extraordinary how differently one plays it with different actresses. Last time I played it was with Claire Bloom. First time I played it with Joan Williams. But they were so different, all three girls, that I played it very differently with all three girls. If you find you have a sentimental actress playing opposite you in that scene and you go too hard, she will burst into tears and be unable to get her words out.

Q: What is the meaning of the play?

A: If it has a meaning at all—that is to say, if Shakespeare meant it to have a meaning outside its entertainment value, and if he consciously tried to—I think he actually put on the stage in one character virtually every emotion of which a man is capable: pity, terror, fear, love, lust, obscenity, virtue, courage, cowardice. Practically everything you can think of is in Hamlet; even homosexuality, if you look for it deep enough. But sometimes he seems incoherently joined up. He seems to have a lot of anachronisms in him—within himself, I mean. It's very difficult, for instance, for an actor to realize the change between "The play's the thing wherein I'll catch the conscience of the King," and then within three minutes—I think it's literally three minutes if you play it in the Folio version—he's back on stage contemplating suicide. The audience has been led to believe, just before, that he's about to start a detective chase of the King; now certainly he's deciding possibly to commit suicide. That kind of inconsistency is enormously difficult for the actor to smooth over. And what it does do, of course, is fascinate scholars and actors alike, because one wonders at the mind of a man behind Hamlet and the man who wrote *Hamlet,* whoever he might have been.

An Interview with

John Gielgud on Hamlet

THIS INTERVIEW *was tape-recorded Sunday, April 12, 1964, in New York.*

Q: What was your first acquaintance with the play?

A: I saw it with H. B. Irving as Hamlet in 1912 in his revival at the Adelphi. I was eight.

Q: How many times have you been associated with the play?

A: I believe this is the sixth. The Old Vic production which moved to the Queens, that was the first. Second was my own production in 1934. There was the American production in 1936, then Elsinore and the Lyceum in 1939, and the Haymarket in 1944.

Q: During that time has your concept of the main character changed?

A: Not exactly changed, no. But one changes the feeling about how it should be played.

Q: Has the play a theme you could summarize?

A: I don't think of it in that way. I just see it as a play. It's a revenge story which Shakespeare adapted into a great philosophical and dramatic poem. But as Shaw said, "You can't state it's meaning on a postcard."

Q: What are the faults of Hamlet's character?

A: He has every man's faults—and he knows them. He's a man of many hobbies and interests and he's certainly very fond of argument. When he comes to the actual mission that he has set to carry out, he finds it difficult to find a way to do it because he's a much more civilized man than all the other people in the play. I think he's doubtful about religion, about whether the Ghost is real or not, whether killing the King is really justified, whether the King has really done the murder, until after the play scene. His belief in the Ghost is always veering from one side to the other.

Q: Is that the reason that he hesitates in killing the King? Or is it that the opportunity does not present itself?

A: Well, when the opportunity does present itself he lets it pass. That's what's so tragic. If he'd only have killed the King at prayers he'd have been all right. And the joke of the thing is that the King wasn't at prayers at all—he couldn't pray! And Hamlet thought he could pray, and didn't want to send him to heaven by killing him at that moment. He was sufficiently Christian or superstitious to think this and so he avoided the issue. But the irony is that if he'd killed him, Claudius would have gone to hell, because he wasn't able to pray. But otherwise Hamlet would not have killed Polonius and the tragedy never would have happened— which is, of course, the turning point of the play.

Q: How would you say your Hamlet is different from Burton's?

A: I think my account of suffering is quite different from his. Mine is much more introverted. His is a more extroverted performance and he suffers in a much bolder way than I can. Perhaps I'm more worried about the inflection, the phrasing, and the diction, which he often changes and varies. My performance is extremely meticulous. His is enormously vigorous—which is awfully valuable.

Q: What is Hamlet's reaction to killing Polonius? Gertrude

later says he weeps for what he's done, yet in the scene he jokes about it.

A: I think he does both. He veers from one side to the other. I think the excitement of the play scene has him so keyed up that he has both a triumph and a horror when he kills Polonius. Sometimes he's turned to love and sometimes to tears. I think that is part of his trouble—he feels too much. Richard is very clever with that. He almost seems to love Polonius at the end of that scene, and I think it's a very clever touch. In some ways Hamlet does love everybody and longs to love them more. Then he finds out their bad qualities and loathes them, as he does with his mother. He even respects the King for his wit and cleverness.

Q: At the end of the closet scene, after he has seemingly made peace with his mother, why does he return to her with a second tirade?

A: It may have been that there were two different ends to the scene that were put together by the actors aferwards. I think it's possible. Most actors end the scene with "I must be cruel only to be kind. Thus bad begins and worse remains behind," which is a couplet which might have signaled the end of the scene. I don't like to cut the last section because it prepares the audience for the episodes with the King and Rosencrantz and Guildenstern and keeps them in the story. It links two parts of the play.

Q: What is Fortinbras' purpose in the play?

A: I suppose it's to show the strength of a man who's without complexes, and to show the sort of prince that Hamlet might have been if his father hadn't been murdered. He's a kind of alter ego to Hamlet. He solves things so simply, leading a good soldiers's life. His motives are quite fine.

Q: Why did you cut the expository lines concerning him in the opening scene?

A: Because I've found that most of the audience doesn't listen to them. It's such a terribly long and difficult political speech.

Q: Why did you cut the King's long aside in the nunnery scene which begins "O, tis too true. How smart a lash that speech doth give my conscience."

A: It's too melodramatic for modern audiences. It's like "It is the poisoned cup. It is too late." All those asides are terribly awkward and difficult to bring off. It's true that the aside in the nunnery scene is the King's first admission of guilt, but by not insisting on it there we keep more excitement in the play scene.

Q: Why is the "To be or not to be" soliloquy placed where it is in the text?

A: Some people think it should come before the "rogue and peasant slave" speech. It's very difficult to know why he put it there except for vocal and poetic reasons. One can play it as depression and emotional exhaustion after the hysteria of "rogue and peasant slave." But your question is quite difficult to answer. Just because it's one of the most famous speeches in Shakespeare doesn't mean that he necessarily put it there with tremendous forethought and deliberation. He may have been suddenly inspired to write it there, like someone putting in a piece of color in a picture. I don't think artists necessarily prepare and elaborate everything. A great genius like Shakespeare is prepared to take risks and put things in all sorts of places.

Q: Do any of the lines of the speech refer specifically to the action of the play?

A: "Pangs of disprized love" probably refers to Ophelia. But it's mainly a self-exploratory scene.

Q: What was Hamlet's former relationship with Ophelia?

A: We don't know whether they were lovers or not. One doesn't feel that Hamlet is a fastidious man who would have a light affair with a girl like Ophelia. Presumably his mother wanted him to marry her, and obviously Polonius would have wanted it too. But one has the feeling that he's only courted her. I don't think that they were lovers, that they had been to bed together. It makes the mad scene more meaningful if they hadn't.

Q: Why did he come to her in her closet "with his doublet all unbraced"?

A: That was the first time he tried to see how the madness would impress. It prepares us for his entrance with the antic disposition. It links the end of the second platform scene with his next entrance in the scene with Polonius and the book.

Q: Why did he break with Ophelia? Because she betrayed him?

A: No. I think he broke with her because she was the person with whom he was most gossiped about. Because he was courting her she would be the first person to spread the rumor of his madness. And immediately, as he intends, she rushes straight to her father, and then he runs and tells the King and Queen. So the idea that he has gone mad is spread round the whole court. Hamlet *wants* them to think that he's gone mad because of her.

Q: Is he ever really mad?

A: I think he is for a moment when the Ghost leaves him, and that gives him the idea of assuming madness. Then once or twice, later on, he goes a bit over the edge—at the end of the play scene, in the closet scene, the nunnery scene, and then again at Ophelia's grave he has the same unbridled temperament which suddenly bursts out and which he can't control. Yet he's still reasonable enough to be very ashamed of his behavior afterwards.

Q: In the graveyard scene why does Hamlet say to Laertes, "What is the reason that you use me thus?" Doesn't he know full well the reason?

A: Yes. The line refers to the actual physical onslaught. Princes aren't used to having people jump at their throats, especially Laertes, who was an old friend.

Q: Does Hamlet suspect that he will die in the duel with Laertes?

A: Not in the duel itself. That's just a game, like football is to us. But he knows the end is at hand. The King very cunningly sent Osric to play the fool in order to divert

Hamlet's suspicion so that the wager will seem trivial and so he won't take it too seriously.

Q: How would you describe the King?

A: Granville-Barker once said he's a cat rather than a dog. He should be an able, charming diplomat—very sensual, heavy drinking. He should be a clever and not an obvious villain. The Queen also has a certain wickedness in her nature, very sensuous, but a kindly, sweet woman who means well and doesn't know about the murder, or she wouldn't have married Claudius. And she changes after she learns of the murder in the last scene. But Shakespeare never overdrew his characters, so that while there's plenty for an actor to play, he didn't draw Ophelia and the Queen in great detail because it would have spoiled their relationship to Hamlet —who is the principal character he was interested in. He only drew the others as far as they affected Hamlet and as Hamlet affected them.

Q: Why does the King keep Polonius in his employ?

A: He's obviously been very clever in helping the King to get the election. Also he's the father of Ophelia, who presumably was going to marry Hamlet. And he's been in with the old guard and knows all the ropes of the court and is a useful spy for the King. He was a very able politician in his day, but rather getting past it now. Also there's no indication that he knows anything about the murder.

Q: Why does the King allow Polonius to listen during the closet scene, when the King knows that Hamlet is on to his guilt and could well reveal it to Polonius?

A: It's Polonius' suggestion. The King doesn't dare refuse him. Polonius puts a lot of the plot in motion. He's really a more active agent against Hamlet than is the King. The King doesn't realize there's any danger until after the nunnery scene, so he's let Hamlet be and thinks having him about the court is quite tactful. He lets Polonius do all the seeking out.

Q: What was Hamlet's former relationship with Rosencrantz and Guildenstern?

A: They were undergraduates together. Though one doesn't quite see those two, Horatio, and Hamlet all having a midnight binge together. They're horrid creatures, really—just toadies to the King. All the people around Hamlet are very second rate, and Hamlet loathes second-rate things. Horatio is the most enigmatic character in the play. I don't know why Shakespeare drew him so strangely. He doesn't tell Hamlet of Ophelia's death. He doesn't appear after the second platform scene until the play scene. Hamlet just conjures him up when he wants to have a heart-to-heart talk. And Horatio really doesn't say anything except "yes" and "no." Still he must be a great character of solidity who makes a wonderful statement to the play of honesty, sweetness, and intelligence.

Q: Were Rosencrantz and Guildenstern at all concerned with what was wrong with Hamlet?

A: Well, they'd have got a jolly good peerage if they'd found that out. I think they're quite prepared to kill Hamlet unnecessarily. By the time they leave for England it was one or the other.

Q: One more question, please. You have played Hamlet more than any other actor of this century. Many distinguished critics have lauded your interpretation as definitive, and you have in your long association with the play solved many of its great mysteries. How then could you remain so free and flexible in your direction of this production?

A: One never really finishes working on any play. When that happens the life is gone from it. What is interesting in directing is how many of your ideas change because the actors seem to be happier doing it another way. With the mad scene, for example, I tried it first as a pretty and charming scene. But that didn't work. For another actress it might have. One tries to suit the scene, has to modify his ideas, to what works best for the actor playing it. You can't force them to do it your way. Even with Richard, who is enormously flexible, I can only urge certain things on him. The suggestions that appeal to him he immediately jumps at and almost always brings them off. But there are other ideas that he doesn't agree with and I never insist on them because his best things he finds himself. You can't plan the details of a play before beginning to work with the cast. And then you've got to approach it as a new play. My first impressions usually come after the first reading with the cast. Actors must be free to improvise and experiment. At every stage of rehearsal a play is continually changing—unpredictably. And I feel it is never too late to alter and improve, and especially to simplify. A great play like *Hamlet* must continually be rediscovered.

ABOUT THE AUTHOR

RICHARD L. STERNE is an actor by profession, and his credits as a young actor are indeed impressive. A graduate of Northwestern University, Mr. Sterne appeared on Broadway in John Gielgud's production of *Hamlet* starring Richard Burton, obtaining first-hand the material for this book. He toured with the National Repertory Theatre under the directorship of Eva Le-Gallienne, appearing in *Liliom* and *She Stoops to Conquer*. Mr. Sterne also appeared with the Oregon Shakespeare Festival, where he played Romeo in *Romeo and Juliet*, as well as other roles in *Love's Labours Lost* and *Henry the Fifth*. He was narrator of the film *Good Night, Socrates*, which won first prize in the Venice Film Festival in 1963.

Acting, however, is only one of Richard Sterne's talents. A musician-composer, he was musical director for the Champlain Shakespeare Festival in Vermont in 1965, and composed some of the music used in Gielgud's production of *Hamlet*.

Mr. Sterne is now living in New York City with his wife, actress Joann Rose, and was recently in Euripides' *The Bacchants* at Lincoln Center.

IN THIS fascinating journal of rehearsals, Richard L. Sterne provides theatre lovers, Shakespearean savants, serious students of drama, and the casual reader with a permanent record of Shakespearean interpretation by two of the most famous actors of our time —John Gielgud and Richard Burton.

When Mr. Sterne was chosen by Sir John Gielgud to play the part of a Gentleman in the now famous Gielgud/Burton production of *Hamlet,* he arrived at the first rehearsal with what seemed to be an unassuming attaché case. Having already secured approval for taking notes at the rehearsals, Mr. Sterne switched on the attaché case-tape recorder, which, unknown to all others, recorded every word of Sir John's direction of Richard Burton, Hume Cronyn, and Alfred Drake. Writing from the transcripts of the tapes and his own journal, Mr. Sterne gives the reader a rare opportunity to witness the artistry, the exhausting experimentation, and the inspiration which went into this unforgettable production.

As well as the journal of rehearsals, this volume includes the prompt-script of Shakespeare's *Hamlet,* with the stage directions, cuts, and emphases Gielgud advised the cast to place on their speeches. The prompt-script is a valuable historical document as well as a fascinating and unusual reading of *Hamlet.* Mr. Sterne also interviewed both Richard Burton and Sir John Gielgud about the play and recorded their own personal and professional interpretations of Hamlet's character and Shakespeare's intention. As a Shakespearean scholar and actor, Mr. Sterne brings his own understanding of the production and thus adds a dimension to *John Gielgud Directs Richard Burton in* **Hamlet** which makes it not only the first such chronicle of the theatre but an outstanding book of English literature.